George Eliot:
A Reference Guide

Constance Marie Fulmer

G. K. HALL & CO., 70 LINCOLN STREET, BOSTON, MASS.

Library of Congress Cataloging in Publication Data

Fulmer, Constance Marie.
  George Eliot : a reference guide.

  (Reference guides to literature)
  1. Eliot, George, pseud., i.e. Marian Evans,
afterwards Cross, 1819-1880--Bibliography.
Z8259.F84 [PR4681] 016.823'8   76-58431
ISBN 0-8161-7859-3

This publication is printed on permanent/durable acid-free paper
MANUFACTURED IN THE UNITED STATES OF AMERICA

For
Edgar Hill Duncan

Contents

Introduction

George Eliot was born Mary Ann Evans on November 22, 1819, at South Farm, Arbury, Warwickshire; she died December 22, 1880, a distinguished writer of fiction. Critical interest in her works has grown steadily during the past quarter of a century.

George Eliot did not begin to publish fiction until she was almost forty years old. Yet for two decades, during her companionship with George Henry Lewes, she was a rather prolific writer, and her works aroused considerable critical comment among her contemporaries. Lewes encouraged her to begin to write, and she always attributed her success to his sympathetic understanding. Her Scenes of Clerical Life appeared in two volumes on January 5, 1858. The three stories which compose the Scenes were originally published separately in Blackwood's Magazine in 1857; the stories are "Amos Barton," "Mr. Gilfil's Love-Story," and "Janet's Repentance." Lewes sent each one to John Blackwood with a recommendation saying they were written by George Eliot, a "clerical friend" of his. Critical interest in George Eliot begins with this work; in subsequent years, each of her new publications was welcomed with enthusiasm and reviewed with meticulous care.

Throughout her productive years George Eliot was almost constantly at work on one novel after another. The novels and their dates of publication are:

1859	Adam Bede
1860	The Mill on The Floss
1861	Silas Marner
1862	Romola in the Cornhill Magazine
1863	Romola in three volumes
1866	Felix Holt, the Radical
1871-1872	Middlemarch in eight installments
1876	Daniel Deronda in eight monthly parts.

Early reviewers commended her for her realistic portrayal of the characters, her clear and simple descriptions, her ability to recreate the local dialect, and her skill in combining humor and pa-

Introduction

thos in depicting ordinary situations. The lively Mrs. Poyser of Adam Bede seems to have been everyone's favorite character.

Although the individual opinions of George Eliot's contemporaries varied, the consensus was that the novels became less and less spontaneous and that the later works were lacking in the vital charm found in the scenes which depict George Eliot's childhood memories and in the descriptions of the local countryside. Her writings became increasingly dull and didactic to the critics as she spent more time analyzing and expounding moral issues. Through the years reviewers continued to compliment her delineation of individual characters, particularly her handling of minor figures, but they observed that the novels became more inartistic in construction and found that the individual parts were more striking than the whole. Middlemarch was pronounced too melancholy and too labored in spite of the excellence of the character analysis; Ladislaw was not considered to be a suitable hero or an adequate companion for Dorothea. Daniel Deronda was also judged to be ineffective as a person and incapable of serving as a moral reformer. The novel was said to fall into two distinct parts; the "Deronda part" or the "Jewish part" was described as a failure because of its lack of action and interest; the "Gwendolen part" was praised for its realistic detail and vitality. However, a number of Jews wrote to commend the accuracy of the sections dealing with Jewish customs and life, and some of George Eliot's contemporaries described Deronda as growing in sympathy and finding a higher religious life that transcended self. By the time George Eliot died in 1880, the main lines of criticism were already established for each novel, and the major critical issues remain the same.

In addition to the novels, George Eliot wrote and published more than two dozen poems and two short stories; in each of these, critics found obvious indications of superfluous moralizing. The Spanish Gypsy, published May 25, 1868, is a verse drama; like the other minor works, it is clearly designed to illustrate her ethical theories. All of her attempts at poetry were described as being too philosophical to be charming, musical, or "poetic." She wrote eleven poems which she called "Brother and Sister Sonnets." The series incorporates poignant memories of her idyllic childhood days with her own brother, Isaac. These sonnets were included in the volume, The Legend of Jubal and Other Poems, 1874. The most well-known of her poems is "O, May I Join the Choir Invisible"; it was read at her funeral, frequently reprinted in her death notices, and used as a Positivist hymn. The two stories were "The Lifted Veil," published in Blackwood's Magazine, July 1, 1859, and described by a reviewer as "woefully somber," and "Brother Jacob," of a more "humorous cast," published in Cornhill Magazine, July, 1864. Critical judgments of these minor works have not changed substantially through the years.

George Eliot's last published work was The Impressions of Theophrastus Such, 1879. It contains eighteen essays which are con-

nected only through the presence of a fictitious narrator who is a
satirical moralist. This volume was at the publisher's when George
Henry Lewes died on November 30, 1878. George Eliot corrected the
proofs of her book for Blackwood, but she refused to write another
word of fiction. She spent her remaining working hours preparing
Lewes's unfinished manuscripts for publication.

Primary materials of various types have been made available to
students of George Eliot with increasing thoroughness. Her letters
were first published in a limited selection which was prepared by
her young husband, J. W. Cross, after her death (1885.A3). Perhaps
the most important single contribution to George Eliot criticism is
the collection of letters prepared by Gordon S. Haight (1954.A1 and
1955.A2). These letters provide the background material for all of
the biographical studies; of the studies of George Eliot's life,
Haight's George Eliot: A Biography (1968.A3) follows the letters
most closely and is the most complete. George Eliot's diaries and
notebooks are also available; many of these have been published and
are listed in this bibliography. For example, seventeen manuscript
pages taken from one of her notebooks were published by Thomas Pinney in the Huntington Library Quarterly (1966.B18). Articles such
as Haight's in the Yale University Library Gazette (1955.B4,
1961.B7, and 1971.B9) describe collections of manuscripts which are
housed in various libraries. A variety of studies based on these
primary materials reveal the growth of George Eliot's mind, the evolution of her artistic criteria, the process by which she rejected
traditional Christianity, and the formulation of her own unorthodox
system of morality.

Before she became George Eliot or began to write fiction, Mary
Ann Evans published a series of sketches called "Poetry and Prose
from the Notebook of an Eccentric" in the Coventry Herald on December 4, 1846. During the early 1850's she published at least sixty
anonymous essays while she was working with John Chapman on the
Westminster Review. Twenty-eight of these have been identified and
collected by Thomas Pinney (1963.A4). The artistic principles which
George Eliot applied in her own fiction were already worked out in
her mind and are stated very distinctly in the early essays. All of
her letters, notebooks, and essays reveal that George Eliot's moral
principles and her artistic credo were clearly defined by the time
she began to write fiction and that they were consistently applied
throughout everything which she wrote.

Even from the beginning of her career in writing fiction, George
Eliot was dissatisfied with the lack of sympathy which the reviewers
expressed for the moral concerns in her writings. On February 11,
1873, she wrote to Charles Ritter and expressed alarm at the reception of Middlemarch. She said: "Though Middlemarch seems to have
made a deep impression in our own country . . . there has not, I be-
lieve, been one really able review of the book in our newspapers and
periodicals." She continued, "What one's soul thirsts for is the

word which is the reflection of one's own aim and delight in writing --the word which shows that what one meant has been perfectly seized, that the emotion which stirred one in writing is repeated in the mind of the reader" (1955.A2, V, 374). She was painfully aware that very few readers made the sympathetic response which she intended to elicic it, but occasionally she received a letter from someone like Freder-Harrison, who wrote to her on January 18, 1866. He said of her poetic drama The Spanish Gypsy that it seemed to him a new thing to find "the highest art for the first time consciously devoted to the deepest moral problems" (1955.A2, IV, 220). She answered his "last little note of sympathy" on January 22 and said of his response, ". . . genuine words from one capable of understanding one's conceptions are precious and strengthening" (1955.A2, IV, 221). And even though George Henry Lewes constantly had his "watchful eye" alert to the possibility of finding encouraging words for George Eliot in the newspapers and periodicals, he was seldom able to locate anyone who was capable of understanding as well as Mr. Harrison her explicit ethical intent.

In all that she wrote, George Eliot had two aims; one was to inspire in her readers a sympathetic understanding of their fellows, and the other was to make a lasting literary contribution to generations to come. The studies listed in this bibliography are ample evidence that she has made an impact on posterity. And although for sixty-five years after her death very little was written which indicated that critics had grown in sympathetic understanding of her writings, during the last twenty-five years, a number of "genuine words" have been written by those who are "capable of understanding" her conceptions as they are embodied in the novels.

During the sixty-five years following her death in 1880, articles about George Eliot and her fiction continued to appear, but virtually no new critical opinions were introduced. General studies covered the same old ground, and chapters on George Eliot were included in histories of English literature. Personal testimonials were written by various individuals who had been acquainted with George Eliot; an anonymous account of Christmas week, 1870, was published (1885.B11) by a fellow-lodger of George Eliot and George Henry Lewes at a country house resort in the Isle of Wight. In 1901 W. C. Brownell was apparently justified in asking, "How long is it since George Eliot's name has been the subject of even a literary allusion?" (1901.B1) He went on to say that the neglect of her writing was due to the fact that contemporary men have "had a surfeit of psychological fiction since George Eliot's day." In spite of the fact that he was embarrassingly incorrect about critical interest in psychological fiction, he seems to have been right about George Eliot's lack of popularity. Not until the late 1940's was anything written which broadened or deepened the contemporary assessments of her novels.

George Eliot's place of central importance in the consideration

Introduction

of the main currents of the thought and belief of her age has remained unquestioned since Basil Willey's Nineteenth Century Studies
appeared in 1949 (1949.B7). He said:

> Probably no English writer of the time, and certainly no novel-
> ist, more fully epitomizes her century; her development is a
> paradigm, her intellectual biography a graph, of its most de-
> cided trend. Starting from evangelical Christianity, the curve
> passes through doubt to a reinterpreted Christ and a religion of
> humanity: beginning with God, it ends in Duty.

The progress in her own life, which Willey describes as a model of
the tendency of the age, is now recognized as being typical of the
pattern of struggle and moral growth which her characters follow in
the novels.

Beginning late in the 1940's, scholars have made a serious attempt to analyze thoroughly the artistic features of the novels and
to relate them to George Eliot's life and way of thinking. Gerald
Bullett's book-length study, George Eliot: Her Life and Books
(1947.A1), and Joan Bennett's George Eliot: Her Mind and Art (1948.A1)
helped to rejuvenate critical concern for the fiction. An article
by Mark Schorer, "Fiction and the Matrix of Analogy," appeared in
the Kenyon Review in 1949 (1949.B4). Schorer discussed her use of
metaphors as explicit symbols of psychological or moral conditions.
This focusing of attention on the significance of the imagery in
George Eliot's fiction was truly the beginning of modern criticism
and represented a major step toward a meaningful appreciation of the
novels.

During the last few years an increasing number of studies have
dealt with her use of imagery, and attempts have been made to point
up different aspects of her artistry. F. R. Leavis has placed her
as securely in the great tradition of English novelists as Basil
Willey did in the intellectual tradition of nineteenth century religious thought. Her place among the great literary artists is unquestioned. F. R. Leavis confidently said, "The great English novelists are Jane Austen, George Eliot, Henry James, and Joseph Conrad." Yet he finds an unsatisfactory element in her work and ob-
serves, "There is something like a unanimity to the effect that it
is distinctive of her, among great novelists, to be peculiarly ad-
dicted to moral preoccupation." These statements appear in The
Great Tradition (1954.B6) although Leavis had written several articles on George Eliot earlier (1945.B3, 1945.B4, 1946.B5).

In his survey of George Eliot criticism (1964.B11), W. J. Harvey
recognized that the interest in her imagery "has generally been related to her personal dilemmas or to her typical moral concerns."
He then went on to say, "No critic, so far as I know, has denied her
a central moral seriousness; the main debate has been on the adequa-
cy or inadequacy of an aesthetic correlative." He also described

INTRODUCTION

the defense of her art as "an increasingly prevailing theme" in general studies on George Eliot. A review by James Wheatley which appeared in the Journal of English and Germanic Philology in 1963 of Harvey's own book (1961.A2) described it as "one long argument to prove that she is really an artist." Such arguments are no longer made, for her artistic achievement is now an accepted fact.

Recent studies of imagery and structure have led to more detailed study of George Eliot's religion, and articles such as those by David R. Carroll and Richard S. Lyons contribute more to an understanding of her morality than previous works ostensibly devoted to her religious ideas. Richard S. Lyons in his study of "The Method of Middlemarch" examined one chapter of the novel (chapter 39, Book 4) and showed how plot becomes the growth in consciousness by which character is defined, and he pointed out a number of significant aspects of the moral growth toward sympathetic understanding which is the philosophic basis of George Eliot's artistic expression (1966.B11). David R. Carroll's "An Image of Disenchantment in the Novels of George Eliot" (1960.B1) sets forth an archetypal pattern for the novels. This study also indicates in specific ways how her artistry and morality are related.

One indication of the increasing interest in George Eliot's writings is the number of book-length studies of scholarly merit which have been published. In 1957 Reva Stump's Movement and Vision in George Eliot's Novels (1959.A5) appeared. Jerome Thale (1959.A6) and Barbara Hardy (1959.A3) have written significant studies; Professor Hardy deserves special recognition for her contributions to George Eliot criticism. W. J. Harvey's The Art of George Eliot (1961.A2) appeared in 1961; in 1964 Walter Allen (1964.A1) published his George Eliot. Books by Bernard J. Paris (1965.A5), Ian Milner (1968.A11), and U. C. Knoepflmacher (1968.A10) deal with George Eliot's ideas and values. Book-length collections of criticism have been edited by Richard Stang (1960.A7), Gordon S. Haight (1965.A2), John Holmstrom and Laurence Lerner (1966.A5), George R. Creeger (1970.A4), Barbara Hardy (1970.A8), and David Carroll (1971.A2). As more extensive and more careful critical treatment is given to George Eliot, her superior quality of mind is revealed, and her artistic aims are seen in the proper perspective.

Middlemarch is a novel which has received the most extensive treatment. There are several specialized studies, such as Jerome Beaty's studies of the manuscript (1960.A1 and 1967.B1). It is generally considered to be George Eliot's "best" novel, and a number of the editions have scholarly introductions. Daniel Deronda has also continued to create a remarkable amount of interest. And although Silas Marner is familiar to far more people than Romola or Felix Holt, it has received less critical attention than any of the novels. The volume Scenes of Clerical Life has stimulated a number of articles and Thomas A. Noble's book (1965.A4).

Introduction

Dissertations have been written on almost every aspect of George Eliot's life and works, and the number written each year seems to grow regularly. Annotations for the dissertations listed in this bibliography are taken from Dissertation Abstracts.

An impressive number and variety of writers who are well-recognized for their own literary accomplishments have written about George Eliot. Many of them have profited from her example and acknowledge her influence on their works. The comparative studies also examine ways in which George Eliot was herself indebted to other writers. She possessed an amazing knowledge of classical, Biblical, and contemporary literature, and everything she has written is a storehouse of literary allusions.

Her works have a continued appeal to readers all over the world. Several significant studies have been written in Hungarian and in a number of languages other than English. All of the critical studies listed in this volume indicate the varied and often contradictory responses which George Eliot's fiction has elicited. Her influence has been extensive, and interest in her life and her writings is still very much alive. This bibliography is a comprehensive list of published critical materials which deal with her writings, 1858-1971. No primary materials are included, and reviews of secondary materials are included only if they are significant criticisms of George Eliot's works. Annotations are provided for the works which were available; in cases where the works were not available the entry is asterisked and a source statement is given. In some cases abbreviations are used to denote the bibliographical source and the year it is published, ie: Cited in ELL(1966). The list in the bibliography incorporates materials from the following bibliographic sources:

ELL   Annual Bibliography of English Language and Literature, 1920-1970. Modern Humanities Research Association.

MLA   Annual Bibliographies published by the Modern Language Association, 1922-1971.

VS   "Victorian Bibliography" in Victorian Studies, 1958-1971.

The New Cambridge Bibliography of English Literature. Volume 3: 1800-1900, edited by George Watson. Cambridge: University Press, 1968, pp. 899-911. 1969.B23.

DA   Dissertation Abstracts.

Marshall, William H. "A Selective Bibliography of Writings About George Eliot to 1965, Part I." Bulletin of Bibliography, 25 (1967), 70-72. 1967.B31.

INTRODUCTION

Marshall, William H. "A Selective Bibliography of Writings About George Eliot to 1965, Part II." Bulletin of Bibliography, 25 (1967), 88-94. 1967.B32.

Harvey, W. J. "George Eliot." Victorian Fiction: A Guide to Research. Ed. by Lionel Stevenson. Cambridge: Harvard University Press, 1964. 1964.B11.

Anderson, John P. "Bibliography," pp. i-xiv. Life of George Eliot by Oscar Browning. London: Walter Scott, 1890. 1890.A1.

"Bibliography," pp. 425-443. George Eliot: A Critical Study by George Willis Cooke. Boston and New York: Houghton, Mifflin and Company; Cambridge: The Riverside Press, 1883. 1883.A2.

The index of this bibliography is divided into four major sections: the first contains titles of George Eliot's works; the second contains titles of the books, articles, and collections of articles about her and her writings; the third contains the names of the authors and editors of these books, articles, and collections of articles; and the fourth contains subjects of the secondary writings. The subjects which are listed are Bibliography, Biography, Comparative Studies, Dissertations, George Henry Lewes, Morality, and Theories of Art.

I would like to acknowledge the deep gratitude I feel to Edgar Hill Duncan, my professor at Vanderbilt University, who inspired my interest in George Eliot and stimulated my enthusiasm for the study of bibliography. I am also indebted to the administrators of David Lipscomb College for making it possible for me to be relieved of my teaching duties during the summer of 1973 to work on this project. My summer's work was facilitated in many ways by the help of Pat Lankford Bradley, who was then a student at Lipscomb. Other David Lipscomb College students who have assisted me with the various stages of the work are Becky Womack Lipe, Carolyn Srite, and Kathleen McCracken. Carolyn Srite, a valuable helper in several crucial stages of the project, has continued to provide inestimable assistance while pursuing a graduate degree at the University of Tennessee in Knoxville.

Writings about George Eliot, 1858-1971

1858 B SHORTER WRITINGS

*1   ANON. Review of <u>Scenes of Clerical Life</u>. <u>Literary Gazette</u>,
        January 23.
            Cited in 1969.B23.

*2   ANON. Review of <u>Scenes of Clerical Life</u>. <u>John Bull's Weekly</u>,
        February 8.
            Cited in 1969.B23.

3   ANON. Review of <u>Scenes of Clerical Life</u>. <u>Saturday Review</u>, 5
        (May 29), 566-567.
            The work of George Eliot's satire is loving; it has pa-
        thos, but the tears make human nature more beautiful. It
        is homely in its pictures, but they are connected with our
        most impassioned sensibilities and our daily duties. It is
        also religious. Reprinted in 1858.B5 and 1971.A2.

4   ANON. Review of <u>Scenes of Clerical Life</u>. <u>Atlantic Monthly</u>,
        May, pp. 890-892.
            To display the candid and inclusive appreciation of life
        and character which is shown in <u>Scenes from Clerical Life</u>
        demands a large intellect and a large heart. Reprinted in
        1971.A2.

*5   ANON. Review of <u>Scenes of Clerical Life</u>. <u>Littell's Living
        Age</u>, 58: 274-278.
            Reprint of 1858.B3. Reprinted in 1971.A2.

*6   ANON. Review of <u>Scenes of Clerical Life</u>. <u>National Review</u>, 7.
            Cited in 1969.B23.

7   LUCAS, SAMUEL. "<u>Scenes of Clerical Life</u>." <u>The Times</u>, January
        2, p. 9.
            Contains speculation as to "who this George Eliot is."
        The suggestion is made that he could even be Crabbe come

1858

back from the grave in a softer mood. Lucas prefers "Mr. Gilfil's Love Story" to the other tales. He finds Mr. Eliot characterized by sobriety and strength, by clear and simple descriptions, and by a combination of humor and pathos in depicting ordinary situations. Reprinted in 1965.A2, 1966.A5, and 1971.A2.

1859 A BOOKS

*1   ANON. Seth Bede, the Methody: His Life and Labors, Chiefly by Himself. London: Tallant and Company.
     Cited in 1883.A2.

1859 B SHORTER WRITINGS

*1   ANON. Review of Adam Bede. Literary Gazette, February 26.
     Cited in 1969.B23.

2   ANON. Review of Adam Bede. Saturday Review, 7 (February 26), 250-251.
     Praises the humor of Mrs. Poyser and the reality of the diary. But suggests a flaw in the manner in which the author intrudes himself in the book. Reprinted in 1971.A2.

3   ANON. Review of Adam Bede. Atlantic Monthly, 4 (October), 521-522.
     Scenes from nature are vividly and tenderly depicted. The characters are drawn with a free and impartial hand, and Mrs. Poyser is a creation for immortality. The epigrams are aromatic.

*4   ANON. Review of Adam Bede. Dublin Review, 47: 33-42.
     Cited in 1969.B23.

*5   ANON. Review of Adam Bede. North British Review, 30.
     Cited in 1969.B23.

*6   ANON. Review of Adam Bede. Westminster Review, n.s. 15: 486-512.
     Cited in 1969.B23.

7   ANON. Review of Scenes of Clerical Life and Adam Bede. Edinburgh Review, 110: 223-246.
     Praises the reality of the characters, quotes long passages from the novel, and speculates as to the identity of the author. The universal question in men's mouths is

"Have you read <u>Adam Bede</u>?" In <u>Scenes of Clerical Life</u> Mr.
Eliot's descriptions of scenery are perfect.

8 [COLLINS, W. L.] "<u>Adam Bede</u>." <u>Blackwood's Magazine</u>, 85
(April), 490-504.
Mr. Eliot dismisses the reader with a lively impression
that self-restraint is better than repentance. Many details of the novel are discussed and praised.

9 DALLAS, ENEAS SWEETLAND. "<u>Adam Bede</u>." <u>The Times</u>, 12 (April),
5.
Considers Mrs. Poyser the gem of the novel. Wonders
about the author. Says, "In the region of latent thoughts,
and unconscious and semi-conscious feelings--in this twi-
light of the human soul our novelist most delights to make
his observations." Reprinted in 1965.A2, 1966.A5 and 1971.A2.

10 [JEWSBURY, G.] Review of <u>Adam Bede</u>. <u>Athenaeum</u>, February 26,
p. 284.
The story is not a story, but a true account of a place
and people who really lived. One or two incidents are too
melodramatic and traditional. Reprinted in 1966.A5.

11 MOZLEY, ANNE. Review of <u>Adam Bede</u>. <u>Bentley's Quarterly Re-
view</u>, 1 (July), 433-456.
<u>Adam Bede</u> has the difficulty of a prominent moral; the
moral is that evil cannot be undone. It also teaches the
value of simple, natural scenes. Praises Mrs. Poyser and
points out Adam's final happiness in passing from pain
into sympathy. Reprinted in 1971.A2.

1860 A BOOKS - NONE

1860 B SHORTER WRITINGS

1 ANON. Review of <u>The Mill on The Floss</u>. <u>Spectator</u>, 33 (April
7), 330-331.
Maggie's love for her brother is thoughtlessly unselfish
and is painted with wonderful minuteness. George Eliot's
children are healthy and rosy, not sickly or queer. And
the mere material facts of the river playing such a great
part in Maggie's life give one the feeling that she is
swept along by a current of circumstances she can neither
resist nor control. The reader is conscious of Maggie's
every thought as her higher faculties are awakened under
the influence of a mind of wider range and finer tone than
her own. Reprinted in 1966.A5 and 1971.A2.

1860

2 ANON. Review of The Mill on The Floss. The Atlas, April 14.
    The notion of predestined calamity is hinted at from the
    very beginning, and when the water brings swift justice and
    everlasting rest, the hand of the artist is apparent. Re-
    printed in 1966.A5.

3 ANON. Review of The Mill on The Floss. The Leader, April 14.
    George Eliot demonstrates the theory that the rare gifts
    of a lively fancy and fertile imagination are fatal to the
    possessor unless accompanied by the strength of mind and
    moral culture necessary to hold them in subjection. No
    wonder Maggie grows into such a wild and contradictory
    creature. Reprinted in 1966.A5.

4 ANON. Review of The Mill on The Floss. Saturday Review, 9
    (April 14), 470-471.
    The whole delineation of passionate love, as painted by
    modern female novelists, is open to very serious criticism.
    These are emotions over which we ought to throw a veil.
    And there is too much painful in the novel. The authoress
    is so far led away by her reflections on moral problems and
    her interest in the phases of triumphant passion that she
    sacrifices her story. Reprinted in 1966.A5 and 1971.A2.

5 ANON. Review of The Mill on The Floss. The Sun, April 23.
    The characters are taken from the ranks of the superior
    workers of the world. Poverty has some advantages. Re-
    printed in 1966.A5.

6 ANON. Review of The Mill on The Floss. Guardian, April 25,
    pp. 377-378.
    The story of The Mill on The Floss is one of the develop-
    ment of character, and the principal influence is that of
    "Kindred." There are two striking faults in the novel.
    One is structure. The last volume seems to be a new book.
    Maggie's passion for Stephen is improbable. At least the
    writer never for an instant loses sight of the sin and
    shame being described. Reprinted in 1966.A5 and 1971.A2.

*7 ANON. Review of The Mill on The Floss. Tait's Magazine, May.
    Cited in 1969.B23.

8 ANON. Review of The Mill on The Floss. Atlantic Monthly, 5
    (June), 756-757.
    The pathos is genuine in the novel, and it presents a
    mental and moral philosophy noble and true. The action
    moves too slowly and tamely in the first three or four
    books. Reading the novel will make the reader wiser and
    better.

9   ANON. Review of The Mill on The Floss. The National Review,
     July.
         The whole of Maggie's relationship to Stephen Guest seems
     a kind of enthusiastic homage to physiological law. It is
     as untrue to nature as it is unpleasant and indelicate.
     Reprinted in 1966.A5.

10 ANON. Review of The Mill on The Floss. Westminster Review,
     74 (July), 13-18.
         The critic congratulates himself for knowing that George
     Eliot is a woman. The separate beauties are numberless.
     The reader seems to be wandering down a long gallery filled
     with masterpieces of Dutch paintings. The denouement is
     altogether melodramatic. Philip Wakem seems to lack vi-
     tality. Reprinted in 1971.A2.

11 ANON. "George Eliot and Nathaniel Hawthorne." North British
     Review, 33: 87-98.
         George Eliot sees things as they are; she can evolve
     great actions and passions, but she dwells with equal com-
     placency on the most trivial events. Hawthorne's imagina-
     tion takes the color of what it feeds on. He starts with
     a moral or intellectual conception and adapts his charac-
     ters to fit that mold.

*12 ANON. Review of The Mill on The Floss. North British Review,
     33.
         Cited in 1969.B23.

13 [COLLINS, W. L.] "The Mill on The Floss." Blackwood's Maga-
     zine, 87 (May), 611-623.
         Begins by pointing out ways in which the novel fails to
     measure up to Adam Bede. The moral is not obtrusive, and a
     playful humor lights up the story throughout.

14 DALLAS, ENEAS SWEETLAND. "The Mill on The Floss." The Times,
     19 (May 19), 10-11.
         George Eliot takes characters from real life in all their
     intrinsic littleness and paints them as she finds them.
     Her description of the life of the child is unique as it is
     painted in all its prosaic reality. The light of the story
     is Maggie, who has a warm heart, abounding in sympathy and
     longing for a return of her affection. Reprinted in
     1965.A2, 1966.A5, and 1971.A2.

15 [JEWSBURY, G.] Review of The Mill on The Floss. Athenaeum,
     April 7, pp. 467-468.
         The workmanship is neither as delicate nor as elaborate

1860

as <u>Adam Bede</u>. Neither is the story comparable in interest or artistic treatment.

16   [ROBERTSON, REV. J. C.] "Review of <u>Scenes of Clerical Life</u>, <u>Adam Bede</u>, and <u>The Mill on the Floss</u>." <u>Quarterly Review</u>, 108 (October), 245-260, 469-499.
      Gives a detailed discussion of each work and finds in each a melancholy ending. George Eliot delights in unpleasant subjects, things which are repulsive, coarse, and degrading. The minds of her readers need to be guarded from impurity and the unnecessary knowledge of evil. The coarse details are designed to fill the mind with details of imaginary vice, distress, and crime.

17   WARE, L. G. Review of <u>The Mill on The Floss</u>. <u>Christian Examiner</u>, 49: 145-147.
      The story is not as interesting, as pleasant, or as artistically told as <u>Adam Bede</u>. The plot is utterly forlorn.

<u>1861 A BOOKS - NONE</u>

<u>1861 B SHORTER WRITINGS</u>

1   ANON. Review of <u>The Mill on The Floss</u>. <u>Dublin University Magazine</u>, 57 (February), 192-200.
      <u>The Mill on The Floss</u> is built on the same faulty principles as <u>Adam Bede</u> and reproduces the same or very similar faults of detail. Let any one read carefully the first volume and then ask himself for what conceivable purpose it was written. The story is suddenly carried off its legs in the flood that drowns poor Maggie. The remaining characters are hustled from the stage at one stroke. It is as if the author and readers were alike glad to be rid of them on any terms. Reprinted in 1971.A2.

*2   ANON. Review of <u>Silas Marner</u>. <u>Literary Gazette</u>, April 6.
      Cited in 1969.B23.

3   ANON. "<u>Silas Marner</u>." <u>The Saturday Review</u>, 11 (April 13), 369-370.
      There does not appear to be a fault in the working out of the plot. The people in the public house proclaim in a few words each a different character and sustain it. Reprinted in 1965.A2, 1966.A5, and 1971.A2.

4   ANON. Review of <u>Adam Bede</u>. <u>London Quarterly Review</u>, 16 (July), 301-307.

The whole of <u>Adam Bede</u> is a vivid picture of the irretrievable effects of wrong doing, and its only morality is to impress self-restraint by a clearer view of those effects. It is an immorality and an irreligion to preach only the consequences of sin while the guilt of yielding is ignored. Reprinted in 1971.A2.

*5   ANON. Review of <u>Silas Marner</u>. <u>Englishwoman's Domestic Magazine</u>, n.s. 3.
          Cited in 1969.B23.

*6   ANON. Review of <u>Silas Marner</u>. <u>London Review</u>, 2.
          Cited in 1969.B23.

7   ANON. Review of <u>Silas Marner</u>. <u>Westminster Review</u>, 76 (July), 280-282.
          The most remarkable peculiarity and distinguishing excellence of <u>Silas Marner</u> is the complete correlation between the characters and their circumstances. Other admirable features are the vivid painting of life itself, the profound remarks on the progress of life, the kindly humor, and the careful construction. Reprinted in 1971.A2.

*8   CLARIGNY, CUCHERAL. Review of <u>Silas Marner</u>. <u>Revue des Deux Mondes</u>, 35 (September), 188-210.
          Cited in 1890.A1.

9   DALLAS, ENEAS SWEETLAND. "<u>Silas Marner</u>." <u>The Times</u>, 29 (April), 12.
          This is a story about a hero whose mind is nearly a blank and whose life is represented as being at the mercy of fate. The picture of his misery and the discipline of his repentance are but a homely, human version of the story of Job. Instead of Deity, a little child comes. She regards life from a high and lofty point and suggests profound reflections. Reprinted in 1965.A2 and 1971.A2.

10   [HUTTON, R. H.] Review of <u>Silas Marner</u>. <u>Economist</u>, April 27, pp. 455-457.
          No element of power is wanting to make <u>Silas Marner</u> more impressive, and no element of beauty is wanting to make it more attractive. All the incidents of the tale work together for good for the poor weaver and restore his faith in man and God. There is nothing more beautiful, humorous, and pathetic in fiction than Dame Winthrop's conversations. Reprinted in 1971.A2.

1861

*11   [JEWSBURY, G.] Review of <u>Silas Marner</u>. <u>Athenaeum</u>, April 6.
        Cited in 1969.B23.

12   LUDLOW, J. M. "<u>Elsie Venner</u> and <u>Silas Marner</u>." <u>Macmillan's</u>
        <u>Magazine</u>, 4 (August), 305-309.
           George Eliot in <u>Silas Marner</u> has reached the very <u>acme</u> of
        artistic power. There is probably nothing in the whole
        realm of fiction more perfect or more touching artistically
        or more true or more instructive morally than Silas's trans-
        formation.

13   LUYSTER, I. M. Review of Three Novels. <u>Christian Examiner</u>,
        70: 227-251. Reviews <u>Scenes of Clerical Life</u>, <u>Adam Bede</u>,
        and <u>The Mill on The Floss</u>.
           The novels display a breadth of culture extraordinary in
        a woman and a painstaking and patience truly admirable.
        The spontaneity of her remarks is refreshing, and the read-
        er never suspects her of contriving incidents merely to
        introduce long reflections.

14   [MULOCK, DINAH.] "To Novelists--and a Novelist." <u>Macmillan's</u>
        <u>Magazine</u>, 3 (April), 441-448.
           <u>The Mill on the Floss</u> is one of the finest imaginative
        works in our language, superior even to <u>Adam Bede</u>. Artis-
        tically the story is perfect. Morally it is severely lack-
        ing. The novel will do no good, lighten no burdened heart,
        help no perplexed spirit, and bring no erring one back
        into the way of peace. Reprinted in 1966.A5 and 1971.A2.

1862 A BOOKS - NONE

1862 B SHORTER WRITINGS

1   ANON. Review of <u>Silas Marner</u>. <u>Dublin University Magazine</u>,
        59 (April), 396-401.
           Finds the work dull. George Eliot's characters were
        never remarkable for pleasantness, but here they are mean,
        boorish, heavy-witted, and fail to touch the heart or the
        fancy. The melodrama is offensive, and there is no suf-
        ficient ending to a disjointed story. Reprinted in
        1971.A2.

1863 A BOOKS - NONE

1863 B SHORTER WRITINGS

1   ANON. Review of <u>Romola</u>. <u>Athenaeum</u>, July 11, p. 46.
     As a novel <u>Romola</u> cannot be called entertaining; it re-
     quires sustained attention. The character of Savonarola
     is the gem of the book. Tito remains vague in image in
     spite of his grace, beauty, and fascination. Reprinted in
     1971.A2.

2   ANON. Review of <u>Romola</u>. <u>Saturday Review</u>, 16 (July 23), 124-
     125.
     Romola seems cut on a bigger scale than there is any oc-
     casion for. She is too much of a goddess to make it fair
     play for such a weak mortal as Tito to have to love her.
     She shows great courage by rising above jealousy and de-
     spair. George Eliot makes the reader feel that he is in
     the hands of a thinker who has thought far down into the
     depths of the religious mind and who has seriously and
     anxiously desired to ascertain the place of religious
     thought in the facts of life. George Eliot has been tempt-
     ed into a field where she is not less than she has been,
     but where her merits are obscured and their effects im-
     paired. Reprinted in 1965.A2 and 1971.A2.

3   ANON. "<u>Romola</u>." <u>Westminster Review</u>, 80 (October), 344-351.
     The author says that it cannot be denied that <u>Romola</u> is
     less popular than its predecessors, but it remains the
     author's greatest work. Yet the best scenes are so philo-
     sophically treated that the reader is in danger of being
     more attracted by the treatment of the moral question than
     interested by its bearing on the fate of those whom it
     affects. Reprinted in 1965.A2 and 1971.A2.

*4   ANON. Review of <u>Romola</u>. <u>British Quarterly Review</u>, 38.
     Cited in 1969.B23.

*5   ANON. Review of <u>Romola</u>. <u>Land We Love</u>, 1: 134.
     Cited in 1883.A2.

*6   ANON. Review of <u>Romola</u>. <u>London Review</u>, 7.
     Cited in 1969.B23.

*7   ANON. Review of <u>Silas Marner</u>. <u>North British Review</u>, 38.
     Cited in 1969.B23.

*8   FORGUES, E. D. Review of <u>Romola</u>. <u>Revue des Deux Mondes</u>, 48:
     939-967.
     Cited in 1890.A1.

1863

9   [HUTTON, R. H.] "Romola." The Spectator, July 18.
       The great artistic purpose of the story is to trace out
the conflict between liberal culture and the more passionate form of the Christian faith in that strange era.
Though the pivot of Romola's character turns on faith, she
does not distinctly show any faith except the faith in
rigid honor, in human pity, and partially also in Savonarola's personal greatness and power. Reprinted in 1966.A5
and 1971.A2.

*10   SCHERER, EDMOND. "Silas Marner." Études Critiques sur la
Littérature Contemporaine, 10 vols. Paris.
       Cited in 1890.A1.

11   [SIMPSON, RICHARD.] "George Eliot's Novels." Home and Foreign Review, 3 (October), 522-549.
       George Eliot is a searching but indulgent moralist who
probes the conscience tenderly. She comes to the critical
question of the relations between passion and duty, reason
and feeling, man and mankind, the soul and God. She
teaches moral and religious lessons which Lewes learned
from Goethe. Reprinted in 1971.A2.

1864 A BOOKS - NONE

1864 B SHORTER WRITINGS

1   FIELD, KATE. "English Authors in Florence." Atlantic Monthly, 14 (December), 660-671.
       The author saw George Eliot at Villino Trollope. The
deep research and knowledge of medieval life and manners
displayed are cause of wonderment to erudite Florentines,
who have lived to learn from a foreigner.

1866 A BOOKS - NONE

1866 B SHORTER WRITINGS

*1   ANON. Review of Felix Holt. Athenaeum, June 23.
       Cited in 1969.B23.

*2   ANON. Review of Felix Holt. Chamber's Journal, August 11,
pp. 508-512.
       Cited in 1969.B23.

3   ANON. "Felix Holt." Contemporary Review, 3 (September), 51-
70.

Discusses each character, compares the novel to George Eliot's early works, and quotes lengthy passages. The reviewer concludes that George Eliot should not be ashamed of Felix Holt, but it will not live and shine above her tomb. The work gives witness of vitality but not of advance.

*4   ANON. Review of Felix Holt. Christian Remembrancer, n.s. 52: 445-468.
     Cited in 1890.A1.

*5   ANON. Review of Felix Holt. Eclectic Review, n.s. 11: 34-47.
     Cited in 1890.A1.

*6   ANON. Review of Felix Holt. London Quarterly Review, 27: 100-124.
     Cited in 1969.B23.

*7   ANON. Review of Felix Holt. London Review, 12.
     Cited in 1969.B23.

*8   ANON. Review of Felix Holt. Westminster Review, n.s. 30: 200-207.
     Cited in 1890.A1.

*9   ANON. Review of Romola. Christian Remembrancer, n.s. 52: 468-479.
     Cited in 1890.A1.

*10 ALCOTT, LOUISE M. "George Eliot." Independent, November 1.
     Cited in 1883.A2.

*11 BROWNE, MATTHEW. "George Eliot and Poetry." Argosy, 2: 437-443.
     Cited in 1890.A1.

12   [COLLINS, W.] "Felix Holt, the Radical." Blackwood's Magazine, 100 (July), 94-109.
     This is a novel of character and not of incident. The reviewer goes through the characters introducing each.

13   DALLAS, ENEAS SWEETLAND. "Felix Holt, the Radical." The Times, 26 (June), 6.
     Announces that a greater than Miss Austen has arisen; she plays with torrents while Miss Austen plays with rills. The secret of her power is found in the depth and range of her sympathies. Reprinted in 1965.A2, 1966.A5, and 1971.A2.

14   [HUTTON, R. H.] Review of Felix Holt. Spectator, 39 (June 23), 692-693.
     This is the brightest, the least penetrated with inner melancholy, of all George Eliot's stories. The great struggle in Felix's mind between political and moral radicalism which gives the thread of unity to the story is

1866

almost over even before the novel opens. With all the no-
bility of his character there is a certain rudeness and
baldness about Felix. Intellectual insight and humor spar-
kle over the whole surface of the story. Reprinted in
1971.A2.

15 JAMES, HENRY. "Felix Holt, the Radical." Nation, 3 (August
16), 127-128.
Describes a broad array of rich accomplishments including
firm and elaborate delineation of individual characters and
extensive human sympathy. But as a story it is clumsily
artificial and singularly inartistic. Reprinted in 1921.B2,
1965.A2, 1966.A5, and 1971.A2.

16 ____. "The Novels of George Eliot." Atlantic Monthly, 18:
479-492.
Comments on the individual novels. Her sentiments are
with the common people, and their passion proves itself
feebler than their consciences. Reprinted in 1908.B1,
1960.A7, 1965.A2, and 1966.A5.

*17 LANCASTER, HENRY H. "George Eliot's Novels." North British
Review, 45 (September), 197-228.
Cited in 1969.B23. Reprinted in 1876.B36.

18 MORLEY, JOHN. "Felix Holt, the Radical." Saturday Review, 21
(June 16), 722-724.
The figure of Felix overshadows any minor defects in
construction. He elevates Esther to a height as lofty as
his own by the subtle force of his own character. Reprinted in 1965.A2, 1966.A5, and 1971.A2.

19 ____. "George Eliot's Novels." Macmillan's Magazine, 14
(August), 272-279.
George Eliot introduces a rich humanness into the popular
conception of religious belief and spreads the conviction
that openness of mind is not inconsistent with religious
devotion. She lets her ideas lie long and ripen in her
mind so that their fruitage of expression is delicate and
diversified. Reprinted in 1866.B20.

20 ____. "George Eliot's Novels." Eclectic Magazine, n.s. 4:
488-495.
Reprint of 1866.B19.

21 [SEDGWICK, A. G.] Review of Felix Holt. North American Review, 103: 557-563.
The plot of Felix Holt cannot be safely disentangled

from the actors who play it. The action is hesitant. She has constantly imitated Dickens. That she should have done so is one of the highest triumphs of Dickens.

22   VENABLES, G. S. Review of Felix Holt. Edinburgh Review, 124 (October), 435-449.
     George Eliot always denotes the intellectual or moral differences of the dullest and most commonplace of mankind by some little idiosyncracy of language or of thought. Felix Holt has some of the defects of ordinary novels, but ordinary novels have none of the merits of Felix Holt. Reprinted in 1866.B23 and 1971.A2.

23   _____. Review of Felix Holt. Littell's Living Age, 91: 432-439.
     Reprint of 1866.B22. Reprinted in 1971.A2.

1868 A BOOKS - NONE

1868 B SHORTER WRITINGS

*1   ANON. Review of The Spanish Gypsy. Saturday Review, July 4.
     Cited in 1969.B23.

*2   ANON. "George Eliot." Tinsley's Magazine, 3: 565-578.
     Cited in 1890.A1.

3   ANON. "George Eliot's Spanish Gypsy." Every Saturday, 6: 1-5.
     Summarizes the poem with lengthy quotes. Closes by saying that this work which gives poetical expression to deep thought will give George Eliot high rank among poets.

*4   ANON. Review of The Spanish Gypsy. British Quarterly Review, 48: 503-534.
     Cited in 1969.B23.

5   ANON. Review of The Spanish Gypsy. Edinburgh Review, 128: 523-538.
     Romola is undoubtedly a finer poem than the Spanish Gypsy. The very abundance of the reflective faculties is against George Eliot's poetical success. "The bark of song is over-freighted with thought." The reviewer tells the story and quotes long passages from the poem; he says that the circumstances are so strange and the situations so violent that they suggest melodrama. The characters are representative passions.

1868

*6   ANON. Review of The Spanish Gypsy. London Quarterly Review,
       31: 160-188.
          Cited in 1969.B23.

*7   ANON. Review of The Spanish Gypsy. St. James Magazine, n.s.
       1: 476-486.
          Cited in 1969.B23.

*8   ANON. Review of The Spanish Gypsy. St. Paul's Magazine, n.s.
       2: 583-592.
          Cited in 1969.B23.

*9   ANON. Review of The Spanish Gypsy. Westminster Review, n.s.
       34: 183-192.
          Cited in 1890.A1.

10   BROWNE, MATTHEW [W. B. RANDS]. "George Eliot As a Poet."
       Contemporary Review, 8: 387-396.
          Her versification often lacks spontaneity and simplicity.
       The reader is set to thinking and feeling; he is agitated
       but not thrilled by any sudden notes. Reprinted in
       1868.B11 and in Volume 17 of the Cabinet Edition of the
       Complete Works. See 1868.B19, 1868.B20.

11   _____. "George Eliot As a Poet." Every Saturday, 6: 79.
          Reprint of 1868.B10. See 1868.B19, 1868.B20.

*12 BROWNE, W. H. Review of The Spanish Gypsy. Southern Review,
       n.s. 6: 383.
          Cited in 1883.A2.

13   [HAMELY, E. B.] "George Eliot's Spanish Gypsy." Blackwood's
       Magazine, 103 (June), 760-771.
          Quotes extensively from the poem and concludes that those
       who read even these specimens will share the conviction
       that the author who holds so lofty a place among novelists
       will take high rank among poets. It is emphatically a
       great poem, in conception and execution.

14   HOWELLS, W. D. Review of The Spanish Gypsy. Atlantic Month-
       ly, 22: 380-384.
          George Eliot betrays her unfamiliarity with the mere
       letter as well as the spirit of poetic art. He gives a
       summary of the poem pointing out various fine effects which
       it does have.

*15 JAMES, HENRY. Review of The Spanish Gypsy. Nation (New
       York), 7 (July 2), 12-14.
          Cited in 1969.B23.

16 ____. "The Spanish Gypsy." North American Review, 107 (October), 620-635.
On first reading the most striking quality is the poem's extraordinary rhetorical energy and elegance. She makes the heroine's predicament a problem in morals. "Its great fault is simply that it is not a genuine poem." Reprinted in 1965.A2.

17 [MORLEY, J.] "The Spanish Gypsy." Macmillan's Magazine, 18 (July), 281-287.
The Spanish Gypsy will be loved not by the crowd but by a select few. George Eliot is most deeply impressive when she brings forth from her treasures the fruits of prolonged moods of brooding and religious meditativeness. Reprinted in 1868.B18.

18 ____. "The Spanish Gypsy." Eclectic Magazine, n.s. 8: 1276-1282.
Reprint of 1868.B17.

19 [RANDS, W. B.] Matthew Browne. "George Eliot As a Poet." Contemporary Review, 8: 387-396. See 1868.B10, 1868.B11, 1868.B20.

20 ____. "George Eliot As a Poet." Every Saturday, 6: 79. See 1868.B10, 1868.B11, 1868.B19.

*21 SKELTON, J. Review of The Spanish Gypsy. Fraser's Magazine, 78 (October), 468-479.
Cited in 1969.B23.

1869 A BOOKS - NONE

1869 B SHORTER WRITINGS

1 McCARTHY, JUSTIN. "'George Eliot' and George Lewes." Galaxy, 7: 801-809.
There seems to be less admiration for George Eliot in New York than in London. Goes on to praise her as the greatest living novelist. Outlines her acquaintance with Lewes and some of his works. Reprinted in 1872.B27.

1870 A BOOKS

1 PATTISON, MARK. Memoirs. Fontwell: Centaur Press.
This facsimile of the original contains the memoirs of a scholar who has been said to be the original of Casaubon.

1870

1870 B SHORTER WRITINGS

*1   ÉTIENNE, LOUIS. Review of The Spanish Gypsy. Revue des Deux
        Mondes, 90: 429-446.
        Cited in 1890.A1.

*2   SCHMIDT, JULIAN. Bilder aus dem Geistigen Leben unserer Zeit.
        4 Bde. Leipzig, 1870-1875. "George Eliot," 1: 344-409.
        Cited in 1890.A1.

1871 A BOOKS - NONE

1871 B SHORTER WRITINGS

 1   ANON. Review of Middlemarch. The Daily News, November 28.
        George Eliot treats Miss Brooke with sly and yet half-
        sympathetic sarcasm. Reprinted in 1966.A5.

 2   ANON. Review of Middlemarch. Athenaeum, December 2, pp. 713-
        714.
           The promise of the greatness of the novel is clear and
        unmistakable. The prose flows smoothly and is polished
        like steel. In the characters she uses a subtle power of
        analysis to trace the windings of a dull common conscience.
        With a few sharp touches she strips a soul and reveals its
        vices and virtues in vivid detail.

*3   ANON. Review of Middlemarch. Examiner, December 2.
        Cited in 1969.B23.

*4   HUTTON, R. H. Essays, Theological and Literary, 2 vols. Lon-
        don: Macmillan and Company. "George Eliot," 2: 294-367.
        Cited in 1969.B23.

 5   [HUTTON, R. H.] "George Eliot's Middlemarch." Spectator, 44
        (December 16), 1528-1529.
           This review of the "mere commencement" of the novel is
        tentative and provisional. The reviewer comments on the
        various characters and commends George Eliot's great charm
        in portraying human weaknesses with friendly sarcasm. Re-
        printed in 1971.A2.

1872 A BOOKS - NONE

1872 B SHORTER WRITINGS

1   ANON. Review of Middlemarch. Athenaeum, February 3, pp. 137-
     138.
          The minor characters of Middlemarch have all of George
     Eliot's own subtle humor. Each character is stereoscopic
     in its distinctness.

*2   ANON. Review of Middlemarch. Examiner, February 3.
          Cited in 1969.B23.

3   ANON. Review of Middlemarch. Athenaeum, March 30, p. 393.
          Through the third installment the novel is a thoughtful
     anatomy of English habits and modes of thought and is full
     of dry, quiet humor.

*4   ANON. Review of Middlemarch. Examiner, March 30.
          Cited in 1969.B23.

5   ANON. Review of Middlemarch. Athenaeum, June 1, p. 681.
          Even though this novel is not "falling off" by the end of
     the fourth installment, it is clear that the mode of pub-
     lication is injudicious. The beauty of the characters is
     revealed in short, distinct scenes.

*6   ANON. Review of Middlemarch. Examiner, June 8.
          Cited in 1969.B23.

7   ANON. Review of Middlemarch. The Daily Telegraph, June 18.
     George Eliot fails to meet the needs of present-day
     readers. The novels should be more lively and exciting.
     She reveals the very thoughts and souls of her characters.
     Reprinted in 1966.A5.

8   ANON. Review of Middlemarch. Athenaeum, July 27, p. 112.
          The plot seriously thickens and incident hurries on in-
     cident; yet happy turns of thought and language are as
     frequent as ever.

*9   ANON. Review of Middlemarch. Examiner, July 27.
          Cited in 1969.B23.

*10 ANON. Review of Middlemarch. Examiner, October 5.
          Cited in 1969.B23.

11   ANON. Review of Middlemarch. The Standard, December 4.
          How George Eliot could represent a man like Lydgate as a
     hero is incomprehensible. He suffers from scandal and mis-
     fortune. Reprinted in 1966.A5.

1872

12 ANON. Review of <u>Middlemarch</u>. <u>Athenaeum</u>, December 7, pp. 725-726.
    After the final volume the reviewer feels that some readers may prefer <u>Romola</u>. All of <u>Middlemarch</u> is tinged with melancholy. The whole is almost too labored. Her power of laying bare the whole anatomy of a soul with a few words is remarkable.

13 ANON. Review of <u>Middlemarch</u>. <u>Examiner</u>, December 7.
    Thinks Ladislaw is almost as bad a husband as Casaubon and wishes Dorothea could have had Lydgate. Reprinted in 1966.A5.

14 ANON. Review of <u>Middlemarch</u>. <u>Saturday Review</u>, 34 (December 7), 733-734.
    Neither talent nor genius can overcome the defect of a conspicuous, constantly prominent lesson. The book is like a portrait gallery. Yet there is too little of that hope which is an essential to the cheerful portraiture of humanity. The religion of the novel is all duty. Reprinted in 1966.A5 and 1971.A2.

15 ANON. Review of <u>Middlemarch</u>. <u>The Saturday Review</u>, December 21.
    For George Eliot the nursery of the ideal woman consists of dignified and distinguished surroundings, which she renounces because all cannot share them. Reprinted in 1966.A5.

16 [COLLINS, W. L.] Review of <u>Middlemarch</u>. <u>Blackwood's Magazine</u>, 112 (December), 727-745.
    Analyzes individual characters and observes that in this, as in all the author's previous works, there is an embarrassing abundance of tempting morsels for extract. Reprinted in 1872.B17, 1872.B18, and 1966.A5.

17 _____. Review of <u>Middlemarch</u>. <u>Eclectic Magazine</u>, n.s. 17: 215-228.
    Reprint of 1872.B16. Reprinted in 1872.B18 and 1966.A5.

18 _____. Review of <u>Middlemarch</u>. <u>Littell's Living Age</u>, 116: 131-145.
    Reprint of 1872.B16. Reprinted in 1872.B17 and 1966.A5.

19 DOWDEN, EDWARD. "George Eliot." <u>Contemporary Review</u>, 20 (August), 403-422.
    The moral significance of George Eliot's novels coalesces with the narrative and lives through the characters. Each

act and each sorrow are dignified and made important by the consciousness of that larger life of which they form a part. The casting away of self becomes a martyrdom for Maggie, Romola, Fedalma, and Armgart. Particular attention is given to Daniel Deronda. Her novels are not didactic treatises; they are works of art. The poems are conspicuously inferior to the novels. Reprinted in 1872.B20, 1872.B21, 1878.B3, 1965.A2, 1966.A5, and 1971.A2.

20   _____. "George Eliot." Littell's Living Age, 115: 100–110.
         Reprint of 1872.B19. Reprinted in 1872.B21, 1878.B3, 1965.A2, 1966.A5, and 1971.A2.

21   _____. "George Eliot." Eclectic Magazine, n.s. 16: 562–573.
         Reprint of 1872.B19. Reprinted in 1872.B20, 1878.B3, 1965.A2, 1966.A5, and 1971.A2.

22   [HUTTON, R. H.] "Middlemarch. Part II." Spectator, 45 (February 3), 147–148.
         The novel is full of noble though too often melancholy sentiment. Dorothea's terror and dread for a husband who has no place in his nature for tenderer sentiments are clearly delineated. Some of the best of the characters from the first section do not appear at all. Reprinted in 1971.A2.

23   _____. "Middlemarch. Part III." Spectator, 45 (March 30), 404–406.
         The novel improves in interest as it goes. This section adds most to the development of Mary Garth, who promises to be one of the author's best characters. The whole tale remains tolerably even and placid, though morbidly intellectual. Reprinted in 1971.A2.

24   _____. "The Melancholy of Middlemarch." Spectator, 45 (June 1), 685–687.
         George Eliot never makes the world worse than it is, but she makes it a shade darker; in this novel she throws cold water on any idealism not based on sympathy and sight. The most spiritual characters appear to be the least happy. Reprinted in 1966.A5 and 1971.A2.

25   _____. "George Eliot's Moral Anatomy." Spectator, 45 (October 5), 1262–1264.
         George Eliot has a speculative philosophy of character that always runs in a parallel stream with her picture of character. The characters are so real they have a life and body of their own quite distinct from her criticisms of

1872

them; however, the power of theoretic moral anatomy adds greatly to the depth and charm of the drawing. Reprinted in 1971.A2.

26   [HUTTON, R. H.] "Middlemarch." Spectator, 45 (December 7), 1554-1556.
       The wealth of the secondary life or provincial life adds greatly to the effect of the well-drawn major characters. The whole tone of the story is thoroughly noble, both morally and intellectually; yet the focus of all light and beauty appears to be dark and cold. Reprinted in 1971.A2.

27   McCARTHY, JUSTIN. "'George Eliot' and George Lewes." Modern Leaders, 8 vol. New York.
       Reprint of 1869.B1. Cited in 1890.A1.

1873 A BOOKS - NONE

1873 B SHORTER WRITINGS

*1   ANON. Review of Middlemarch. Canadian Monthly, 3: 549-552.
       Cited in 1890.A1.

 2   ANON. Review of Middlemarch. London Quarterly Review, 40: 99-110, 178-195.
       Dorothea's spiritual and physical beings are in complete unison. The two qualities which mark George Eliot as a prominent representative of English literature are her realism and her dignity. Her most serious defect is a want of enthusiasm.

*3   BENTZON, TH. Review of Middlemarch. Revue des Deux Mondes, 103: 667-690
       Cited in 1890.A1.

 4   BROOME, FREDERICK NAPIER. Review of Middlemarch. The Times, March 7.
       The reader of Middlemarch is impressed, and perhaps depressed, by its cruel likeness to life. Reprinted in 1966.A5.

*5   BROWNE, W. H. Review of Middlemarch. Southern Monthly, 12: 373.
       Cited in 1883.A2.

 6   COLVIN, SIDNEY. Review of Middlemarch. Fortnightly Review, 19 (January 19), 142-148.

George Eliot has the perpetual application of her own intelligence to the broad problems and conclusions of modern thought. And she possesses a sympathetic insight into the workings of human nature. She also uses her knowledge of science and physiology to illustrate the spiritual progress of her characters. She handles skillfully the physical looks and gestures of her characters and excels in all that pertains to the passions of the individual. Reprinted in 1966.A5 and 1971.A2.

7   [DICEY, A. V.] "Middlemarch." Nation, 16 (January 23), 60-62.
The parts of the novel are much more striking than the whole. Will is the least satisfactory character in the book. The book is an effort in a bad as well as in the good sense of the word. The brilliancy of the epigrams and the power of analysis leave in the mind a sense of strain. Reprinted in 1971.A2.

8   ____. "Middlemarch." Nation, 16 (January 30), 76-77.
The defect of the book is that the parts are more striking than the whole. She aimed at two different objects. She gives a successful picture of existence in an English country town, but the form of the story makes it impossible for the reader to center his interest on any one character. Reprinted in 1971.A2.

9   HERRICK, MRS. S. B. "The Genius of George Eliot." Southern Review, n.s. 13: 205-235.
George Eliot truly possesses an intellect which is so far above ordinary womanhood as to include the strength and grasp, the critical acumen of a man. Yet she has the tenderness and purity of a woman. The morality in her books is so pure and high it is obviously the morality of the Bible. The chief artistic merit of Middlemarch is its unity.

10 [HOUGHTON, LORD.] Review of Middlemarch. Edinburgh Review, 137: 246-263.
There seems to be an abundance of aphorism, a weight of wit, which may become burdensome to the ordinary reader. Yet in Middlemarch another volume is added to the noble series of British works of fiction which is at once acceptable to girls and men. Reprinted in 1966.A5.

11 [HUTTON, R. H.] Review of Middlemarch. British Quarterly Review, 57: 407-429.
The book is a little tame in plot with melancholy as its essence. Noble natures struggle hard against a poor kind

of world. Yet it is clear that even during that low ebb of trust in the supernatural element of religion, there was no want of ardent belief in the spiritual obligations of purity and self-sacrifice.

12 [JAMES, HENRY.] Review of Middlemarch. Galaxy, 15 (March), 424-428.
    Middlemarch is a treasure-house of details, but it is an indifferent whole. The dramatic current stagnates as the elaborate solemnity with which Dorothea's struggle is depicted becomes almost ludicrously excessive. Ladislaw is a failure; he remains vague and impalpable to the end. Rosamond is a rare psychological study, and Bulstrode's comely wife is the happiest reality. Reprinted in 1953.B8, 1957.B16, 1965.A2, 1966.A5, and 1971.A2.

13 [LAING, R.] Review of Middlemarch. Quarterly Review, 134: 336-369.
    George Eliot condemns alike license and lassitude. She counsels resignation when she cannot impart peace. The reviewer looks back at her life and other works. He finds Middlemarch lacking in enthusiasm and exuberance.

14 [LAWRENNY, H.] EDITH SIMCOX. "Middlemarch." Academy, 4 (January), 1-4.
    See 1873.B18. Reprinted in 1965.A2, 1966.A5, and 1971.A2.

15 [McCARTHY, J.] "The Story of Two Worlds." Catholic World, 17 (September), 775-792.
    George Eliot takes the community of Middlemarch up as a scientist would take a basin of water from the sea to examine it, not for the sake of that sample only, but with a view to the whole. Christianity has practically gone from her world; only the sham and cant of it remain. This is a comparison between George Eliot and Fleurange.

16 [PERRY, T. S.] Review of Middlemarch. North American Review, 116: 432-440.
    George Eliot aimed to tell the story of certain aspects of life and to show certain sorts of human lives which bear within them the elements of tragedy from the incongruity between their aspirations and the possibility of attaining them under the conditions imposed on them by their surroundings. He wonders if a reader not familiar with the modes of life she portrays can appreciate the wonderful accuracy of the picture.

17   SEDGWICK, A. G. Review of <u>Middlemarch</u>. <u>Atlantic Monthly</u>, 31 (April), 490-494.
        George Eliot's idea of fate is the compounded destiny of natural laws, character, and accident. Man is a part of nature. This fate assumes a moral color that is sad, ironical, and undogmatically didactic.

18   SIMCOX, EDITH [H. LAWRENNY]. "<u>Middlemarch</u>." <u>Academy</u>, 4 (January), 1-4.
        The material circumstances of the outer world are made subordinate and accessory to the artistic presentation of a definite passage of mental experience; it is a profoundly imaginative psychological study. Reprinted in 1965.A2, 1966.A5, and 1971.A2. <u>See</u> 1873.B14.

*19   SMITH, GEORGE B. Review of <u>Middlemarch</u>. <u>St. Paul's Magazine</u>, 12: 592-616.
        Cited in 1969.B23.

*20   SPAULDING, H. G. Review of <u>Middlemarch</u>. <u>Old and New</u>, 7: 352-356.
        Cited in 1883.A2.

1874 A BOOKS - NONE

1874 B SHORTER WRITINGS

*1   ANON. Review of <u>The Legend of Jubal and Other Poems</u>. <u>Saturday Review</u>, 37 (June 13), 75.
        Cited in 1969.B23.

2   ANON. "Two Cities: Two Books." <u>Blackwood's Magazine</u>, 116 (July), 72-91.
        Consuelo, George Sand's simple-hearted singer, is to Venice what Romola is to Florence. Consuelo belongs to the opinions of the past. Romola is a better representative of her city. Even though Consuelo is more conventional, she is more charming and interesting as a person.

3   HOWELLS, W. D. Review of Poems. <u>Atlantic Monthly</u>, 34 (July), 102-104.
        Discusses several of the poems that appear in the 1874 volume, <u>The Legend of Jubal and Other Poems</u>. He has no doubt but that they give the worthiest proof to date of the author's right to make verse. But there is not much hope that they will be treated with exacter justice than her former poetic attempts. Her great fame as a novelist stands between her and the critic.

1874

4   JAMES, HENRY. "George Eliot's The Legend of Jubal." North
American Review, 119 (October), 484-489.
    James finds it necessary to see her poetry and novels as
all of one piece. "The author's verses," he says, "are a
narrow manifestation of her genius, but they are an unmis-
takable manifestation." They are characteristic products
of the same intellect. He discusses individual poems. Reprinted in 1965.A2.

5   LATHROP, GEORGE P. "The Growth of The Novel." Atlantic
Monthly, 33 (June), 684.
    Discusses George Eliot in a survey of the history of the
novel. She presides too watchfully over the progress of
the reader and keeps before him always the stern effort she
is making not to swerve from strict analysis.

*6   [MINTO, W.] Review of The Legend of Jubal and Other Poems.
Examiner, May 16.
    Cited in 1969.B23.

*7   [SIMCOX, G. A.] Review of The Legend of Jubal and Other Poems.
Academy, 5 (May), 33.
    Cited in 1969.B23.

*8   SPIELHAGEN, FREIDRICH. Review of Middlemarch. Die Gegenwart,
Nos. 10-12.
    Cited in 1883.A2.

9   WILKINSON, W. C. "The Literary and Ethical Quality of the
Novels of George Eliot." Scribner's Monthly, 8: 685-703.
    George Eliot is more than simply a great writer. She is
a prime elemental literary power. He discusses each novel
suggesting that she believes what she teaches with her
head; yet her heart demurs and rebels. Reprinted in
1874.B10.

10   _____. "The Literary and Ethical Quality of the Novels of
George Eliot, "in A Free Lance in the Field of Life and Letters.
    Reprint of 1874.B9.

1875 A BOOKS - NONE

1875 B SHORTER WRITINGS

1   CARPENTER, J. E. "Religious Influences in Current Literature:
George Eliot." Unitarian Review, 3: 357-373.

More than any other writer of fiction she has clearly
discerned what a part is played in life by the spiritual
forces which lie beneath its surface and mold and direct
its individual growth. She stands apart from any of the
existing organizations of religion.

*2   FIELD, MRS. HENRY M. "The Author of Adam Bede in Her Own
      Home." Home Sketches in France and Other Papers. New York:
      G. P. Putnam's Sons, p. 208.
          Cited in 1883.A2.

*3   HATTON, JOSHUA [GUY ROSLYN]. "George Eliot." London Society,
      27: 311-319, 439; 28: 20-27.
          Cited in 1969.B23. Reprinted in 1876.A1. See 1875.B5.

*4   MacCRIE, GEORGE. The Religion of Our Literature. Essays
      Upon Thomas Carlyle, Robert Browning, Alfred Tennyson; In-
      cluding Criticisms Upon the Theology of George Eliot. Lon-
      don.
          Cited in 1890.A1.

*5   [ROSLYN, GUY] JOSHUA HATTON. "George Eliot." London Society,
      27: 311-319, 439; 28: 20-27.
          Cited in 1969.B23. Reprinted in 1876.A1. See 1875.B3.

1876 A BOOKS

*1   HATTON, JOSHUA [GUY ROSLYN]. George Eliot in Derbyshire: A
      Volume of Gossip About Passages and People in the Novels of
      George Eliot. Alterations, Additions, and Introduction by
      George Barnett Smith. London: Ward, Lock, and Tyler.
          Cited in 1969.B23. Contains a reprint of 1875.B3. See
      1876.A2.

*2   [ROSLYN, GUY] JOSHUA HATTON. George Eliot in Derbyshire: A
      Volume of Gossip About Passages and People in the Novels of
      George Eliot. Alterations, Additions, and Introduction by
      George Barnett Smith. London: Ward, Lock, and Tyler.
          Cited in 1969.B23. Contains a reprint of 1875.B3. See
      1876.A1.

1876 B SHORTER WRITINGS

1   ANON. Review of Daniel Deronda. Athenaeum, January 29, p.
      160.
          The reviewer finds the first section unsatisfying. There

is no hint of what the rest of the story will be, and there
are no individual passages which may be presented as attractive gems.

2   ANON. Review of Daniel Deronda. Examiner, January 29.
        Gwendolen is more like one of Ben Jonson's "humorous"
than a real human being. George Eliot always grasps the
individuality of her characters, but she fails to invest
them with the attributes of common humanity. Reprinted in
1966.A5.

3   ANON. "Daniel Deronda." Academy, 9 (February 5), 120.
        Written after the appearance of the first number, this
review finds Gwendolen already cast for the role of demon.
But Deronda's role is not as clear; there does seem to be
something hopefully unpredictable about his returning Gwendolen's necklace. Reprinted in 1966.A5 and 1971.A2.

4   ANON. Review of Daniel Deronda. Athenaeum, March 4, p. 327.
        The second part of the novel is better than the first
and contains one scene almost worthy of the author. Deronda's drifting down the river is described in a passage of
great beauty.

*5   ANON. Review of Daniel Deronda. Examiner, March 4.
        Cited in 1969.B23.

*6   ANON. Review of Daniel Deronda. Examiner, April 1.
        Cited in 1969.B23.

7   ANON. Review of Daniel Deronda. Athenaeum, April 24, p. 461.
        In the third book Deronda has not yet become the chief
character. The same pedantry and clumsiness remain; yet
Gwendolen's character is strengthened and begins to have a
certain interest.

8   ANON. Review of Daniel Deronda. Athenaeum, April 29, pp.
593-594.
        The fourth part of the novel is full of interest; how-
ever, the plan of publication in parts again spoils the
effectiveness of the story.

9   ANON. Review of Daniel Deronda. Athenaeum, June 3, p. 762.
        There is no "action" in the fifth book but much develop-
ment of character, and it is again divided into two parts
which have little or no connection with each other.

*10   ANON. Review of Daniel Deronda. Examiner, June 3.
        Cited in 1969.B23.

11   ANON. Review of <u>Daniel Deronda</u>. <u>Athenaeum</u>, July 1, p. 14.
     The Jewish scenes in the sixth book are completely want-
     ing in interest, but the admiration Gwendolen has for
     Deronda arouses a more marked interest in the "story."

12   ANON. Review of <u>Daniel Deronda</u>. <u>Athenaeum</u>, July 29, p. 143.
     The novel has been a magnificent financial success, but
     Book VIII can never redeem it from literary failure.

*13 ANON. Review of <u>Daniel Deronda</u>. <u>Examiner</u>, August 5.
     Cited in 1969.B23.

14   ANON. Review of <u>Daniel Deronda</u>. <u>Athenaeum</u>, September 2, p.
     303.
     By the last book the reviewer feels that George Eliot was
     as tired of the story as her readers. The whole novel he
     calls the least good and the least interesting of her works.

15   ANON. Review of <u>Daniel Deronda</u>. <u>Examiner</u>, September 2.
     Gwendolen's state at the end of the novel is appropriate.
     If she were poor or in physical misery, the reader would
     not have the same assurance of the reality of her moral
     regeneration. Reprinted in 1966.A5.

16   ANON. Review of <u>Daniel Deronda</u>. <u>Saturday Review</u>, 42 (Septem-
     ber 16), 356-358.
     The reader finds an utter want of sympathy with George
     Eliot's motive and the leading idea of the story. He feels
     perpetually called away from the action of the persons in
     the drama to investigate the theme. It seems to be a re-
     ligious novel without a religion. Reprinted in 1966.A5 and
     1971.B2.

17   ANON. Review of <u>Daniel Deronda</u>. <u>Saturday Review</u>, 42 (Septem-
     ber 23).
     Gwendolen has a root of conscience in her, but it has
     never been aroused until Deronda's eye is resting on her.
     Reprinted in 1966.A5.

18   ANON. Review of <u>Daniel Deronda</u>. <u>The Jewish Chronicle</u>, Decem-
     ber 15.
     George Eliot gauges the religious depth of the Jew's ho-
     liest feelings. The old prophetic and Messianic strains
     are heard. Reprinted in 1966.A5.

*19 ANON. "George Eliot and George Sand." <u>Saturday Review</u>, 42:
     561-562.
     Cited in 1890.A1. Reprinted in 1877.B5.

20   ANON. Review of Daniel Deronda. British Quarterly Review,
        44: 224-234.
            The prominent characters in Daniel Deronda are so full of
        meaning that they perhaps render the by-play of incident or
        humor less fully than most of George Eliot's novels. The
        reader will find a moral lesson of the highest nature. Re-
        printed in 1876.B22.

*21   ANON. Review of Daniel Deronda. Canadian Monthly, 9: 250-
        251, 343-344; 10: 362-364.
            Cited in 1883.A2.

22   ANON. Review of Daniel Deronda. Eclectic Magazine, 87: 657-
        667.
            Reprint of 1876.B20.

23   ANON. Review of Daniel Deronda. Edinburgh Review, 144: 442-
        470.
            Anyone who ventures to express disapproval of George Eli-
        ot's works requires a large amount of sincere stupidity or
        confidence. This reviewer expresses his disappointment in
        Daniel Deronda. Man seems to have become for her a crea-
        ture to be analyzed rather than a being made primarily for
        life.

*24   CLARKE, E. "The Clergy As Drawn By George Eliot." Charing
        Cross, n.s. 4: 293-304.
            Cited in 1890.A1.

25   [COLVIN, SIDNEY.] Review of Daniel Deronda. Fortnightly Re-
        view, 26 (November 1), 601-616.
            George Eliot's religious and moral ardor influences all
        that she writes. She has a stern sense of the conse-
        quences and responsibilities of human action. She is
        severe with her characters and in sympathy with the in-
        exorable. Daniel himself seems constructed rather than
        created. Reprinted in 1966.A5.

*26   DE PRIEUX, G. "George Eliot." Le Correspondant, 104: 672-
        683.
            Cited in 1890.A1.

27   DICEY, A. V. "Daniel Deronda." Nation, 23 (October 19), 230-
        231, 245-246.
            The superfluous moralizing in the novel becomes painful.
        She over-analyzes in the vivisection of Deronda's physical
        and moral qualities. But when dealing with the minor
        characters, George Eliot becomes carried away by the stress

of the drama and falls back on artistic instinct and paints with a bold hand. Reprinted in 1971.A2.

28   FRANCILLON, R. E. Review of Daniel Deronda. Gentleman's Magazine, 17 (October), 410-427.
     Daniel Deronda is a romance and is not to be compared with her other novels. Romance is the form of fiction which grapples with fact upon its whole ground and deals with the more occult wisdom. Deronda is a nineteenth century knight errant. Reprinted in 1971.A2.

29   [HUTTON, R. H.] "Armgart." The Spectator, February 12.
     In "Armgart" there is all the Miltonic tone of feeling applied to measure the standard of a woman's ambition and devotion. George Eliot always indulges more neutrality of feeling in relation to men than she does in relation to women. Her men lack earnestness. Reprinted in 1966.A5.

30   _____. Review of Daniel Deronda. The Spectator, April 8.
     Herr Klesmer is a remarkable character. His conception of art as a great calling and Gwendolen's conception of art as a mode of gaining admiration and gaining a living present a double contrast. Reprinted in 1966.A5.

31   _____. "The Hero of Daniel Deronda." The Spectator, June 10.
     The character Daniel Deronda seems to be something of a problem to the author herself. His moral grandeur is based on his desire to lavish sympathy on others; yet about him there remains a noble vagueness and wax-like tentativeness. Reprinted in 1966.A5.

32   _____. "The Strong Side of Daniel Deronda." The Spectator, July 29.
     In this novel George Eliot has presented a faith in the larger purpose which molds men into something higher than anything into which they could mold themselves. Reprinted in 1966.A5.

33   HUTTON, RICHARD HOLT. "Daniel Deronda." The Spectator, 49 (September), 1131-1133.
     Compared to Middlemarch, the novel's "summits are higher, but its average level of power is very much lower." No book of hers has contained so many fine characters and betrayed so subtle an insight into the modes of growth of a better moral life within the shrivelling buds and blossoms of the selfish life which has been put off and condemned. Reprinted in 1965.A2 and 1971.A2.

1876

34   JAMES, HENRY. "Daniel Deronda: A Conversation." Atlantic
      Monthly, 38: 684-694.
           Constantius, Theodora, and Pulcheria carry on a conversa-
      tion about the strengths and weaknesses of the novel.
      Deronda.is described as "a lay father-confessor," and Gwen-
      dolen is said to be too light and too flimsy to be tragic.
      Constantius concludes, "I think there is little art in
      Deronda, but I think there is a vast amount of life." Re-
      printed in 1888.B6, 1960.A7, 1965.A2, 1970.A4, and 1971.A2.

35   _____. "Daniel Deronda." Nation, 22 (February 24), 131.
           Welcomes the novel after the first installment. Finds
      the "sense of the universal" constant, omnipresent, perhaps
      even conscious and overcultivated. Reprinted in 1965.A2
      and 1971.A2.

*36   LANCASTER, HENRY HILL. "George Eliot's Novels." Essays and
      Reviews. Edinburgh, pp. 351-398.
           Cited in 1969.B23. Reprint of 1866.B17.

37   PICCIOTTO, JAMES. Review of Daniel Deronda. Gentleman's Mag-
      azine, 17 (November), 593-603.
           To make a Jew the hero of a story was contrary to the
      canons of fiction. There is a far greater purpose in Dan-
      iel Deronda than the tale of a woman's life and the devel-
      opment of her soul. It is the vindication of a long mal-
      igned race against ignorant misrepresentation or willful
      aspersion, the defense of Jews and Judaism against fanati-
      cism and prejudice. Reprinted in 1971.A2.

*38   RICHARDSON, A. S. Review of Daniel Deronda. Victoria, 28:
      227-231.
           Cited in 1890.A1.

39   SAINTSBURY, GEORGE. Review of Daniel Deronda. Academy, 10
      (September 9), 253-254.
           Points out the strengths of Gwendolen's characterization
      and the weaknesses of the portrayal of the Jews. He con-
      cludes that the characters are designed to illustrate doc-
      trine and that no perfect novel can be designed to illus-
      trate a theory, moral or immoral. Reprinted in 1971.A2.

*40   SPENCE, MISS C. H. "George Eliot." Melbourne Review, April,
      pp. 141-163.
           Cited in 1890.A1.

1877 A BOOKS

1 SOLOMON, HENRY. Daniel Deronda from a Jewish Point of View.
     London.
          Cited in 1890.A1.

1877 B SHORTER WRITINGS

1 ANON. "Deronda's Mother." Temple Bar, 49: 542-545.
          Finds a prototype for Deronda's mother, Leonora, Princess
     of Halm-Eberstein, in Mrs. Disraeli, mother of Benjamin
     Disraeli. Reprinted in 1877.B2 and 1877.B3.

2 ANON. "Deronda's Mother." Eclectic Magazine, 78: 751-753.
          Reprint of 1877.B1. Reprinted in 1877.B3.

3 ANON. "Deronda's Mother." Living Age, 133: 248-250.
          Reprint of 1877.B1. Reprinted in 1877.B2.

*4 ANON. "George Eliot and Comtism." London Quarterly Review,
     94: 446-471.
          Cited in 1969.B23.

*5 ANON. "George Eliot and George Sand." Eclectic Magazine,
     n.s. 25: 111-114.
          Reprint of 1876.B19.

6 ANON. Review of Daniel Deronda. Church Quarterly Review, 5:
     91-119.
          The morals of Daniel Deronda are suspect. The author
     professes a severe morality, but her morals are not Chris-
     tian. Human and divine love are confused. There is not a
     single character actuated by religion as a motive.

7 BOWKER, R. R. Review of Daniel Deronda. International Re-
     view, 4 (January), 68-76.
          George Eliot is always dealing with the most profound of
     practical religious questions. Her vocabulary is too dif-
     ficult for the general reader. Deronda is a Messianic man;
     he is strong with man's strength and tender with the ten-
     derness of woman. He touches no life that he does not
     lighten and inspire. Reprinted in 1971.A2.

8 DOWDEN, EDWARD. "Middlemarch and Daniel Deronda." Contem-
     porary Review, 29 (February), 348-369.
          In Daniel Deronda the poetical or ideal element is de-
     cidedly preponderant. The entire work possesses an air of

spiritual prescience. As a chosen and anointed priest, Deronda finds a higher, religious life that transcends self. Reprinted in 1878.B3, 1965.A2, and 1971.A2.

9   HEYWOOD, JOSEPH CONVERSE. "An Ingenious Moralist: George Eliot." How They Strike Me, These Authors. Philadelphia: J. B. Lippincott and Company, pp. 57-77.
        George Eliot is eminently practical, a teacher of charity and fellow-feeling. She wants us to sympathize with the fictitious so that we will sympathize with the real.

10 JACOBS, JOSEPH. "Mordecai: A Protest Against the Critics." Macmillan's Magazine, 36 (June), 101-111.
        The first thing for a Jew to say about Daniel Deronda is an expression of gratitude for the wonderful completeness and accuracy with which George Eliot has portrayed the Jewish nature. Reprinted in 1877.B11 and 1966.A5.

11 _____. "Mordecai: A Protest Against The Critics." Living Age, 134: 112-121.
        Reprint of 1877.B10. Reprinted in 1966.A5.

*12 KAUFMAN, DAVID. "George Eliot and Judaism: An Attempt to Appreciate Daniel Deronda." Translation of a three-part article in Monatschrift für Geschichte und Wissenschaft. Cited in 1969.B23.

*13 SCHERER, WILHELM. Review of Daniel Deronda. Deutsche Rundschau, 10 (February 7), 240-255.
        Cited in 1890.A1.

14 SIKES, WIRT. Review of Daniel Deronda. Appleton's Journal, n.s. 3: 274.
        Gives a long analysis of the derivation of the name Gwendolen.

15 SWINBURNE, ALGERNON CHARLES. A Note on Charlotte Brontë. London: Chatto and Windus, pp. 6-53.
        Charlotte Brontë is a woman of the first order of genius, but George Eliot is of the first order of intellect. Reprinted in 1965.A2 and 1971.A2.

16 WHIPPLE, EDWIN P. Review of Daniel Deronda. North American Review, 124: 31-52.
        Daniel Deronda is a novel of both incident and character; it exhibits a wealth of subtle, deep, and comprehensive thought. George Eliot is not what is technically

styled "a believer," yet she is incomparably skillful in
exhibiting the interior moods of all classes of believers.
She has an equal power of reproducing from the rustic life
of her youth and the gentry and upper middle classes of
provincial England. She has anticipated and answered in
the book itself most of the criticisms which have been made
upon it since its publication. The chief defect in the
story is that it suddenly stops rather than artistically
ends. Reprinted in 1887.B10.

1878 A BOOKS - NONE

1878 B SHORTER WRITINGS

*1   ANON. "George Eliot." Victoria Magazine, 31: 56-60.
        Cited in 1890.A1.

*2   ANON. "The Later Manner of George Eliot." Canadian Monthly,
        11: 261-268.
        Cited in 1890.A1.

3   DOWDEN, EDWARD: "Middlemarch and Daniel Deronda." Studies in
        Literature, 1789-1877. London: Paul.
          Contains reprints of 1872.B19 and 1877.B8.

*4   DU QUESNOY, PIERRE. "The Work of George Eliot." Le Corres-
        pondant, 113: 438-470, 660-682, 826-847.
        Cited in 1890.A1.

5   JAMES, HENRY. "'The Lifted Veil' and 'Brother Jacob.'" Na-
        tion, 26 (April 25), 277.
          "The Lifted Veil" appeared in Blackwood's Magazine in
        1859, and "Brother Jacob" in Cornhill in 1860. The two
        stories are extremely different. "Brother Jacob" is of a
        humorous cast. "The Lifted Veil" is more metaphysical and
        woefully somber. Reprinted in 1965.A2.

*6   SCHERER, EDMOND. "Daniel Deronda." Études Critiques sur la
        Littérature Contemporaine, 10 vols. Paris. 5: 287-304.
        Cited in 1890.A1.

*7   SIMCOX, G. A. Review of Poems. Every Saturday, 16: 667.
        Cited in 1883.A2.

1879 A BOOKS - NONE

1879

1879 B SHORTER WRITINGS

*1 ANON. Review of Impressions of Theophrastus Such. Examiner,
June 7.
Cited in 1969.B23.

2 ANON. Review of Impressions of Theophrastus Such. Nation
(New York), 28 (June 19), 422-423.
In this book George Eliot has dropped the pretense of
story. Theophrastus is a satirical moralist who could wear
out the best-natured of novel-readers and make them wish
she had put her wise saws into an appendix.

3 ANON. "George Eliot's Ideal Ethics." Littell's Living Age,
142 (July 12), 123-125.
The truth and depth of her knowledge of character, the
genuineness of her love for what is pure and what is noble,
the breadth of her charity and the earnestness of her in-
dignation against all that is either cruel or mean or soft-
ly selfish and insincere, would put to shame too many
Christian moralists. The defect of her positivist morality
is that it tries to deduce morality from the principle of
human co-operation not from the relation of the soul to
God. Reprint of 1879.B6.

*4 ANON. Review of Impressions of Theophrastus Such. Fraser's
Magazine, 100 (July), 103-124.
Cited in 1969.B23.

5 ANON. Review of Impressions of Theophrastus Such. Westminster Review, 112 (July), 185-196.
Treats Theophrastus as a character who has dipped his pen
into rather bitter ink to make "pleasant fooling" for the
reader's meager smiles out of his friends and acquaintances
who do not come up to his standard of intellectual or moral
perfection.

6 ANON. "George Eliot's Ideal Ethics." Spectator, 52: 751.
Reprinted in 1879.B3.

7 ANON. Review of Impressions of Theophrastus Such. British
Quarterly Review, 70: 126-127, 240-242.
The book divides itself into two sections. The first is
truly dramatic and significant of human nature. The other
is purely analytical or scientific. The portions of the
book which are most spontaneous and most congenial to the
reader are precisely those in which there is no effort
after intellectual distinction.

*8   ANON. Review of Impressions of Theophrastus Such. Canadian
      Monthly, 16: 333-335.
         Cited in 1890.A1.

9   [ALLEN, GRANT.] Review of Impressions of Theophrastus Such.
      Fortnightly Review, 32 (July), 144-149.
         In spite of all its admirable writing, it is not probable
      that Theophrastus Such will be popular. To appreciate such
      delicate psychological studies, the reader must himself pos-
      sess at least a sympathy with their analytic mode of treat-
      ment. Many readers will be bewildered and annoyed by the
      fine subtlety of George Eliot's typical dissections and
      will regard the absence of a story a breach of contract
      with the public.

10   BOODLE, R. W. Review of Impressions of Theophrastus Such.
      Unitarian Review, 12: 292-303.
         The tone of all eighteen chapters is practical and con-
      servative. George Eliot takes exception to the established
      scope imposed upon the terms morals and morality. The book
      is tentative and suggestive and does not claim to be in any
      sense a regular system of morals.

11   COURTHOPE, W. J. "The Reflections of English Character in
      English Art." The Quarterly Review, 147 (January), 43-60.
         The novel Daniel Deronda takes the reader into a world
      of mystery, philosophy, emotion, and crime. It has two
      perfectly distinct plots, which scarcely anywhere touch
      each other and never blend. It demonstrates the mistake of
      sacrificing action to analysis and manners to metaphysics.

*12   DOWNS, MRS. ANNIE. "A Visit to George Eliot." The Congrega-
      tionalist, May 28.
         Cited in 1883.A2.

*13   EGGLESTON, E. Review of Impressions of Theophrastus Such.
      North American Review, 129: 510-513.
         Cited in 1969.B23.

*14   MAGUIRE, FRANCIS, JR. "George Eliot." International Review,
      7 (July), 17.
         Cited in 1883.A2.

15   MALLOCK, W. H. Review of Impressions of Theophrastus Such.
      Edinburgh Review, 150 (October), 557-586.
         Points out the ways in which George Eliot has failed as
      a novelist. The composition of her stories is rude and
      faulty. Yet "her eyes are occupied with the high and deep

1879

places of the human spirit, and the larger and profounder
questions of human destiny." Her philosophy has triumphed
over her art. She remains a gloomy pessimist. To many
people her works are like Bibles and are read with reverence to discover truths about life. Yet she is the first
godless writer of fiction to appear in England. Partially
reprinted in 1971.A2.

*16   [SAINTSBURY, G.]   Review of Impressions of Theophrastus Such.
Academy, June.
      Cited in 1969.B23.

17   [SHAND, A. I.]   "Contemporary Literature: Novelists."   Blackwood's Magazine, 125 (March), 335-337.
      Praises George Eliot's sense of truth and her portrayal
of an ideal. She is a living protest against the deteri-
oration of modern literature.

*18   WOODBERRY, G. E.   Review of Impressions of Theophrastus Such.
Nation (New York), 28 (June 19), 422.
      Cited in 1969.B23.

1880 A BOOKS - NONE

1880 B SHORTER WRITINGS

1   ANON.   "Early Life of George Eliot."   Pall Mall Gazette, December 30.
      Gives a review of the facts of George Eliot's life up to
1851 when she began to help Dr. Chapman with the Westminster Review.   Reprinted in 1881.B10.

2   AXON, WILLIAM E. A.   "George Eliot's Use of Dialect."   English
Dialect Society, Miscellanies, no. 4.   London: Trübner and
Company, pp. 37-43.
      Comments on George Eliot's use of dialect to give point
and finish to "the personages of rural life who live and
breathe in her pages."   Reprinted in 1965.A2.

3   BROWNELL, W. C.   "George Eliot."   Nation, 31: 456-457.
      Perhaps George Eliot would have done better to have re-
lied less on a woman's empirical observation of life and
the world and more upon the natural force of an uncommon
genius.

*4   FRANCILLON, ROBERT E.   The Pen.
      Cited in 1883.A2.

*5   MILNER, GEORGE. "George Eliot as Poet." Papers of the Man-
        chester Literary Club, 7 (1880-1881), 108-115.
            Cited in 1883.A2.

6   RUSKIN, JOHN. "Fiction--Fair and Foul." Nineteenth Century,
        7 (June), 941-963.
            Expresses amazement that the catastrophe of The Mill on
        The Floss turns upon the lack of common self-command on the
        part of the young lady and gentleman; this restraint was
        taught to respectable young men and women. Reprinted in
        1971.A2.

*7   SUTTON, CHARLES W. "George Eliot: A Bibliography." Papers
        of the Manchester Literary Club, 7: 97-107.
            Cited in 1967.B31.

8   TAYLOR, BAYARD. "George Eliot." Critical Essays and Literary
        Notes. New York: G. P. Putnam's Sons, pp. 339-347.
            In Daniel Deronda George Eliot has probably reached the
        climax of her popularity. None of her former novels so
        distinctly present the quality of her intellect. The plot
        of the work falls short of absolute proportion; it lacks
        the highest artistic coherence. Yet its charm derives from
        her profound yet delicate psychological insight.

1881 A BOOKS

*1   MORGAN, WILLIAM. George Eliot: A Paper Read Before the
        "Portsmouth Literary and Scientific Society." March 29.
        London: Hamilton and Company.
            Cited in 1890.A1.

1881 B SHORTER WRITINGS

1   ANON. "George Eliot." Athenaeum, January 1, pp. 20-21.
            The Christmas season is darkened by the death of George
        Eliot. Reviews her career from the translations through
        Impressions of Theophrastus Such. She applied herself con-
        sciously to ethical teaching. She has done a great deal
        for the cause of woman by direct teaching, but she has done
        most by giving the world assurance of the possibilities of
        woman's excellence. Reprinted in 1891.B1.

*2   ANON. "George Eliot." The Academy, 19 (January 8), 27.
            Cited in 1883.A2.

1881

*3   ANON. "George Eliot." Fraser's Magazine, 103 (February), 263.
          Cited in 1883.A2.

*4   ANON. "Life in Geneva." Le Livre, April 10.
          Cited in 1883.A2.

*5   ANON. "George Eliot." Modern Review, 2 (April), 399.
          Cited in 1883.A2.

*6   ANON. "George Eliot." East and West, 1 (June), 203.
          Cited in 1883.A2.

7   ANON. "Three Letters to Professor D. Kaufmann." Athenaeum,
          November 26, pp. 703-704.
              In the first two she expresses her gratification at his
          estimates of Daniel Deronda. The letters are signed "M. E.
          Lewes."

8   ANON. "Account of George Eliot's Early Life and of Her Funer-
          al: A Personal Sketch." Eclectic Magazine, March, pp.
          353-361.
              Begins by examining the influence of Herbert Spencer on
          George Eliot's life. The second part describes her funer-
          al; it includes a copy of the funeral oration and a list of
          the mourners who attended. This part is from The London
          Daily News, December 30, 1880. The third section is an es-
          timate of her works from The Spectator.

*9   ANON. "Catholic View of George Eliot." Month, 42: 272-278.
          Cited in 1890.A1.

10   ANON. "Early Life of George Eliot." Littell's Living Age,
          148: 381-383.
              Reprint of 1880.B1.

11   ANON. "George Eliot, with Portrait." The Century, 23: 47-
          48.
              Tells of the portraits which were done of George Eliot.
          The one presented is by Frederick W. Burton. The picture
          was exhibited at the Royal Academy in 1867. It belonged to
          Lewes then to J. W. Cross. M. Paul Rajon produced the
          etching which has often been reproduced. The portrait is
          opposite page 1.

12   ANON. "George Eliot." Church Quarterly Review, 12: 242-267.
              George Eliot dealt with human character and conduct in
          its whole extent. Compares her to Shakespeare and Goethe

and then discusses the individual works. The two main qualities of the works are sympathy and moral force.

*13   ANON. "George Eliot." The Congregationalist, 10: 293-299. Cited in 1890.A1.

14   ANON. "George Eliot." Littell's Living Age, 148: 318-320. George Eliot tries to illustrate the true facts and laws of human nature with ideal feelings. Yet she often mars her finest moral effects by the skeptical atmosphere with which she permeates them.

*15   ANON. "George Eliot." London Quarterly Review, 57: 154-176. Cited in 1969.B23.

16   ALLARDYCE, ALEXANDER. "George Eliot." Blackwood's Magazine, 129 (February), 255-268.
       This is an affectionate tribute to the memory of a brilliant genius. Her deep and Catholic love for humanity in its broadest and best sense was the strongest motive of her genius and will maintain her influence in the future. Traces the main current of her life and thought through the novels. Reprinted in 1881.B17, 1881.B18, and 1966.A5.

17   _____. "George Eliot." Eclectic Magazine, 33: 433-443. Reprint of 1881.B16. Reprinted in 1881.B18 and 1966.A5.

18   _____. "George Eliot." Littell's Living Age, 148: 664-674. Reprint of 1881.B16. Reprinted in 1881.B17 and 1966.A5.

19   BARRY, WILLIAM FRANCIS. "The Genius of George Eliot." Dublin Review, 5: 371-394, 433-464.
       George Eliot's true calling was to distil from the facts of science the true religion of mankind and to frame her own experience into an epic whole. Reprinted in 1909.B1.

*20   BAYNE, PETER. "George Eliot." Literary World, n.s. 23: 25-26, 40-42, 56-58, 72-74, 89-91, 104-106, 120-122, 136-138, 152-154, 168-170, 184-186, 200-202, 216-218, 232-234, 245-250, 264-266, 280-281, 296-298, 312-314, 328-330, 344-346, 377-379, 390-392; 24: 8-10, 73-75, 88-90, 104-105, 120-122, 136-137, 152-154, 169-171, 184-186, 200-201, 232-233. Cited in 1890.A1.

21   BELLOWS, JOHN A. "Religious Tendencies of George Eliot's Writings." Unitarian Review, 16: 125-134, 216-229.
       Every great writer is a religious teacher. George Eliot preaches the inevitable consequences of sins. Her religion

1881

is full of a mighty faith in humanity, in the close depen-
dence of human beings on one another, and in the high service which may be rendered by a noble soul. As a Positivist she emphasizes the duty which must be done for our fel-
lowmen.

*22   BRUCE, MRS. M. E. "George Eliot." The Christian Leader, Oc-
      tober 27.
         Cited in 1883.A2.

23   BRYCE, J. "George Eliot and Carlyle." Nation (New York), 32
      (March 3), 201-202.
         Carlyle was remote from the feelings and ideas of the
      present generation. But no writer has more completely rep-
      resented the tone of intellectual society than George Eliot.

24   CALL, W. M. W. "George Eliot: Her Life and Writings." West-
      minster Review, n.s. 60: 154-198.
         This is a detailed biographical summary with a discussion
      of each novel. George Eliot was above all an artist. With
      the exception of only Goethe, she is supreme in classical
      attainments and culture.

*25   EGGLESTON, EDWARD. "George Eliot and the Novel." Critic (New
      York), 1: 9.
         Cited in 1890.A1.

*26   HUET, COENRAAD BUSKEN. "George Eliot." Litterarische Fan-
      tasien en Kritieken. Haarlem, pp. 105-134.
         Cited in 1890.A1.

27   KEBBEL, T. E. "Village Life According to George Eliot."
      Fraser's Magazine, 103: 263-276.
         In Scenes of Clerical Life, Adam Bede, Silas Marner, and
      The Mill on The Floss, the reader can find a picture of
      rural England as it was before the days of reformers and
      agitators and philosophers. Kebbel traces the details of
      her description. Reprinted in 1881.B28.

28   ____. "Village Life According to George Eliot." Littell's
      Living Age, 148: 608-617.
         Reprint of 1881.B27.

*29   LIPPINCOTT, MRS. "The Great Women." The Independent, Febru-
      ary 17.
         Cited in 1883.A2.

*30   MORTIMER, JOHN. "George Eliot As a Novelist." <u>Papers of the Manchester Literary Club</u>.
        Cited in 1883.A2.

31   MYERS, F. W. H. "George Eliot." <u>Century Magazine</u>, 23: 57-64.
        Religious and moral ponderings made the basis of George Eliot's life. Follows the circumstances of her life in a biographical sketch. Relates his conversation at Cambridge on <u>God</u>, <u>Immortality</u>, and <u>Duty</u> with George Eliot in the garden of Trinity. Every one of her works is a commentary on the text that man is a very God to man. "The Legend of Jubal" is the sublimation of all she had to say. Reprinted in 1885.B26 and 1921.B3.

32   PAUL, C. K. "George Eliot." <u>Harper's New Monthly Magazine</u>, 62 (May), 912-923.
        Relates the details of her life for those who have not had the opportunity to know her. The article contains several photographs.

*33   PORTER, NOAH. "George Eliot." <u>Christian Union</u>, February.
        Cited in 1883.A2.

*34   RAE, W. FRASER. "Life and Writings of George Eliot." <u>International Review</u>, 10 (May and June), 447, 497.
        Cited in 1883.A2.

35   RUSKIN, JOHN. "Fiction--Fair and Foul." <u>Nineteenth Century</u>, 10 (October), 516-531.
        In <u>The Mill on the Floss</u> interest is stimulated in the vulgar reader for the vilest character because the author describes so carefully blotches, burrs, and pimples in which the paltry nature resembled her own. There is no girl alive, fairly clever, half-educated, whose life has not at least as much in it as Maggie's to be described and pitied. Reprinted in 1971.A2.

*36   SARSON, G. "George Eliot and Thomas Carlyle." <u>Modern Review</u>, 2: 399-413.
        Cited in 1969.B23.

37   SIMCOX, EDITH. "George Eliot." <u>Nineteenth Century</u>, 9: 778-801.
        She begins by saying she is disabled to speak in appreciation of the writer or her books by an overpowering sense of personal loss. There follows an account of George Eliot's life and works with several enlightening observations. She thinks <u>Middlemarch</u> will be ranked as the greatest of her works. Reprinted in 1881.B38.

1881

38 SIMCOX, EDITH. "George Eliot." Littell's Living Age, 149:
    791-805.
        Reprint of 1881.B37.

39 STEPHEN, LESLIE. "George Eliot." Cornhill Magazine, 43 (Feb-
    ruary), 152-168.
        The poor woman was not content simply to write amusing
    stories. She is convicted upon conclusive evidence of hav-
    ing indulged in ideas. She ventured to speculate upon hu-
    man life and its meaning, and still worse, she endeavored
    to embody her convictions in imaginative shapes, and proba-
    bly wished to infect her readers with them. Written a few
    weeks after George Eliot's death, this is a tribute to her
    greatness. Reprinted in 1881.B40, 1881.B41, 1899.B2,
    1960.A7, 1965.A2, and 1971.A2.

40 ____. "George Eliot." Littell's Living Age, 148: 731-742.
        Reprint of 1881.B39. Reprinted in 1881.B41, 1899.B2,
    1960.A7, 1965.A2, and 1971.A2.

41 ____. "George Eliot." Eclectic Magazine, 33: 443-455.
        Reprint of 1881.B39. Reprinted in 1881.B40, 1899.B2,
    1960.A7, 1965.A2, and 1971.A2.

*42 SULLIVAN, MARGARET F. "George Eliot." Dial (Chicago), 1:
    181-183.
        Cited in 1890.A1.

*43 SULLY, JAMES. "George Eliot's Art." Mind, 6: 378-394.
        Cited in 1969.B23.

44 SWINBURNE, ALGERNON CHARLES. "The Deaths of Thomas Carlyle
    and George Eliot." Athenaeum, 30 (April), 591.
        A little poem is printed commemorating their deaths; he
    says George Eliot "found in love of loving-kindness light."

*45 WARD, R. "Scepticism in George Eliot." Journal of Science,
    18.
        Cited in 1969.B23.

46 [WEDGWOOD, J.] "The Moral Influence of George Eliot." Con-
    temporary Review, 39 (February), 173-185.
        This farewell to George Eliot is signed "One Who Knew
    Her." He says, "No preacher of our day, we believe, has
    done so much to mould the moral aspirations of her con-
    temporaries as she has, for none had both the opportunity
    and the power. In losing her we have lost the common in-
    terest of the intellectual ranks most widely separated."

She sympathizes with the love of man to man, the love which gathers up the whole being. Reprinted in 1881.B47.

47   . "The Moral Influence of George Eliot." Littell's Living Age, 148: 561-571.
     Reprint of 1881.B46.

1882 A BOOKS

*1   RUSSELL, G. W. E. George Eliot: Her Genius and Writings. Woburn: H.G. Fisher.
     Cited in 1969.B23.

1882 B SHORTER WRITINGS

1   ANON. "George Eliot as a Moral Teacher." Westminster Review, 117 (January), 65-81.
     George Eliot reveals a fine perception of the value of inward over outward things in human life. One of the most healthful, because the most natural, pictures of middle-class poverty in literature is the home of the Garths. Reprinted in 1966.A5.

2   ANON. "George Eliot and Emerson." The Century, 23 (February), 619-621.
     The renunciation of belief in God and immortality wrought in George Eliot a profound and abiding sadness. Yet hers was the great endowment of a noble sympathy with mankind and a keen susceptibility to beauty and grandeur. She was still mastered by disbelief, and her life became a redutio ad absurdum of the philosophy she accepted. Emerson sees divinity in everything. He goes deeper than any conviction about man's futurity to that absolute trust in all-ruling good which is the heart of spiritual faith.

3   BULKLEY, L. "Dinah Morris and Mrs. Elizabeth Evans." Century, 24: 550-552.
     Relates an "eye-witness account" of Mrs. Evans' life and death. George Eliot represented her faithfully and fully in Dinah Morris. The real Dinah married Seth Bede (Samuel Evans). Adam was George Eliot's father, Robert Evans.

4   MATHESON, ANNIE. "Children in the Novels of George Eliot." Macmillan's Magazine, 46: 488-497.
     George Eliot's children are not impossible cherubs, or wingless fairies, or idealized precocities. She creates

1882

the vivid individuality of real children. She draws on her own memories of childhood. The article contains quotations from the novels as the children "speak for themselves." Reprinted in 1882.B5 and 1882.B6.

5   MATHESON, ANNIE. "Children in the Novels of George Eliot." Eclectic Magazine, n.s. 36: 822-830.
       Reprint of 1882.B4. Reprinted in 1882.B6.

6   _____. "Children in the Novels of George Eliot." Littell's Living Age, 155: 211-219.
       Reprint of 1882.B4. Reprinted in 1882.B5.

7   PHELPS, ELIZABETH STUART. "Last Words from George Eliot." Harper's Magazine, 66 (March), 568-571.
       Takes extracts from George Eliot's letters. George Eliot answered the request of Elizabeth Stuart Phelps to provide biographical material for a study which she was conducting.

*8 SHEPARD, WILLIAM. "George Eliot." Pen Pictures of Modern Authors: The Literary Life. (Authors and Authorship). New York: G. P. Putnam's Sons, pp. 41-57.
       Cited in 1890.A1.

*9 TUCKERMAN, BAYARD. A History of English Prose Fiction From Sir Thomas Malory to George Eliot. New York: G. P. Putnam's Sons.
       Cited in 1883.A2.

10 WELSH, ALFRED H. Development of English Literature and Language. 2 vols. Chicago: S. C. Griggs and Company. "George Eliot," 2: 470-487.
       Discusses George Eliot's life and each work. One section contains a list of moral truths which the reader would do well to ponder. She was a moral teacher of the purest and noblest tone.

1883 A BOOKS

1   BLIND, MATHILDE. George Eliot. Boston: Roberts Brothers.
       Begins with George Eliot's own remarks on women novelists. Then devotes several chapters to the facts of her life with one entire chapter on Lewes. Then she does an analysis of each novel and of the poems. Reprinted in 1904.A1.

2   COOKE, GEORGE WILLIS. George Eliot: A Critical Study. Boston: J. R. Osgood; New York: Houghton Mifflin and Company. Contains a bibliography of writings; selections, translations and portraits; biographies; general criticism; discussions of her teachings; and studies of individual works. His discussion is very interesting on the various works and on her religious tendencies.

1883 B SHORTER WRITINGS

*1   ANON. Sonnet on George Eliot. Temple Bar, 67: 123.
Cited in 1890.A1. Reprinted in 1883.B2.

*2   ANON. Sonnet on George Eliot. Eclectic Magazine, 38: 80.
Cited in 1890.A1. Reprint of 1883.B1.

3   [BAYNE, P.] "Shakespeare and George Eliot." Blackwood's Magazine, 133 (April), 524-538.
Says that if Shakespeare had lived during the Victorian era he would have written novels. The article suggests cases in which it would have been satisfactory if George Eliot had written out a Shakespearean drama into a novel. Shakespeare could not improve on the portraits of Dorothea and Celia or touch more subtly on the roots of self-love than George Eliot does. Reprinted in 1883.B4.

4   _____. "Shakespeare and George Eliot." Eclectic Magazine, n.s. 37: 743-754.
Reprint of 1883.B3.

*5   BROOKE, STOPFORD A. "George Eliot and Thomas Carlyle." The Independent, March 24.
Cited in 1883.A2.

*6   BRUNETIÈRE, FERDINAND. "English Naturalism: A Study of George Eliot." Le Roman Naturaliste.
Cited in 1883.A2.

7   DICKSON, J. A. "An Afternoon at Ashbourne." Lippincott's Magazine, 31 (May), 510-514.
Tells of visiting the cottage in which George Eliot wrote Adam Bede. The inn opposite is the "Donnithorne Arms" of the story. Much of the scenery of the book is the graphic picture of the village of Mayfield and its surroundings.

*8   HAZELTINE, MAYO WILLIAMSON. "George Eliot." Chats About Books, Poets, and Novelists. New York: C. Scribner's

1883

Sons, pp. 1-13.
Cited in 1890.A1.

9   HENRY, MARIA LOUISE. "The Morality of Thackeray and George
Eliot." Atlantic Monthly, 51 (February), 243.
Both writers leave an impression of sadness and discour-
agement. George Eliot's creed is a kind of modern stoicism.
She thinks the only life worth living is one of infinitely
active compassion. Intellectually she was of her age.

10   KEBBEL, T. E. "Miss Austen and George Eliot." National Review, 2 (October), 259-273.
George Eliot can never equal Miss Austen in giving individuality to her common-place characters. George Eliot's
admirers have confused the word "common" with "common-
place." Her characters are prosy, unromantic, and essen-
tially vulgar.

*11   PAUL, C. KEGAN. "The Rustic of George Eliot and Thomas Hardy."
Merry England, 1 (May), 40-51.
Cited in 1883.A2.

*12   ROBERTSON, ERIC SUTHERLAND. "George Eliot." English Poetess-
es: A Series of Critical Biographies. London: Cassell
and Company, pp. 327-334.
Cited in 1890.A1.

*13   ROBERTSON, J. "George Eliot." Progress, 1: 381-384; 2: 57-
61, 117-123.
Cited in 1890.A1.

*14   SHEPPARD, NATHAN. "George Eliot's Analysis of Motives." Li-
brary Magazine, 7: 84. Reprinted as an introduction to
George Eliot's Essays. New York: Funk and Wagnalls.
Cited in 1883.A2.

15   TILLEY, ARTHUR. "The New School of Fiction." National Review, April, pp. 257-268.
George Eliot often sacrifices artistic considerations to
moral; in each successive novel the moral element becomes
more predominant. James and Howells are of a new school
which has improved on George Eliot. They are before all
things artists.

*16   TROLLOPE, ANTHONY. An Autobiography.
Her imagination acts in analyzing rather than creating;
everything that comes before her is pulled to pieces so
the inside may be seen. Chapter 13 reprinted in 1965.A2.

1884 A BOOKS

*1   ANON. <u>The Round Table Series, II. George Eliot, Moralist and Thinker</u>. Edinburgh.
     Cited in 1890.A1.

1884 B SHORTER WRITINGS

*1   ANON. "On the Gospel." <u>Christian World</u>, February 28.
     Cited in 1890.A1.

*2   ANON. "George Eliot As a Christian." <u>Contemporary Pulpit</u>, 2: 179-183.
     Cited in 1890.A1.

*3   ADAMS, WILLIAM HENRY DAVENPORT. <u>Celebrated Englishwomen of the Victorian Era</u>. 2 vols. London: F. V. White and Company. "George Eliot," 2: 86-182.
     Cited in 1890.A1.

*4   BRAY, CHARLES. "Miss M. A. Evans." <u>Phases of Opinion and Experience During a Long Life: An Autobiography</u>. London: Longmans and Company, pp. 72-78.
     Cited in 1890.A1.

*5   ESTES, DANA. "George Eliot and Mr. Lewes." <u>Critic</u>, March 1, pp. 103-104. Reprinted from <u>The Boston Herald</u>.
     Cited in 1890.A1.

1885 A BOOKS

1   BROWN, JOHN CROMBIE. <u>The Ethics of George Eliot's Works</u>. "Introduction" by Charles Gordon Ames. Philadelphia: George H. Buchanan and Company.
     George Eliot is studied as a moral teacher. Brown finds in each of her works "the doctrine of the cross" as the symbol of the spirit and the law of self-sacrifice or self-giving which merges the individual life in universal ends. "Among all fictionists she stands out as the deepest, broadest and most Catholic illustrator of the true ethics of Christianity."

2   CLEVELAND, ROSE ELIZABETH. <u>George Eliot's Poetry and Other Studies</u>. New York: Funk and Wagnalls.
     Says the poetry shows too much effort to be successful and explains that George Eliot fails as a poet because of her agnosticism.

1885

3   CROSS, J. W. George Eliot's Life as Related in Her Letters
      and Journals. New York: Harper and Brothers; Edinburgh
      and London: William Blackwood and Sons.
        Claims that "the life has been allowed to write itself in
      extracts from her letters and journals." And "each letter
      has been pruned of everything that seemed to me irrelevant
      to my purpose--of everything that I thought that my wife
      would wish to be omitted." Adds a sketch of her girlhood
      at the beginning.

1885 B SHORTER WRITINGS

*1   ANON. "The Religion of George Eliot." Christian World, Janu-
       ary 29.
         Cited in 1890.A1.

2   ANON. "The Humour of George Eliot." Spectator, January 31,
       pp. 146-147.
         George Eliot's imagination was the origin of her humor
       and that only through the exercise of the will. In most
       cases her humor is a pale irony. She herself takes life
       gravely and drearily. Reprinted in 1885.B9.

3   ANON. Review of J. W. Cross, The Life and Letters of George
       Eliot. Saturday Review, 59 (February 7), 181-182.
         The reviewer of 1885.A3 says, "Of the actual events of
       George Eliot's not very eventful life these volumes tell
       little that was not known before, but as a commentary on
       her works, they are simply invaluable." Reprinted in
       1971.A2.

*4   ANON. "The Morality of George Eliot." Christian World, Feb-
       ruary 12.
         Cited in 1890.A1.

5   ANON. "A Week With George Eliot." Critic (New York), March
       7, pp. 116-117.
         Reprint of 1885.B11. Reprinted in 1885.B12.

*6   ANON. "Adam Bede's Library." Book-Lore, 2: 96-99.
         Cited in 1890.A1.

7   ANON. "George Eliot." British Quarterly Review, 81: 316-
       333.
         Warns against the personal example of George Eliot's
       life. The central fact of her life's history was not
       merely regrettable but confused in her admirers the lines
       of right and wrong. This is a review of 1885.A3.

*8   ANON.   "George Eliot."   <u>Temple Bar</u>, 73:   512-524.
       Cited in 1890.A1.

9   ANON.   "The Humour of George Eliot."   <u>Littell's Living Age</u>,
       164:   638-640.
       Reprint of 1885.B2.

*10   ANON.   "Opinions About Religion."   <u>Month</u>, 53:   473-482.
       Cited in 1890.A1.

11   ANON.   "A Week With George Eliot."   <u>Temple Bar</u>, 73:   226-232.
       Christmas week of 1870 the author was one of a party of
       four in a pleasant country house in the Isle of Wight.   Two
       of the other guests were George Eliot and George Henry
       Lewes.   This is an account of the week.   Reprinted in
       1885.B2 and 1885.B12.

12   ANON.   "A Week With George Eliot."   <u>Littell's Living Age</u>, 164:
       743-746.
       Reprint of 1885.B11.   Reprinted in 1885.B2.

13   ACTON, JOHN.   "George Eliot's Life."   <u>Nineteenth Century</u>, 17:
       464-485.
       Describes George Eliot as affectionate, proud, and sensi-
       tive in the highest degree.   From her renunciation of re-
       ligion until her death, no misgiving favorable to Christi-
       anity ever penetrated her mind or shook for an instant its
       settled unbelief.   Reprinted in 1965.A2 and 1971.A2.

*14   DOLMAN, F.   "The Politics of George Eliot."   <u>Eclectic Maga-</u>
       <u>zine</u>, n.s. 42:   675-679.
       Cited in 1890.A1.   Reprinted in 1885.B15.

*15   _____.   "The Politics of George Eliot."   <u>Gentleman's Magazine</u>,
       259:   294-300.
       Cited in 1890.A1.   Reprint of 1885.B14.

*16   DRUSKOWITZ, H.   "George Eliot."   <u>Drei Englische Dichterinnen</u>.
       Berlin, pp. 149-242.
       Cited in 1969.B23.

17   EVERETT, C. C.   Review of J. W. Cross, <u>George Eliot's Life as</u>
       <u>Related in Her Letters and Journals</u>.   <u>Andover Review</u>, 3:
       519-539.
       This reviewer of 1885.A3 comments that it is remarkable
       that humor plays no greater part in the letters.   Yet
       through the volumes the reader does come to know the sweet
       and strong nature here portrayed.   The tragic lives which

1885

    George Eliot describes in the novels are in striking con-
trast with the success of her own.

18   JAMES, HENRY. "The Life of George Eliot." <u>Atlantic Monthly</u>,
     55: 668-678.
      The world was, first and foremost, for George Eliot, the
moral, the intellectual world; the personal spectacle came
after. He says, "She had all the initiation of knowledge
and none of its dryness, all the advantages of judgment and
all the luxuries of feeling." Review of 1885.A3. Reprinted in 1888.B7, 1960.A7, and 1971.A2.

*19 JOHNSTON, R. M. "Married People of George Eliot." <u>Catholic</u>
     <u>World</u>, 40: 620-634.
      Cited in 1890.A1.

20   KINGSLEY, ROSE G. "The Country of George Eliot." <u>Century</u>
     <u>Magazine</u>, 30: 339-352.
      Describes the Elizabethan side of Warwickshire and pro-
vides sketches and photographs. Concludes by saying, "Our
castles--our parks--were historical. Now our farmhouses--
our 'Rainbows'--our very cottages--have become immortal
through the genius of George Eliot."

*21 MARTIN, MRS. J. "George Eliot." <u>Sunday Magazine</u>, pp. 231-235.
      Cited in 1890.A1.

*22 MONTÉGUT, ÉMILE. "George Eliot." <u>Écrivains modernes de</u>
     <u>l'Angleterre</u>, Series I. Paris: Hachette, pp. 3-180.
      Cited in 1969.B23.

23   MORLEY, JOHN. "The Life of George Eliot." <u>Macmillan's Maga-</u>
     <u>zine</u>, 51 (April), 241-256.
      In fiction, as the years go by, readers crave more fancy,
illusion, and enchantment than the quality of her genius
allowed. But the loftiness of her character is abiding,
and it passes nobly through the ordeal of an honest biography (1885.A3). Reprinted in 1885.B24 and 1885.B25.

24   _____. "The Life of George Eliot." <u>Eclectic Magazine</u>, 104:
     506-520.
      Reprint of 1885.B23. Reprinted in 1885.B25.

25   _____. "The Life of George Eliot." <u>Littell's Living Age</u>,
     164: 533-546.
      Reprint of 1885.B23. Reprinted in 1885.B24.

26   MYERS, F. W. H. <u>Essays--Modern</u>. London: Macmillan.
      Contains a reprint of 1881.B31. Reprinted in 1921.B3.

*27 PROCTOR, R. A. "On Mental Decay." Knowledge, August 14, pp. 127-129.
Cited in 1890.A1.

*28 SCHERER, EDMOND. "George Eliot." Études Critiques sur la Littérature Contemporaine, 10 vols. Paris. 8: 187-242.
Cited in 1890.A1.

*29 THOMSON, J. R. "Life of George Eliot: Illustrative of the Religious Ideas of Our Time." British and Foreign Evangelical Review, 34: 517-543.
Cited in 1890.A1.

30 WHIPPLE, EDWIN P. "The Private Life of George Eliot." North American Review, 141: 320-330.
This review of Cross (1885.A3) expresses the complaint that Cross tells so little of his own opinions, things which he must have thoroughly known, and which he must have felt his readers wanted to know. Whipple goes on to tell the facts of George Eliot's life and make speculations as to their significance. Reprinted in 1887.B10.

*31 WOLZOGEN, E. VON. George Eliot: eine biographische kritische Studie. Leipzig.
Cited in 1969.B23.

*32 [YONGE, C. M.] "George Eliot and Her Critics." Monthly Packet, May.
Cited in 1969.B23.

1886 A BOOKS

*1 AMES, CHARLES GORDON. George Eliot's Two Marriages. Philadelphia: G. H. Buchanan and Company.
Cited in 1890.A1.

*2 LONSDALE, MARGARET. George Eliot: Thoughts Upon Her Life, Her Books, and Herself. London: Paul. 32 pp.
Cited in 1969.B23.

3 WOOLSON, ABBA GOOLD. George Eliot and Her Heroines. New York: Harper and Brothers.
George Eliot saw sympathy for others as an individual's chief obligation to the race. Her theory of life and morals tends to rob the soul of its noblest attributes. Her novels will stand as glowing transcripts of such phases of woman's advancement as belong to the history of the

1886

nineteenth century. Her heroines ascertain, rather than feel, the difference between right and wrong; they ponder, deliberate, and are lost. Her men lack strength and dislike stern and disagreeable things. In all cases the heroines fail utterly in attaining what they seek; the young men also fail universally. There is not a single instance of a wholly suitable or happy marriage. This is the result of her advocacy of a peculiar pessimistic philosophy and of her unsound ethical bias.

1886 B SHORTER WRITINGS

*1   ANON. "George Eliot and Kingsley." Literary World, October 15.
       Cited in 1890.A1.

*2   ANON. "George Eliot's Criticisms on Contemporaries." Lippincott's Magazine of Literature, 37: 19-20.
       Cited in 1890.A1.

*3   ANON. "George Eliot." Victorian Era: Queens of Literature of the Victorian Era. London, pp. 185-258.
       Cited in 1890.A1.

*4   BLACKIE, W. G. "Surrender of Faith by George Eliot." British and Foreign Evangelical Review, 35: 38-65.
       Cited in 1890.A1.

*5   DAWSON, W. J. "George Eliot." Quest and Vision: Essays in Life and Literature. London: E. Stock, pp. 158-195.
       Cited in 1969.B23.

*6   DRONSART, MARIE. "George Eliot." Portraits d'Outre-Manche. Paris, pp. 213-289.
       Cited in 1890.A1.

 7   HARRISON, FREDERIC. The Choice of Books and Other Literary Pieces. London: Macmillan.
       Mentions George Eliot several times.

1887 A BOOKS

*1   CONRAD, HERMANN. George Eliot: Ihr Leben und Schaffen Dargestellt nach ihren Briefen und Tagebüchern. Berlin: Georg Reimer.
       Cited in 1969.B23.

GEORGE ELIOT: A REFERENCE GUIDE

1887 B SHORTER WRITINGS

*1   BARINE, ARVÈDE. Portraits de Femmes: Madame Carlyle, George
      Eliot, Une Dé traguée [Mary Wollstonecraft]. Paris.
      Cited in 1969.B23.

*2   BLASHFIELD, E. H. and E. W. "In Florence with Romola."
      Scribner's Magazine, 2: 693-721.
      Cited in 1890.A1.

3   BOLTON, SARAH K. "George Eliot." Lives of Girls Who Became
      Famous. New York: Thomas Y. Crowell and Company, pp. 213-
      239.
         The article is prompted by reading Cross's Life (1885.A3).
      She reviews George Eliot's life and works recognizing that
      she was affectionate, gentle, and tender. Yet she pos-
      sessed scholarship that few men can equal.

*4   BUCHANAN, ROBERT. A Look Around Literature. London: Ward
      and Downey. "A Talk With George Eliot," pp. 218-226;
      "George Eliot's Life," pp. 314-321.
      Cited in 1890.A1.

*5   FENTON, FERRAR. "Adam Bede and Parson Christian." Gentle-
      man's Magazine, 262: 392-407.
      Cited in 1890.A1.

6   GRISWOLD, HATTIE TYNG. "George Eliot." Home Life of Great
      Authors. Chicago: A. C. McClurg and Company, pp. 351-362.
         Since George Eliot's death, interest has been constantly
      increasing. She looked too deeply into life to make of it
      a mere thing of daily bread, of common homely joys and
      trifling labors. Gives a summary of the life, commending
      Mr. Cross's wisdom in carefully pruning her letters
      (1885.A3).

7   HUTTON, R. H. Essays on Some of the Modern Guides of English
      Thought in Matters of Faith. London: Macmillan and Com-
      pany, pp. 145-258, Chapter IV, "George Eliot As Author";
      pp. 259-300, Chapter V, "George Eliot's Life and Letters."
         George Eliot was in the highest sense her own God, her
      own moral Providence, her own conscience, her own lawgiver,
      her own judge, her own Savior. Those who try in her novels
      to swim against the stream of their past are neutralized
      and paralyzed in the vain effort. Hutton concludes that
      George Eliot's skepticism is one of the greatest limita-
      tions of her genius.

1887

8 OGDEN, R. "George Eliot's Religious Transition." <u>Nation</u>, 45:
   68-70.
      Finds premonitions of the change in George Eliot's re-
   ligious thinking throughout her early life in which her
   "power of acquirement, stimulated by insatiable desire was
   sure to bring her into contact with writings broader than
   her sect." He concludes, "No one but the dupe of a Hindu
   juggler can suppose that the flower bursts into bloom ten
   minutes after the seed is sown."

9 TOWNE, EDWARD C. "George Eliot's Religious Views." <u>Nation</u>,
   45: 92.
      This is a letter which attempts to clarify the few days
   following November 2, 1841, in which George Eliot's mind
   was engaged on the inquiries which resulted in her change
   of faith. He uses evidence from her letters.

10 WHIPPLE, E. P. <u>Recollections of Eminent Men</u>. Boston: Tick-
   nor and Company. "Daniel Deronda," pp. 344-379; "George
   Eliot's Private Life," pp. 380-397. Reprints of 1877.B16
   and 1885.B30.

1888 A BOOKS

*1 PARKINSON, S. <u>Scenes from the "George Eliot" Country</u>. With
    Illustrations. Leeds: R. Jackson.
       Cited in 1890.A1.

*2 SEGUIN, LISBETH GOOCH. <u>Scenes and Characters from the Works
    of George Eliot. A Series of Illustrations by Eminent
    Artists</u>, with introductory essay and descriptive letter-
    press by L. G. Seguin. London: A. Strahan.
       Cited in 1890.A1.

1888 B SHORTER WRITINGS

*1 ANON. "George Eliot." <u>National Review</u>, 11: 191.
       Cited in 1883.A2.

*2 BELL, J. <u>George Eliot as a Novelist</u>. Aberdeen.
       Cited in 1969.B23.

3 BROWNING, OSCAR. "The Art of George Eliot." <u>Fortnightly Re-
   view</u>, n.s. 43: 538-553.
      Decides he likes <u>Adam Bede</u> better than George Eliot's
   other novels and explains why. She was profoundly

conscious of the little thought and value which many people
set on life. The keynote of her art is painting the lives
of those about her, to describe their joys and sorrows.

*4   CONE, HELEN GRAY, and JEANNETTE L. GILDER. Pen-Portraits of
      Literary Women. 2 vols. New York: Cassell and Company.
      "George Eliot," 2: 245-292.
          Cited in 1890.A1.

5   IRELAND, ANNIE E. "George Eliot and Jane Welsh Carlyle."
      Gentleman's Magazine, 264: 229-238.
          Both George Eliot and Jane Welsh Carlyle endured serious
      physical and mental suffering. Excerpts from their cor-
      respondence are given indicating their various discomforts.
      She even speculates as to what the two would have been had
      motherhood been added to their respective crowns of glory.

6   JAMES, HENRY. "Daniel Deronda: A Conversation." Partial
      Portraits. London: Macmillan.
          Reprint of 1876.B34. Reprinted in 1960.A7, 1965.A2,
      1970.A4, and 1971.A2.

7   ____. "The Life of George Eliot." Partial Portraits. Lon-
      don: Macmillan.
          Reprint of 1885.B18. Reprinted in 1960.A7 and 1971.A2.

8   STEPHEN, LESLIE. "Cross, Mary Ann, or Marian (1819-1880)."
      Dictionary of National Biography, 13: 216-222.
          Gives an account of her life and works.

1889 A BOOKS - NONE

1889 B SHORTER WRITINGS

1   CROSS, WILBUR L. "The Psychological Novel." The Development
      of the English Novel. New York and London: Macmillan,
      pp. 237-251.
          Her moral discernments, often clothed in the language of
      positivism, are nevertheless embedded everlastingly in the
      inherited thought of the ages.

*2   DE HEUSSEY, ROBERT DU PONTAVICE. "George Eliot." Le Livre,
      January, pp. 16-32.
          Cited in 1890.A1.

*3   HAMLEY, E. Shakespeare's Funeral and Other Papers. Edin-
      burgh: William Blackwood and Sons.
          Cited in 1969.B23.

1889

4   NEWDIGATE, ANNE EMILY. The Cheverels of Cheverel Manor. London: Longmans and Company.
    The correspondence of Sir Roger and Lady Newdigate.

5   PHILIPSON, DAVID. "Daniel Deronda." Jew in English Fiction. Cincinnati: Robert Clarke and Company, pp. 122-156.
    Says that Daniel Deronda is the only English novel in which the Jew is treated as he should be. Mordecai is not a representative of Jewish thought today. The perfection of his character is due to the working of a noble soul with intuitions of lofty ideals.

*6 TYTLER, SARAH. "George Eliot." Atalanta, July, pp. 682-686.
    Cited in 1890.A1.

1890 A BOOKS

1   BROWNING, OSCAR. Life of George Eliot. London: Walter Scott.
    This contains J. P. Anderson's checklist of early literature as an appendix. Relates her life to the composition of the fiction. Includes personal details such as, "She told me at a later period she always read some of the Iliad before beginning her work, in order to take out of her mouth the taste of the modern world." He gives a personal account of having attended her funeral. Pp. 147-167 reprinted in 1965.A2.

1890 B SHORTER WRITINGS - NONE

1891 A BOOKS

*1 NEGRI, G. George Eliot: la sua Vita e i suoi Romanzi, 2 vols. Milano.
    Cited in 1969.B23.

1891 B SHORTER WRITINGS

1   JACOBS, JOSEPH. "George Eliot." George Eliot, Matthew Arnold, Browning, Newman. Essays and Reviews from the 'Athenaeum.' London: D. Nutt, pp. 3-73.
    In his "Introduction" Jacobs tells of the fear and ardent reverence with which he approached the Pirory, North Bank, one Sunday afternoon in 1877. Ten years after George Eliot's death her reputation had declined. There is a general tendency against taking intellectual nourishment in anything but small doses. She aimed and claimed to be a teacher. Contains a reprint of 1881.B1.

2   SCHERER, EDMOND. Essays on English Literature, trans. George
     Saintsbury. New York: Charles Scribner's Sons, pp. 1-12.
     In character-drawing George Eliot's superiority is es-
     pecially manifest. The reader is calmed by her lofty chari-
     ty.

1892 A BOOKS - NONE

1892 B SHORTER WRITINGS

 *1   WHITING, MARY BRADFORD. "George Eliot as a Character Artist."
      Westminster Review, 138: 406-415.
          Cited in 1969.B23.

1893 A BOOKS

 *1   BENDER, H. George Eliot: ein Lebensbild. Hamburg.
          Cited in 1969.B23.

1893 B SHORTER WRITINGS

 *1   DAMON, L. T. "George Eliot's Theory of Realism." Harvard
      Monthly, 15.
          Cited in 1967.B31.

 *2   SCHERER, WILHELM. "George Eliot und das Judentum." Kleine
      Schriften, Vol. II. Berlin: Weidmann Buchhandlung.
          Cited in 1967.B31.

1894 A BOOKS

 *1   WESTERMARCK, H. George Eliot och den Engelska Naturaliska
      Romanen. Helsingfors.
          Cited in 1969.B23.

1894 B SHORTER WRITINGS - NONE

1895 A BOOKS - NONE

1895 B SHORTER WRITINGS

 1   HARRISON, FREDERIC. "George Eliot's Place in Literature."
      Forum, 20: 66-78.
          George Eliot was a most thoughtful artist, but she was

1895

more of a thinker than an artist; she was always more the
artist when she was least the teacher.

2   HARRISON, FREDERIC. Studies in Early Victorian Literature.
London: E. Arnold, pp. 205-224.
    Until nearly the age of forty, George Eliot was known
only as a critical and philosophical writer; she was the
equal of the first minds of her time. At the same time she
had very rare talents as an artist and a worker in the
sphere of imagination and creation. At times her intellectual powers seriously mar her artistic gifts. Reprinted in
1901.B2.

*3 LILLY, WILLIAM SAMUEL. Four English Humourists of the Nine-
teenth Century. London: John Murray.
    Cited in 1969.B23.

4   SAINTSBURY, GEORGE. Corrected Impressions: Essays on Victorian Writers. New York: Dodd, Mead, pp. 162-172.
    George Eliot's experience and assimilated impressions
came out in novels; at first they were simple and then ex-
tremely powerful. Then they grew less simple and yet in-
geniously reproductive of current phases of thought and
sentiment. The last were expressions of will-worship,
which she had taken up to replace the faith that she had
cast out.

1896 A BOOKS - NONE

1896 B SHORTER WRITINGS

1   RUSSELL, G. W. E. "George Eliot Revisited." Contemporary Review, 69 (March), 357-373.
    George Eliot deserves first rank among the benefactors of
mankind for making the sublime creeds of duty and self-
sacrifice lovely and attractive. Yet as an artist she remains "a little lower than the angels."

1897 A BOOKS

*1 DAVIDSON, HANNAH AMELIA. The Study of Romola: Topics and
References Arranged for Literary Circles. Albany, New
York.
    Reprinted in 1902.A1. Cited in 1969.B23.

1897 B SHORTER WRITINGS

1 LANIER, SIDNEY. The English Novel: A Study in the Development of Personality. New York: Charles Scribner's Sons,
pp. 152-176, 197-302.
  This work contains twelve lectures delivered at Johns
Hopkins University in the winter and spring of 1811. The
lectures trace the growth of human personality from Æschy-
lus to George Eliot. He says, "If I were asked for the
most significant, the most tender, the most pious and al-
together the most uplifting of modern books it seems to me
I should specify Daniel Deronda."

1898 A BOOKS - NONE

1898 B SHORTER WRITINGS

*1 RICKETT, ARTHUR COMPTON. Prophets of This Century. London:
Ward, Lock and Company.
Cited in 1969.B23.

1899 A BOOKS - NONE

1899 B SHORTER WRITINGS

1 OLIPHANT, JAMES. Victorian Novelists. New York: Ames Press,
pp. 78-142.
  George Eliot's life is proof that a burning enthusiasm
for all that is good does not depend on supernatural sanc-
tions and that tolerance reaches its ideal in the pro-
foundest sympathy with every earnest endeavor of struggling
humanity to understand the truth by which it lives. He
goes on to discuss each novel.

2 STEPHEN, LESLIE. "George Eliot." Hours in a Library, III.
London: Smith, Elder, Company; G. P. Putnam's Sons.
  Reprint of 1881.B39. Reprinted in 1881.B40, 1881.B41,
1960.A7, 1965.A2, and 1971.A2.

1901 A BOOKS

*1 THOMSON, CLARA. George Eliot. London: Kegan Paul Trench
Trübner and Company (The Westminster Biographies).
Cited in 1969.B23.

1901

1901 B SHORTER WRITINGS

   1   BROWNELL, W. C. Victorian Prose Masters. New York: Charles
      Scribner's Sons, pp. 99-145, 249-250.
         Says that George Eliot has fallen into neglect. In her
      time the novelty of psychological fiction was a powerful
      source of attraction, but since that time readers have had
      a surfeit of psychological fiction. It is as a moralist
      that she makes her real contribution to literature. Re-
      printed in 1965.A2.

   2   HARRISON, FREDERIC. Studies in Early Victorian Literature.
      London: E. Arnold, pp. 205-224.
         Reprint of 1895.B2.

*3   HOWELLS, W. D. Heroines of Fiction. 2 vols. New York: Har-
      per and Brothers Publishers.
         Cited in 1969.B23.

1902 A BOOKS

*1   DAVIDSON, HANNAH AMELIA. The Study of Romola: Topics and
      References Arranged For Literary Circles. Boston: Puritan
      Press.
         Cited in 1969.B23. Reprint of 1897.A1.

   2   STEPHEN, LESLIE. George Eliot. London: Macmillan and Com-
      pany.
         Discusses her life and also discusses each novel and The
      Spanish Gypsy separately. The combination of an exquisite-
      ly sympathetic and loving nature with a large and tolerant
      intellect is manifest throughout her works. Her pathos is
      powerful because it is always under command. There is a
      personal element and a revelation of her knowledge of the
      human heart. She believed that a work of art must exert an
      ethical influence, and reading George Eliot's novels af-
      fects the reader in the same way as an intimacy with the
      woman herself.

1902 B SHORTER WRITINGS

   1   BONNELL, HENRY H. "George Eliot's Language." Charlotte
      Brontë, George Eliot, Jane Austen: Studies in Their Works.
      New York: Longmans, Green and Company.
         George Eliot has the happy selective ability to find the
      one correct word to describe what must otherwise be

George Eliot: A Reference Guide

described by circumlocution. She is not a constant neolo-
gist nor is she a pedant. Reprinted in 1965.A2.

1903 A BOOKS

*1   STOWELL, R. S. <u>A Study of Romola</u>. Boston: The Poetlore Com-
      pany.
         Cited in 1969.B23.

1903 B SHORTER WRITINGS – NONE

1904 A BOOKS

1   BLIND, MATHILDE. <u>George Eliot</u>. Boston: Roberts Brothers.
        The 1904 "new edition" has a bibliography appended. Re-
     print of 1883.A1.

1904 B SHORTER WRITINGS

1   GOULD, GEORGE M. <u>Biographic Clinic: The Origin of the Ill-
     Health of DeQuincy, Carlyle [and others]</u>, 6 vols. Phila-
     delphia: P. Blakiston's Sons, 1903–09. Vol. 2.
        Assumes that each of these suffered from eyestrain of one
     type or another. Dr. Gould assigns to presbyopia the speci-
     fic reason for the deaths of George Eliot and George Lewes.

1905 A BOOKS

1   MOTTRAM, WILLIAM. <u>The True Story of George Eliot in Relation
     to "Adam Bede" Giving the Real Life History of the More
     Prominent Characters</u>. London: F. Griffiths: T. Fisher
     Unwin.
        The author claims to be the grand nephew of Adam and Seth
     Bede and cousin to George Eliot. He gives a detailed ac-
     count of the people and places included in the novel and
     publishes a number of photographs taken by his sons. Re-
     printed in 1906.A1.

1905 B SHORTER WRITINGS

1   DAWSON, W. J. <u>The Makers of English Fiction</u>. New York:
     Fleming H. Revell Company, pp. 145–163.
        Philosophic insight, the keenest analysis of spiritual

1905

emotion, and the finest and most sympathetic painting of country manners find their perfection in George Eliot. She was greater as a moralist and teacher than as an artist.

1906 A BOOKS

1   MOTTRAM, WILLIAM. The True Story of George Eliot in Relation to "Adam Bede." Giving the Real Life History of the More Prominent Characters. Chicago: A. C. McClurg and Company. Reprint of 1905.A1.

1906 B SHORTER WRITINGS

1   HUTTON, R. H. Brief Literary Criticisms, ed. E. M. Roscoe. Selected from The Spectator. London: Macmillan and Company. "George Eliot," pp. 175-183; "The Idealism of George Eliot and Mr. Tennyson," pp. 184-191.
        Soon after George Eliot's death, Hutton says that largeness of mind and largeness of conception are her first characteristics in matters of reason and imagination. She draws patient and powerful studies of social manners from the dumbest provincial life to life of the highest self-knowledge.

2   JOHNSON, M. L. "George Eliot and George Combe." Westminster Review, 156: 557-568.
        Any one acquainted with the philosophical opinions and literary style of George Combe's phrenological writings cannot fail to be impressed by the strong bias which they have given to the character of George Eliot's genius. Her creations assimilate the principles of psychological and physiognomical law as enunciated by him.

*3   PAUL, HERBERT WOODFIELD. Stray Leaves. London; New York: John Lane.
        Cited in 1969.B23.

1907 A BOOKS

*1   RICHTER, H. George Eliot: fünf Aufsätze. Berlin.
        Cited in 1969.B23.

1907 B SHORTER WRITINGS - NONE

1908 A BOOKS - NONE

1908 B SHORTER WRITINGS

1   JAMES, HENRY. "The Novels of George Eliot." <u>Views and Re-</u>
     <u>views</u>. Boston: Ball Publishing Company.
        Reprint of 1866.B16. Reprinted in 1960.A7, 1965.A2, and
     1966.A5.

1909 A BOOKS - NONE

1909 B SHORTER WRITINGS

1   BARRY, WILLIAM FRANCIS. "The Genius of George Eliot." <u>Her-</u>
     <u>alds of Revolt: Studies in Modern Literature and Dogma</u>.
     London: Hodder and Stoughton, pp. 1-29.
        Reprint of 1881.B19.

2   BURTON, RICHARD. "George Eliot." <u>Masters of the English</u>
     <u>Novel</u>. New York: Henry Holt and Company, pp. 218-243.
        Discusses George Eliot as a meliorist with a brief look
     at each of her works.

1910 A BOOKS

1   OLCOTT, CHARLES S. <u>George Eliot: Scenes and People in Her</u>
     <u>Novels</u>. New York: Thomas Y. Crowell.
        Contains photographs and a discussion of the scenes and
     people connected with each novel. Three other chapters
     are the first, "Warwickshire," about George Eliot's youth,
     and the last two, "George Eliot and Mr. Lewes" and "The
     Womanliness of George Eliot." Includes twenty-four photo-
     graphs of people and places, and a list of characters from
     <u>Scenes of Clerical Life</u> are identified with specific people
     and places.

1910 B SHORTER WRITINGS - NONE

1912 A BOOKS

1   GARDENER, CHARLES. <u>The Inner Life of George Eliot</u>. London:
     Sir I. Pitman and Sons, Ltd.
        Calls <u>Daniel Deronda</u> George Eliot's "supreme achievement"
     and suggests in his preface that all who think otherwise
     are "ephemeral faddists who deride but do not read her."

1912

1912 B SHORTER WRITINGS - NONE

1913 A BOOKS

   *1   DEAKIN, MARY H. The Early Life of George Eliot. Manchester:
       University Press.
         Harvey in Victorian Fiction: A Guide to Research
       (1964.B11) says that this biography became, as much as
       Cross's Life and Letters (1885.A3), the source of later bi-
       ographies. He says the aim is to show "how the sensitive,
       passionate child, with so eager a longing for love, grew
       into the pious, introspective maiden."

1913 B SHORTER WRITINGS

   1   CLIFFORD, LUCY. "Remembrance of George Eliot." Nineteenth
       Century, 74: 109-118.
         In America, Lucy Clifford says, she was often asked to
       comment on what George Eliot looked like, what her home and
       surroundings were like, and about Lewes. She then gives a
       detailed account of her personal acquaintance with George
       Eliot during the last four years of her life.

   2   FAIRLAY, E. "The Art of George Eliot in Silas Marner." Eng-
       lish Journal, 2: 221-230.
         Silas Marner is complete in design and admirable in con-
       struction, a masterpiece in which critics may study George
       Eliot in small compass. She insists on the value of char-
       acter, the necessity of right conduct, and a vision of the
       moral order of the world which showed an answer to the
       problems of human destiny.

   *3   ISEBARTH, MAX. "Die Psychologie der Charaktere in George Eli-
       ot's The Mill on the Floss." Die Neueren Sprachen, 21:
       511-533.
         Cited in 1967.B31.

1915 A BOOKS

   *1   RHOTERT, C. Die Frau bei George Eliot. Berlin.
         Cited in 1969.B23.

1915 B SHORTER WRITINGS - NONE

1917 A BOOKS - NONE

1917 B SHORTER WRITINGS

1 BERLE, LINA WRIGHT. George Eliot and Thomas Hardy: A Con-
    trast. New York: Mitchell Kernnerley.
        Concludes by saying of George Eliot, "After a brief sea-
    son of high esteem, she has lost prestige as a thinker,
    while retaining the doubtful glory of artistic achievement
    in an unfashionable style." Of the works she says that her
    treatment of sexual relationships is much to be preferred
    to Hardy's stories dealing with "the mating, mismating, and
    unmating of men and women, ignoring the existence of any
    other motives as determining factors in human intercourse."

2 WARD, SIR A. W. "The Political and Social Novel." Ch. 11,
    The Nineteenth Century, 13, The Cambridge History of Eng-
    lish Literature. New York: G. P. Putnam's Sons, pp. 423-
    446.
        Outlines her life in connection with her works. Of her
    poems, he says, "They are full of brilliant turns of
    thought, and the poet had acquired a mastery of meter which
    made her delight in putting her ideas into a form well-
    suited to gnomic utterances." Discusses The Impressions of
    Theophrastus Such, a work devoid of gaiety.

1918 A BOOKS - NONE

1918 B SHORTER WRITINGS

1 BLOCK, LOUIS JAMES. "The Poetry of George Eliot." Sewanee
    Review, 26: 85-91.
        Block discusses The Spanish Gypsy and The Legend of Ju-
    bal. Says that in plot and construction the poems are no
    less successful than the novels. She could demand recog-
    nition as a poet on the basis of The Legend of Jubal alone.
    Elias Baptist Butterworth in "A Minor Prophet" is one of
    her passionate seers. The "College Breakfast Party" is a
    remarkable imaginative tour de force and a discussion of
    man's highest good and the social order.

2 TOMLINSON, MAY. "Dodsons and Tullivers." Sewanee Review, 26:
    319-327.
        Explains the novel as "a consummate exposition of small-
    mindedness." The unenlightened mind characterized by nar-
    rowness of imagination and intellect seems to have come
    under George Eliot's close observation.

1918

3   TOMLINSON, MAY. "Rosamond and Lydgate." <u>South Atlantic Quarterly</u>, 17: 320-329.
    The tragedy of Lydgate's life consists in his failure to do what he meant to do and in his unfortunate matrimonial choice. Rosamond's self-image completely blocks her vision of self-blame. Dorothea is a perfect foil to her. Lydgate matures as he is initiated into the life of suffering.

1919 A BOOKS

*1 ZUBER, ELISABETH. <u>Kind und Kindhert bei George Eliot</u>. Frauenfeld: Drück von Haber.
    Cited in 1969.B23.

1919 B SHORTER WRITINGS

1   GARDNER, CHARLES. "George Eliot." <u>London Quarterly Review</u>, 132: 170-182.
    George Eliot went back to the ethics of Judaism and found the great moral sanctions in the ties of family and race. Her stories are full of poetry, loving humor, and a sad music.

2   JOHNSON, R. BRIMLEY. <u>The Women Novelists</u>. Freeport, New York: Books for Libraries Press, Inc., pp. 204-225, 278-281.
    George Eliot is a moral realist; her realism is inspired by sympathy with life. For many years she influenced thought and culture among the middle-classes more widely, and perhaps more profoundly, than any other writer. Women have always been realistic and parochial. Her outlook remains thoroughly emotional and feminine. "Her heart and her genius are those of a woman, womanly." Reprinted in 1967.B21.

3   MINCHIN, H. C. "George Eliot: Some Characteristics.". <u>Fortnightly Review</u>, 112: 896-903.
    The most outstanding feature of George Eliot's character was her power of sympathy. Serious in the main, her novels are full of lofty and uplifting sentiment.

4   PARRY, EDWARD A. "The Humour of George Eliot." <u>Fortnightly Review</u>, 112: 883-895.
    The humor in each of the <u>Scenes of Clerical Life</u> is used to strengthen the effect of a serious and almost tragic story. The reader is amused by the self-deceptions, the vanity in fancied gifts, and the conceit of vain

imaginings. Mrs. Poyser in <u>Adam Bede</u> is undoubtedly her greatest humorous character. In <u>Romola</u>, <u>Middlemarch</u>, and <u>Daniel Deronda</u>, George Eliot was striving to express great truths wherein humor had no part to play.

5   ROWLAND-BROWN, LILLIAN. "The Boys of George Eliot." <u>The Nineteenth Century</u>, 86: 859-869.
    Tom Tulliver is solid flesh and blood. But Daniel Deronda proves that George Eliot knew nothing of boyhood in the stately homes of England. She goes along commenting on the various young boys which appear in the novels.

6   TOMLINSON, MAY. "The Beginning of George Eliot's Art: A Study of <u>Scenes of Clerical Life</u>." <u>Sewanee Review</u>, 27: 320-329.
    George Eliot discovers in this initial effort many of the excellencies which characterize her work in general and many of the tendencies now recognized as the permanent features of her art. The similes from nature, the use of description as a means of emphasizing mental and spiritual moods, the skill with which "little intervals are filled up," the portrayal of children, the sensitivity to the tones of the human voice, the fun and wit, the depiction of "comfortable sights," and the concern with the serious aspects of life all are already apparent.

7   WOOLF, VIRGINIA. "George Eliot." <u>Times Literary Supplement</u>, 18 (November), 657-658.
    Herbert Spencer exempted her novels, as if they were not novels, when he banned all fiction from the London library. Her <u>Middlemarch</u> is one of the few English novels written for grown-up people. Her heroines bring out the worst in her; their problem is that they can not live without religion. But they want something incompatible with the facts of human existence. Reprinted in 1925.B8, 1960.A7, and 1965.A2.

1920 A BOOKS

*1   CHAFFURIN, LOUIS. <u>Les amours de George Eliot</u>. <u>Grande Revue</u>, Juillet-September.
    Cited in ELL (1920).

1920 B SHORTER WRITINGS

1   CROSS, WILBUR L. "George Eliot in Retrospect." <u>Yale Review</u>, 9: 256-270.

1920

Reviews her life and works in general and decides that "even George Eliot's early novels are somehow out of tune with the present. Even they are too reflective." But he hopes the pendulum will swing back towards a more closely organized art of fiction having dramatic vitality and that novelists will discover George Eliot.

2   ELTON, OLIVER. <u>A Survey of English Literature, 1830-1880</u>. 2 vols. London: Edward Arnold, Ltd., pp. 258-275.
George Eliot's art cannot be separated from the ethical habit of her mind. In <u>Middlemarch</u> the interest of crime passes into that of casuistry. She shows a real power of pinning down a moral problem. She has a lawyer's grasp of the facts and a psychologist's vision of the motives. Reprinted in 1965.A2.

3   TOMLINSON, MAY. "The Humor of George Eliot." <u>The Texas Review</u>, 5: 243-248.
Stupidity is the chief substance to attract her humor. Artistically her sense of humor was her solution. It lies in the excellence of her description of queer modes of thought and expression and the skill with which she presents various phases of mentality. She portrays irrelevance, garrulity, inflexibility, complacency, self-conceit, and self-deception. Discusses scenes which embody these things.

4   VINCENT, LEON H. "A Note on George Eliot." <u>Methodist Review</u>, 103: 712-722.
The writer tells of seeing the house on Foleshill Road where George Eliot lived. Written on the one-hundredth anniversary of her birth, this praises her dialogue and description, her analysis of character and philosophy, and her humor and pathos.

1921 A BOOKS

*1   SMALLFIELD, P. S. <u>Notes on "Romola."</u> 5th ed. revised. Whitcombe and Tombs.
Cited in ELL(1921).

1921 B SHORTER WRITINGS

*1   GROOT, J. C. J. "George Eliot en haar romans." <u>Studiën</u>, 95 (March).
Cited in ELL(1921).

GEORGE ELIOT: A REFERENCE GUIDE

2 JAMES, HENRY. "Felix Holt, the Radical." Notes and Reviews.
     Cambridge: Dunster House.
       Reprint of 1866.B15. Reprinted in 1965.A2, 1966.A5,
     and 1971.A2.

3 MYERS, F. W. H. "George Eliot." Essays Classical and Modern.
     London: Macmillan.
       Reprint of 1881.B31 and 1885.B26.

4 WALKER, HUGH. The Literature of the Victorian Era. Cambridge:
     University Press, pp. 728-747.
       George Eliot's very greatness of mind lifts her so far
     above her reader that the personal relationship is chilled.
     No one before her had so combined profound culture in
     philosophy with insight into character and keen observation.

1922 A BOOKS - NONE

1922 B SHORTER WRITINGS

1 GOSSE, EDMUND. "George Eliot." Aspects and Impressions. New
     York: Charles Scribner's Sons, pp. 1-16.
       Saw George Eliot several times including at the concert
     where she took the cold which brought on her death, but he
     never spoke to her. Discusses contemporary reactions to
     her, but he feels that she has been rashly awarded too
     high a place by these infatuated admirers. After all he
     says, "We are sheep that look up to George Eliot and are
     not fed by her ponderous moral aphorisms and didactic ethi-
     cal influence."

2 HELLMAN, GEORGE SIDNEY. "Unpublished Letters." The Century,
     104 (September), 643-648.
       The letters are begun to Elizabeth Stuart Phelps in ac-
     knowledgement of the American woman's words of appreciation
     of Middlemarch. Their continued correspondence reveals two
     women in close mental and temperamental contact.

3 KAWA, MARIE E. "The Women of George Eliot's Novels." English
     Studies, 4: 185-191, 217-223.
       Too much of a portrait of one of George Eliot's acquain-
     tances is in Milly Barton. This is not true of Dinah Mor-
     ris; her ideal nature does arouse some doubt as to its re-
     ality. There is nothing stifled or affected in Mrs. Win-
     throp. Other "altruistic women" are discussed and that
     "beautiful little sinner" Hetty Sorrel. Daniel Deronda's
     mother behaves much like Hetty. Rosamond's selfishness is

1922

of a different kind. In the second installment of the article she discusses Gwendolen, Esther, Romola, and Maggie;
they die to self and give up high and pure joy and the
happiness to which they cling with passionate impulse.
This renunciation is not easy to them.

4   LAW, FREDERICK HOUK. "Main Street and Silas Marner." Inde-
     pendent, 108: 263-265.
        George Eliot paints the "real" main street. Her English
     Raveloe is more like an American village than the crude
     caricature of the American Gopher Prairie.

5   SANDWITH, MRS. HAROLD. "Maggie Tulliver and La Dame aux Camé-
     lias." Nineteenth Century, 91: 782-790.
        Finds parallels between Maggie and Marguerite Gautier,
     the lady of the camelias, of Dumas.

*6   WENLEY, R. W. "Marian Evans and George Eliot." Washington
     University Studies, 9: 3-34.
        Cited in 1969.B23.

*7   ZUBER, ELISABETH. "George Eliot als Gelehrte, Dichterin und
     Frau." Neophilologus, 7: 109-125.
        Cited in ELL(1922).

1923 A BOOKS

*1   J., A. C. Notes on the Influence of Sir Walter Scott on
     George Eliot. Edinburgh: Baxendine.
        Cited in 1969.B23.

1923 B SHORTER WRITINGS

1   ANON. "A Collection of George Eliot MSS and Books." Times
     Literary Supplement, July 5, p. 460.
        A comment is made on a Sotheby's sale of George Eliot
     MSS; her portraits were sold, her notebooks, and some of
     her books with inscriptions from Lewes.

2   BALD, MARJORY A. Women-Writers of the Nineteenth Century.
     Cambridge: The University Press, pp. 166-208.
        Four things must be considered in understanding George
     Eliot. She was a woman, a student; she stood apart from
     dogmatic Christianity; and she formed an "irregular" con-
     nection with Lewes. She sought the impersonal life of art
     as a fundamental religion. It was a channel to escape from

self. Her humor may be directed toward scorn or toward
fellow-feeling or compassion. Discusses the poetry with
respect. But "George Eliot plodded too much to be a great
poet."

*3   CAZAMIAN, MADELEINE L. Le Roman et les Idées en Angleterre:
     L'Influence de la Science (1860-1890). Strasburg: Li-
     brairie Istra; New York: Oxford University Press.
          This is a study of Dickens, Disraeli, Mrs. Gaskell, and
     Kingsley. Cited in 1969.B23.

*4   HUMPHREY, GRACE. The Story of the Marys. Philadelphia:
     Pennsylvania Publishing Company.
          Cited in ELL (1923).

1924 A BOOKS

1   MUDGE, ISADORE GILBERT, and M. E. SEARS. A George Eliot Dic-
     tionary. London: George Routledge and Sons; New York:
     H. W. Wilson Company.
          There is a chronological list of the novels, short stor-
     ies, and poems followed by synopses of these works. The
     dictionary itself consists of the characters of the novels,
     stories, and poems arranged alphabetically.

1924 B SHORTER WRITINGS

1   SPEARE, MORRIS EDMUND. "George Eliot and Radicalism." The
     Political Novel: Its Development in England and in America.
     New York: Oxford University Press, pp. 221-236.
          George Eliot attempts to discover in Felix Holt the pa-
     thos, the blindness, and the injustice of conduct and the
     heroism of the 1832 Reform Bill. Felix sounds the holiness
     of labor and has the asceticism and practical wisdom of the
     Puritan. He embodies the doctrines of Thomas Carlyle. The
     endowed classes hold the precious inheritances of the past
     in their hands. Yet George Eliot is convinced that no
     political reforms can amount to much if they are the result
     of moral reforms.

1925 A BOOKS - NONE

1925

1925 B SHORTER WRITINGS

1   GARDNER, CHARLES. "George Eliot's Quarries." Atlantic Month-
        ly, 136: 659-665.
            On Wednesday, June 27, 1923, at Sotheby's, three of
        George Eliot's notebooks were among the sales. One is the
        quarry for Middlemarch. The other two are for Romola; one
        of them is written entirely in Italian. Among the manu-
        scripts of Mrs. Ouvry, Lewes's granddaughter, was a sketch
        for a new novel and an independent jotting which may have
        been for another tale. Gardner's description of these MSS
        is followed by his own account of her life and his evalua-
        tion of her novels as being rather heavy, the work of a
        magnificent intelligence.

2   HALDANE, ELIZABETH S. "A Victorian Novelist." Saturday Re-
        view of Literature, 2: 97-98.
            The younger generation these days has little use for her
        high-brow view of life. George Eliot just missed being a
        pedant because of her enormous sympathy with actual human
        beings. There is humor in that she saw the inherent ab-
        surdity of much that passes as serious in ordinary life.
        Her great lesson is that the spiritual is all that counts.

*3   IMELMANN, R. ed. "Briefe Lord Actons über George Eliot."
        Festschrift für Johannes Hoops. Probleme d. engl. Sprache
        u. Kultur. Festschr. Johannes Hoops zum 60. Geburtstag.
        Hrsg. von W. Keller. Heidelberg: Winter.
            Cited in ELL(1925).

4   MUENIER, PIERRE-ALEXIS. "Lettres Inédites de Carlyle et de
        George Eliot." Revue de Littérature Comparée, 5: 499-505.
            Prints the text of George Eliot's letter of July 2, 1859,
        to Émile Montégut.

5   ROYCE, JOSIAH. "George Eliot As a Religious Teacher." Fugi-
        tive Essays. Cambridge: Harvard University Press, pp.
        261-289.
            The essay was written in 1880 and discusses the influence
        on George Eliot of Strauss, Feuerbach, Hegel, Spinoza, and
        Comte. Says that her personal views burst forth in her
        essay on Young. She never finished an abstract statement
        of doctrine, partly because she was at her best as an ar-
        tist, not a philosophic systematizer, and partly because
        she was too intensely skeptical to accept any one formula.

6   WADE, MABEL CLAIRE. "George Eliot's Philosophy of Sin." Eng-
        lish Journal, 14: 269-277.

72

George Eliot leaves no doubt of the hideousness of sin and its deadly effect on character. Her God is an illusion. Immortality is the effect of the lives of her characters on posterity. The characters suffer, but they can not be saved.

7   WEYGANDT, CORNELIUS. "The Higher Provincialism of George Eliot." A Century of the English Novel. New York: The Century Press.
    Feels that George Eliot's experience with life was so scant that she was soon written out. All of her writing in which there is joy and beauty is based on the same experience of life on a Warwickshire farm.

8   WOOLF, VIRGINIA. "George Eliot." The Common Reader. New York: Harcourt, Brace and World, Inc.
    Reprint of 1919.B7. Reprinted in 1960.A7 and 1965.A2.

1926 A BOOKS - NONE

1926 B SHORTER WRITINGS

1   LUSSKY, A. E. "George Eliot's The Mill on the Floss and Storm's Immensee." Modern Language Journal, 10: 431-433.
    Suggests strong similarities between passages in The Mill on the Floss and the tale "Immensee" (1849) by the German writer Theodor Storm. He presents evidence of George Eliot's intimate acquaintance with German literature contemporary with her own.

2   WILLIAMS, ORLO. "Adam Bede." Some Great English Novels: Studies in the Art of Fiction. London: Macmillan and Company, pp. 179-204.
    The novel is what publishers call a "strong" love story; there is the warning that moral weakness leads to disaster, the performance of duty to satisfaction, thoughtless pleasure-seeking to remorse, and humble virtue to a rich reward. Hetty is like an unfortunate character in Greek tragedy involved in the workings of immutable law. George Eliot cannot bring herself to a total condemnation of Hetty's beauty.

1927 A BOOKS

1   HALDANE, ELIZABETH S. George Eliot and Her Times. New York: D. Appleton and Company.

1927

> The purpose is to consider how the relations of George
> Eliot's work to the general aim and effort of her epoch
> appear after the lapse of nearly half a century. Wants to
> see in what form her ideas commended themselves to her con-
> temporaries and were rejected by her successors.

*2 POND, E. J. Les Idées Morales et Religieuses de George Eliot.
    Paris: Les Presses Universitaires.
    Cited in 1969.B23.

1927 B SHORTER WRITINGS

*1 CLIFFORD, W. K. "George Eliot: Some Personal Recollections."
    Bookman (London), October.
    Cited in 1969.B23.

*2 MUIR, P. H. "A Bibliography of First Editions of the Books of
    George Eliot." Bookman's Journal, Suppl., 4: 41-58.
    Cited in 1967.B31.

1928 A BOOKS

1 PATERSON, ARTHUR. George Eliot's Family Life and Letters.
    London: Selwyn and Blount; Boston: Houghton Mifflin.
      Largely a collection of letters telling domestic news
    from George Eliot and "Pater" to Lewes's sons. There are
    letters from Lewes, and a few are included from Lewes's
    sons. A biographical memoir accompanies the letter to give
    a vivid picture of George Eliot's affectionate personality
    and of their family life.

1928 B SHORTER WRITINGS

*1 LÖSCH, OLGA. "Das Naturgefühl bei George Eliot und Thomas
    Hardy." Beiträge zur Erforschung der Sprache und Kultur
    Englands und Nordamerikas, 5: 88-180.
    Cited in ELL (1928).

1929 A BOOKS

*1 SIMON-BAUMANN, LOTTE. Die Darstellung der Charaktere in
    George Eliots Romanen. Leipzig: Tauchnitz.
    Cited in 1969.B23.

1929 B SHORTER WRITINGS

1 DEVONSHIRE, MARION G. English Novel in France, 1830-1870.
London: Frank Cass and Company, pp. 365-375.
Adam Bede, Silas Marner, and La famille Tulliver were
well received in France. The French ranked her among the
greatest novelists of her time. They did not agree with
her views on realism and art, did not approve of her later
works, and deplored her lengthy dialogues which interfered
with the action. Reprinted in 1967.B11.

1930 A BOOKS

*1 KABOTH, KLARA. George Eliots Beziehungen zu Frankreich.
Breslau: Inaugural dissertation.
Cited in 1969.B23.

*2 MAY, JAMES LEWIS. George Eliot. London; Indianapolis: The
Bobbs-Merrill Company.
Harvey in Victorian Fiction: A Guide to Research
(1964.B11) says that this work is "honest and well inten-
tioned but often inaccurate and not worth serious study."

*3 PFEIFFER, SIBILLA. George Eliots Beziehungen zu Deutschland.
Anglistische Forschungen, Heft 60. Amsterdam: Swets und
Zeitlinger N.V., 1967, 309 pp; Heidelberg: Winter.
Contains a significant bibliography. Cited in 1930.ELL.

1930 B SHORTER WRITINGS

1 ANON. "Autograph MSS of George Eliot." Times Literary Supplement, April 24, p. 356.
A Sotheby's sale of the correspondence of G. H. Lewes
from Dickens and other of George Eliot's manuscripts is
reported with the items and prices given individually.

2 ANON. "George Eliot and Dr. Chapman." Times Literary Supplement, September 11, p. 720.
Describes Chapman's diaries about George Eliot, 1860.

3 BASSETT, J. J. "Purpose in George Eliot's Art." Anglia, 54
(November), 338-350.
George Eliot felt that fiction should teach the truth
about life through truths embodied in the story itself and
also by moral teachings added as side remarks.

1930

4   PARLETT, MATHILDE. "George Eliot and Humanism." Studies in
       Philology, 27: 25-46.
          Romola traces out the conflict in Renaissance Florence
       between Greek culture and the humanitarianism that Positiv-
       ism shares with Christianity. The humanist's life appears
       to be futile, and the Greek ethic is inadequate. George
       Eliot takes exception to the conception of antique culture
       as an unfailing and everlasting solace from sorrows; to the
       derivative idea that antique culture should be the basis of
       education; and to the assumption that humanities are eso-
       teric.

1931 A BOOKS

1   BUCKROSE, J. E. [ANNIE EDITH JAMESON]. Silhouette of Mary
       Ann. A Novel About George Eliot. London: Hodder and
       Stoughton; New York: Stokes.
          A fanciful fictional account of George Eliot's life.
       See 1931.A2.

2   [JAMESON, ANNIE EDITH] J. E. BUCKROSE. Silhouette of Mary Ann.
       A Novel About George Eliot. London: Hodder and Stoughton;
       New York: Stokes. See 1931.A1.

*3   TOYODA, MINORU. Studies in the Mental Development of George
       Eliot in Relation to the Science, Philosophy, and Theology
       of Her Day. Tokyo: Kenkyusha Company.
          In Victorian Fiction: A Guide to Research (1964.B11),
       Harvey says this study is naïve, though "painstaking."

1931 B SHORTER WRITINGS

1   KNIGHT, GRANT C. The Novel in English. New York: Richard
       R. Smith, Inc., pp. 187-198.
          Compares The Scarlet Letter to Adam Bede and The Marble
       Faun to Romola. Also contrasts their moral views. Her
       works are clinics in soul diseases; she never wrote a word
       in her novels of which her father could have complained
       that it violated scriptural teachings.

*2   SIMON-BAUMANN, LOTTE. "George Eliot über Heinrich Heine."
       Anglia, 55: 311-320.
          Cited in 1969.B23.

3   SPARROW-SIMPSON, W. J. "George Eliot's Religion." Church
       Quarterly Review, 224 (July), 233-247.

> She is aware of the power which accompanies definite con-
> viction. She was not in the smallest degree exclusive in
> her choice of the type of religion from which help may come.
> But not one of her characters achieves high moral excel-
> lence from an exclusively philosophic speculation.

1932 A BOOKS

1   ROMIEU, EMILIE and GEORGES. The Life of George Eliot. Trans-
    lated from the French by Brian W. Downs. New York: E. P.
    Dutton and Company.
       A fictionalized biography which portrays her as: "A gen-
    ius, a lofty, beautiful soul, assuredly, but above all a
    woman."

*2   ROSENBERG, ROSE SCHORR. "George Eliot: A Study in Conflicts."
    (University of Pittsburgh).
       Cited in ELL (1932).

1932 B SHORTER WRITINGS

1   LOVETT, ROBERT MORSS, and HELEN SAND HUGHES. A History of the
    Novel in England. Cambridge, Massachusetts: Houghton
    Mifflin Company, pp. 376-379.
       George Eliot's work represents the highest and sincerest
    development of fiction with a purpose. Those who live and
    suffer are able to compensate for evil in her system of
    ethics.

2   MACY, JOHN. "George Eliot: Victorian Queen." American Book-
    man, 75: 16-25.
       Reviews the facts of her progress toward "free-thinking"
    and her relationship with Lewes. Her later books are a
    descent from her greatest. Her emotional energy seems to
    have run out. She sits enthroned in a domestic Sunday af-
    ternoon court, as near to a salon as could be in England.

3   PURDY, R. L. "Journals and Letters of George Eliot." Yale
    University Library Gazette, 7: 1-4.
       Reviews what is available of George Eliot's letters and
    diaries in comparison to what Cross chose to print. Among
    the materials available the future biographer should be
    able to trace a new George Eliot and reveal her passionate
    intellectual curiosity and that age-old conflict of the
    flesh and the spirit.

1932

4   SACKVILLE-WEST, VICTORIA. "George Eliot." <u>The Great Victori-</u>
    <u>ans</u>. Edited by H. J. and Hugh Massingham. Garden City:
    Doubleday, Doran, pp. 185-195.
        Says that "<u>Romola</u> should not be read by anyone over the
    age of seventeen. <u>Romola</u> was a freak in an otherwise or-
    derly intellectual existence."

<u>1933 A BOOKS</u>

1   BOURL'HONNE, P. <u>George Eliot: Essai de Biographie Intellec-</u>
    <u>tuelle et Morale, 1819-1854</u>. Paris: Champion.
        Suggests that the spirit of Feuerbach, and especially his
    views on friendship and marriage, may have contributed
    towards making George Eliot's union with Lewes possible.
    She never attained true humility although she was con-
    stantly denouncing spiritual pride and indulging in self-
    abasement. Her inspiration is optimistic; yet her works
    are pessimistic.

2   FREMANTLE, ANNE. <u>George Eliot</u>. London: Duckworth; New York:
    Macmillan.
        Concludes that "she had no sense of form and no love of,
    nor gift for handling words nor much dramatic power, but
    she has an almost unparalleled power of description, and
    her characterization is unequaled." And "Her attempt to
    carry ethical purpose and erudition into art nearly ruined
    that art." She includes the fact that George Eliot's poem,
    "O May I Join the Choir Invisible" was used as a Positivist
    hymn and was read at the end of George Eliot's funeral.

3   KITCHEL, ANNA THERESA. <u>George Lewes and George Eliot: A Re-</u>
    <u>view of Records</u>. New York: The John Day Company.
        Recreates the early career of Lewes, 1840-1860, and fol-
    lows "as intimately as possible" Lewes's life with George
    Eliot. His whole personality was of a quality complemen-
    tary to her own. The Appendices contain lists of Lewes's
    works and an excerpt from the novel, <u>The Autobiography of</u>
    <u>Christopher Kirkland</u>, 1885, by Mrs. Eliza Lynn Linton,
    which is a reminiscence of Lewes's break with his wife.

<u>1933 B SHORTER WRITINGS</u>

1   GARY, FRANKLIN. "In Search of George Eliot: An Approach
    Through Marcel Proust." <u>Symposium</u>, 4: 182-206.
        There is no cult of George Eliot; her wide circle of
    readers died with the Victorian age. She seems to have had
    no influence on contemporary novelists. Yet she appears to
    have affected Proust. Attempts to explain what appealed to

Proust in her novels. He found in her treatment of memory a point of view already congenial to him. She has made incarnate in her novels a humanist view of the universe.

*2 PARLETT, MATHILDE M. "George Eliot and the English Literary Periodical." University of North Carolina Record: Research in Progress, July 1932–July 1933. Chapel Hill: University of North Carolina Press.
       Cited in ELL(1933).

3 _____. "The Influence of Contemporary Criticism on George Eliot." Studies in Philology, 30: 103–132.
       The critical appreciation of her later works grows as those who claim preeminence for the early novels become fewer. The first group includes Scenes, Adam Bede, The Mill on the Floss, and Silas Marner. Their material is drawn largely from her own experience. The characters are simple, plain people, motivated by the elemental drives of universal human nature. The second group includes Romola, Felix Holt, Middlemarch, and Daniel Deronda. These characters are drawn mainly from her own imagination. There is so much dissection and interpretation that the characters are not dramatically present. Miss Parlett then explains her reasons for thinking George Eliot changed the type of novels after reading the contemporary criticism.

4 PARRISH, M. L. Victorian Lady Novelists: George Eliot, Mrs. Gaskell, the Brontë Sisters. First Editions in the Library at Dormy House. New Jersey. London: Constable, pp. 3–51.
       Says it is quite incomprehensible that an exhaustive bibliography of George Eliot has not been made. Gives complete information about George Eliot's first editions and includes pertinent letters.

1934 A BOOKS

*1 LEMKE, FREDERICK D. "George Eliot and Her Predecessors in Village Literature." (University of Illinois).
       Cited in ELL(1935).

*2 MÖLLES, ALFRED. George Eliots Beschäftigung mit dem Judentum und ihre Stellung für Judenfrage. Hamburg: P. Brandel.
       Cited in 1967.B31.

1934 B SHORTER WRITINGS

1 CECIL, LORD DAVID. Early Victorian Novelists: Essays in Revaluation. London: Constable, pp. 309–336.

1934

    George Eliot brings characters alive by penetrating to the secret mainsprings of their actions. She exposes all the complex writhings of a spirit striving to make itself at ease on the bed of a disturbed conscience and the desperate casuistry by which it attempts to justify itself. Reprinted in 1935.B1, 1960.A7, and 1965.A2.

2   MASEFIELD, MURIEL. Women Novelists From Fanny Burney to George Eliot. Freeport, New York: Books for Libraries Press, Inc.

    One chapter is called "Life of George Eliot," and one is "George Eliot's Novels." She is typical of a period when even the atheists were religious. Her works bear too clearly the marks of conscientious intellectual labor. Reprinted in 1967.B33.

3   MOORE, VIRGINIA. Distinguished Women Writers. New York: Dutton, pp. 205-218.

    George Eliot strove all her life to tell people what they should be and do. But she stands today as a monumental and all but terrifying example of what a novelist should not be and do. An account of her life follows this proclamation.

1935 A BOOKS

*1   BERTI, LUIGI. Considerazioni sul realismo morale di G. Eliot. Florence: Nuovo Italia, Novembre.

    Cited in 1969.B23.

1935 B SHORTER WRITINGS

1   CECIL, LORD DAVID. Early Victorian Novelists: Essays in Revaluation. New York: Bobbs-Merrill Co.

    Reprint of 1934.B1.

2   CLARKE, ISABEL C. Six Portraits. Freeport, New York: Books for Libraries Press, Inc., pp. 137-192.

    A biographical sketch, this attributes to Lewes much of George Eliot's success. He gave her the love and appreciation she craved most. Reprinted in 1967.B5.

3   D., F. "Daniel Deronda: 'Organ Stop.'" Notes and Queries, 169: 175-176.

    "Organ pause" as George Eliot uses it is simply a translation of the French "point d'orgue."

4   WILLIAMS, BLANCHE COLTON. "George Eliot and John Chapman: A
     Fragment." Colophon, n.s. 1: 65-70.
        Contains a history of the relationship between George Eli-
     ot and John Chapman with a reprinting of some of their let-
     ters.

1936 A BOOKS

*1   DAVIES, RUTH G. "George Eliot: A Study in Mid-Victorian Pes-
     simism." Doctoral Dissertations Accepted by American Uni-
     versities, no. 3, p. 85. (Ohio State University).
        Cited in ELL (1936).

2   EUWEMA, BEN. The Development of George Eliot's Ethical and
     Social Theories. Private Edition. Chicago: The Univer-
     sity of Chicago Libraries. 40 pp.
        Describes George Eliot's emancipation from Christian dog-
     ma, and discusses the influences which lead her to religious
     rationalism. She comes to promise the virtuous the immor-
     tality sanctioned by the Religion of Humanity; the dead
     live in minds made better by their presence. Euwema lists
     "the dogmas of Calvinism" and gives her symbolic interpre-
     tation of each of them.

3   WILLIAMS, BLANCHE COLTON. George Eliot. New York: The Mac-
     millan Company.
        Based in part on an acquaintance with living relatives of
     George Eliot and Lewes. Also came to know Cross's niece
     and various friends. She has visited her childhood haunts.
     The book contains a number of photographs.

1936 B SHORTER WRITINGS

1   DIEKHOFF, JOHN S. "The Happy Ending of Adam Bede." English
     Literary History, 3: 221-227.
        He finds a contradiction between the happy ending and the
     "main moral bias" of the novel. The marriage of Dinah and
     Adam, which was added to the original plan of the novel out
     of deference to Lewes's mistaken judgment, is out of har-
     mony with the tone of the whole and untrue to the charac-
     ters. The wedding, Adam's forgiveness of Arthur, and the
     pardon of Hetty are all gestures which show her dependence
     on his judgment. Until the ending, the novel is a sermon
     on the unhappy consequences of sin which affect the inno-
     cent as well as the guilty. That the wrongs are righted in
     the end is artistically untrue.

1937

1937 B SHORTER WRITINGS

1   BAKER, ERNEST A. "George Eliot." The History of the English
       Novel. London: H. F. & G. Witherby, Ltd.; New York:
       Barnes and Noble, 8: 221-273.
         She abandoned dogmas which gave Evangelical principles
       authority and sanctity and erected those moral principles
       into a religion which she believed to be established, rati-
       fied, and sanctified by the admonitions of life itself.
       Middlemarch is a characteristic study of human solidarity;
       the highest possible development of personality becomes a
       religion.

2   DAVIS, JESSIE. "George Eliot and Education." Educational
       Forum, 1: 201-206.
         George Eliot was interested in education because of its
       moral implications. She was particularly concerned about
       the education of women. Her views are set forth most
       clearly in The Mill on the Floss. She admired idealists,
       but she also saw the value of the woman who was of practi-
       cal use either in the home or out.

3   H., J. "The Schoolteacher's Novel: Silas Marner." Saturday
       Review of Literature, 15 (March 20), 13.
         George Eliot's worst novel is her most important. One
       part melodrama and one part Sunday School moralizing make
       it the perfect schoolteacher's idea of the novel to teach.
       Silas utters no dirty words. Teaching Silas Marner is a
       good example of the failure to prevent the teaching of
       public school English exclusively by old maids.

4   MURRAY, EDWARD C. "Samuel Laurence's Portrait of George
       Eliot." British Museum Quarterly, 11: 11-13.
         Describes the portrait of George Eliot by Samuel Laurence.
       He met her because he was so delighted with Adam Bede. In
       the early months of 1861 Lewes commissioned the painter to
       make a drawing of her. She gave him repeated sittings at
       his studio at 6 Wells Street, London. Then Lewes refused
       to take the drawing.

1938 B SHORTER WRITINGS

1 ANON. "Dickens to George Eliot; Unpublished Letters." Dickensian, 34: 268-269.
   Two letters from Dickens are printed in full. The first was written in January, 1858. He begins, "Dear Sir," but says he would address the writer as a woman if left to his own devices. The second was written in July, 1859, after she revealed her identity to him. He is very complimentary of Adam Bede.

2 BACON, JANE. "George Eliot." Dickensian, 34: 264-267.
   This account of the life of George Eliot closes with the observation, "Her genius is undeniable, but one cannot help wishing that she had known laughter and that in walking with intellectual kings, she had not lost the common touch."

3 BETHELL, S. L. "The Novels of George Eliot." Criterion, 18 (October), 39-57.
   Sees her use of scientific metaphor as characteristic of a dominant tendency of her age. Discusses several novels.

4 PHELPS, WILLIAM LYON. The Advance of the English Novel. New York: Dodd, Mead and Company, pp. 113-115.
   Reports (with no citation) a conversation between Lewes, Professor Bogesen of Columbia, and Turgenev on which was her best book. Lewes declared for Daniel Deronda, Bogesen for Middlemarch, and Turgenev for The Mill on the Floss.

5 STRACHAN, L. R. M. "George Eliot as Reviewer." Notes and Queries, 174: 14.
   Four of George Eliot's reviews which were contributed to the Westminster Review were reprinted in Essays and Leaves from a Notebook edited by Charles Lee Lewes. Her other contributions to the Westminster Review are listed here.

6 WILLIAMS, BLANCHE C. "George Eliot: Social Pressure on the Individual." Sewanee Review, 46: 235-241.
   Everything in George Eliot's novels results from causes. The characters reap what they sow. Her relationship with Lewes had a great influence on her work. She began to write because of the social pressures she felt and because of the needs of his family.

1939 A BOOKS

*1 DEWES, SIMON. Marian: The Life of George Eliot. London: Rich and Cowan.

1939

Harvey in Victorian Fiction: A Guide to Research
(1964.B11) refers to this study as "a vulgar dramatization,
frequently inaccurate and generally worthless."

1939 B SHORTER WRITINGS

*1   ANSON, H. "The Church in Nineteenth Century Fiction: George
      Eliot." Listener, May 25.
         Cited in 1969.B23.

2   C., T. C. "Middlemarch: A Classical Reference." Notes and
      Queries, 176: 44.
         A passage describing Dorothea refers to words of Herodo-
      tus I, 188 and 191, concerning the march of Cyrus against
      Babylon.

3   MODDER, MONTAGU FRANK. "Daniel Deronda." The Jew in the
      Literature of England. Philadelphia: The Jewish Publica-
      tion Society of America.
         George Eliot was attracted by Disraeli's idea of a res-
      toration of a national center for the Jewish people. Dan-
      iel Deronda reveals this sympathetic attitude and is re-
      ported to have played a considerable part in predisposing
      certain elements of European Jewry in favor of a Zionist
      movement.

1940 A BOOKS

*1   DOREMUS, ROBERT. "George Henry Lewes: A Descriptive Biogra-
      phy." Doctoral Dissertations Accepted by American Univer-
      sities, no. 7, p. 104. 2 vols. (Harvard University).
         Cited in 1940. Doctoral Dissertations.

2   HAIGHT, GORDON S. George Eliot and John Chapman. With Chap-
      man's Diaries. New Haven: Yale University Press.
         George Eliot met Chapman in 1842 when he was absorbed
      in phrenology. He became someone for her to lean on and
      gave her the opportunity to devote herself wholly to some-
      one she loved. Chapman edited the Westminster Review for
      forty-three years. He lived a life of "deliberate sensu-
      ality." He was always silent about his relationship with
      George Eliot. This outlines their relationship and prints
      materials from the years which Cross (1885.A3) intention-
      ally omitted. Reprinted in 1969.A8.

1940 B SHORTER WRITINGS

1   MALY-SCHLATTER, F. The Puritan Element in Victorian Fiction:
     With Special Reference to the Works of George Eliot, Dick-
     ens, and Thackeray. Zurich: A. G. Gebr. Leeman and Com-
     pany.
         George Eliot treats Maggie's spiritual experience and
     Hetty's actual physical sin; the girls have her sympathy,
     but she knows from her own experience the great price a
     Victorian has to pay for sexual freedom. Feminine delicacy
     demanded that ladies be unconscious of passion. Weakness
     is the basis of evil for George Eliot. Contemporary re-
     viewers were shocked because she acknowledged passion in a
     woman. The scene in Hetty's bed chamber is unmistakably
     and frankly sensual. George Eliot was wholly under the
     spell of Hetty's charm, yet even so she is forced to punish
     her for the consequences of her comeliness.

2   SACKVILLE-WEST, EDWARD. "Books in General." New Statesman,
     20 (November 23), 518-520.
         Stresses the idea that George Eliot is a novelist-philos-
     opher with an underlying conflict between feeling and in-
     tellect. The immense seriousness of tone is the most
     striking thing about Middlemarch. Her theme concerns the
     problem of fidelity; it is illustrated by the Casaubons and
     the Lydgates.

1941 A BOOKS

*1   RYAN, MARION A. "George Eliot As A Literary Critic." Doctor-
     al Dissertations Accepted by American Universities, no. 8,
     p. 116. (Boston University).
         Cited in ELL (1941).

1941 B SHORTER WRITINGS

1   WRIGHT, WALTER F. "George Eliot as Industrial Reformer."
     Publications of the Modern Language Association, 56: 1107-
     1115.
         In Felix Holt George Eliot was first of all interested
     in finding out to what extent men and women were responsi-
     ble for their own fate and to what extent one should expect
     progress in the moral, social, and intellectual worlds.
     She was trying to fit economic and social progress into a
     cosmic pattern, slowly evolutionary and yet directed.

1942

1942 A BOOKS - NONE

1942 B SHORTER WRITINGS

    1   GEROULD, GORDON HALL. The Patterns of English and American Fiction. Boston: Little Brown and Company, pp. 367-376.
        George Eliot was a passionate creature and a keenly sensitive one. She tried to show the operation of the inexorable laws by which men's lives are governed.

    2   HAIGHT, GORDON S. "George Eliot Letters." Times Literary Supplement, January 3, p. 7.
        Reports excerpts of letters published in 1894 by Poet-Lore. They were written by George Eliot to her school friend Martha Jackson.

    3   PRITCHETT, V. S. "Books in General." New Statesman, n.s. 24 (October 31), 291-292.
        A general, complimentary treatment of the novel in which Pritchett suggests that George Eliot persuades the reader to take her philosophy of life seriously.

1943 A BOOKS - NONE

1943 B SHORTER WRITINGS

    1   ANNAN, NOEL. "Books in General." New Statesman, 26 (November 27), 355.
        George Eliot valued her abilities as an intellectual and a moralist far above her gifts as a novelist. Yet her compassion pervades Middlemarch through her humor as she shows how the search for the true and the good brings suffering and sorrow.

    2   G., E. "Henry James on George Eliot." Notes and Queries, 185 (July 31), 76.
        Answers Alice Meynell's account of the "foolishness" of Ruskin and Brown (1943.B4) with Henry James' tribute in his Preface to "Princess Casamassima" (1908).

    3   HENRY, JOHN. "Henry James on George Eliot." Notes and Queries, 185: 235-236.
        When Henry James proclaimed Felix Holt a masterpiece, Nation, August 16, 1866, he was obviously immature and unwise.

4   P., B. J.   "Dr. John Brown and Ruskin on George Eliot."   <u>Notes
    and Queries</u>, 184 (April 24), 251-252.
        <u>Dr. Brown</u> found in <u>Middlemarch</u> and <u>The Mill on the Floss</u>
    the taint of sexuality and sensuality. Ruskin ridiculed
    the flight and return of Maggie. He gets at both opinions
    through Alice Meynell.

5   WAGENKNECHT, EDWARD.   "The 'New' Novel: George Eliot."   <u>Caval-
    cade of the English Novel</u>. New York: Henry Holt and Com-
    pany, pp. 319-335.
        Discusses her break with the traditions of her youth.
    She was the first major English novelist who did not pro-
    fess the Christian religion. Yet none other has set forth
    the Christian ethic with such intellectual power. She
    never made the loss of faith the principal theme of a novel.
    A bibliography is included, pp. 601-602.

*6 YOUNG, PERCY M.   "George Eliot and Music."   <u>Music and Letters</u>,
    24: 92-100.
        Cited in 1969.B23.

<u>1944 A BOOKS - NONE</u>

<u>1944 B SHORTER WRITINGS</u>

1   LIPTZIN, SOL.   "Heine, the Continuation of Goethe: A Mid-
    Victorian Legend."   <u>Journal of English and Germanic Philol-
    ogy</u>, 43: 317-325.
        George Eliot and Matthew Arnold are primarily responsible
    for Heine's mid-Victorian fame. Her essay on Heine ap-
    peared in the <u>Westminster Review</u> in 1856, about a month be-
    fore his death. It was reprinted in the <u>Eclectic Magazine</u>,
    in <u>Littell's Living Age</u>, and in later editions of her works.
    She knew Heine well and was the first English writer of
    eminence to appraise him as a lyric genius equalled by none
    save Goethe.

2   PRITCHETT, V. S.   "Books in General."   <u>New Statesman</u>, 28: 170.
        Calls George Eliot the great schoolmistress who has more
    to teach the modern novelists than any Victorian. She
    teaches the interest of massive writing, of placing people,
    of showing how even the minds of characters must be placed
    among other minds.

<u>1945 A BOOKS - NONE</u>

1945

1945 B SHORTER WRITINGS

1 BISSON, L. A. "Proust, Bergson, and George Eliot." Modern
Language Review, 40: 104-114.
   Compares passages in The Mill on the Floss to Proust's
conception and literary treatment of the affective or in-
voluntary memory and its mode of operation in A la re-
cherche du temps perdu. In this novel George Eliot dwells
on unsought reawakening, not conscious remembering, of the
experiences of childhood. She translates the Bergsonian
formulas of time and memory into terms of lyric sentiment.

2 DeBANKE, CÉCILE. "Week end with Middlemarch." Queen's Quarterly, 52: 346-351.
   A comment on the entertainment value of the novel.

3 LEAVIS, F. R. "Revaluations (XV): George Eliot, I." Scrutiny, 13: 172-187.
   George Eliot's moral preoccupations leave a large established blur across the reader's field of vision. At her
best she has the impersonality of a genius, but there is
characteristic work of hers that is rightly felt to have
intimate relations with her weakness. Silas Marner closes
the first phase of her creative life. Romola might well
have justified the opinion that her creative life was over.

4 _____. "Revaluations (XV): George Eliot, II." Scrutiny, 13:
257-271.
   Discusses Romola, Felix Holt, and Middlemarch. Romola is
unreadable; Felix Holt is exasperating and characteristic
of her, and only Middlemarch represents her mature genius.

1946 A BOOKS - NONE

1946 B SHORTER WRITINGS

1 BULLETT, GERALD. "George Eliot." Times Literary Supplement,
March 23, p. 139.
   He advertises the writing of his critical biography and
asks for relevant information.

2 DODDS, M. H. "George Eliot and Charles Dickens." Notes and
Queries, 190: 143-145.
   Bleak House seems to have influenced George Eliot in
writing Felix Holt. Both involve a Chancery suit. She
seems to use the same story. Her characters are more realistic.

1946

3   HALSTEAD, FRANK G. "George Eliot: Medical Digressions in
       Middlemarch, and Eliot's State of Health." Bulletin of the
       History of Medicine, 20: 413-425.
         George Eliot's evaluation of Xavier Bichat is realistic
       and as far as it goes, accurate. In modern pathology a
       diseased organ is diseased only in that one or more of its
       several tissues are affected. Her choice of Bichat is
       quite fitting. Halstead goes on to explain that instead of
       dying of eyestrain as Dr. Gould has suggested that she more
       than likely died of an inflammation of the pericardium.

4   HINKLEY, LAURA L. Ladies of Literature. New York: Hastings
       House, pp. 279-351.
         Proclaims George Eliot "the greatest lady who has appeared
       in literature."

5   LEAVIS, F. R. "Revaluations (XV): George Eliot, III." Scru-
       tiny, 14: 15-26.
         Continues the discussion of Middlemarch. The emotional
       "fulness" represented by Dorothea depends for its power on
       an abeyance of intelligence and self-knowledge, and the
       situations offered by way of "objective correlative" have
       only a day-dream relation to experience; they have no ob-
       jectivity, no vigor of illusion.

6   _____. "George Eliot: Daniel Deronda and The Portrait of a
       Lady." Scrutiny, 14: 102-131.
         In no other of George Eliot's works is the association of
       the strength with the weakness so remarkable or so unfor-
       tunate as in Daniel Deronda. He discusses the novel in
       terms of the Deronda part and the Gwendolen part. The dif-
       ference between James and George Eliot is largely a matter
       of what he left out. He derives much more from George Eli-
       ot than he suspects. Isabel Archer has neither a more in-
       tense nor a richer moral significance than Gwendolen Har-
       leth, but very much the reverse.

7   McCULLOUGH, BRUCE. "The Psychological Novel: George Eliot's
       Middlemarch." Representative English Novelists: Defoe to
       Conrad. New York: Harper and Brothers, pp. 197-214.
         George Eliot took a broad view of conduct and, in examin-
       ing the motives of her protagonists, attempted to evaluate
       the relative influence of internal and external factors.
       She joined the worlds of inward propensity and visible cir-
       cumstance and showed both. What happens to Dorothea and
       Lydgate is symbolic of what happens to us all. The read-
       er's interest in the community is incidental to his inter-
       est in those who are seriously at odds with community
       ideals.

1946

8 PARSONS, COLEMAN O. "Background Material Illustrative of
Silas Marner." Notes and Queries, 191: 266-270.
Relates the story of Silas to miser-lore as found in Bal-
zac's Maître Cornélius, 1831; a ghost story in Harper's,
1857; and Dickens' "A Christmas Carol," 1843. Yet George
Eliot goes beyond these to present a full-length portrait
with enough detail to attain full emotional force.

9 PRITCHETT, V. S. The Living Novel. London: Chatto and Windus.
George Eliot is one of the first to give an intellectual
direction to the English novel. Hers is a world where conscience and self-interest keep down the passions like a
pair of gamekeepers. Reprinted in 1947.B3. The section on
George Eliot is reprinted in 1960.A7 and 1965.A2.

1947 A BOOKS

1 BULLETT, GERALD. George Eliot: Her Life and Books. London:
Collins.
Discusses the novels only in a general way. Makes comments such as "If you are a character in a George Eliot
novel, the chief thing you have to fear is your author's
unqualified moral approval. If that cannot destroy your
pretension to reality, nothing can." He suggests that the
success she does attain is "beyond her conscious intention." Reprinted in 1948.A2.

*2 FUKUHARA, RINTARO. "Romola." Fujingaho (Japan), no. 8.
Cited in ELL (1947).

*3 SAKSENA, P. K. The Novels of George Eliot. Lucknow Univer-
sity.
Cited in ELL (1947).

1947 B SHORTER WRITINGS

1 BAILY, F. E. Six Great Victorian Novelists. London: MacDon-
ald and Company, pp. 113-142.
A simple biographical "story," this includes judgments
such as that her stories, naturally, had to be anonymous.
No publisher would dare to publish a novel signed by Mary
Ann, who was living in sin.

2 COHEN, ISRAEL. "Comments on Daniel Deronda." Times Literary
Supplement, August 23, p. 427.

Cohen writes a letter saying Lewes was acquainted in
Paris with a German Jew, Moses Hess. They no doubt discussed the basis of Jewish nationalism.

3   PRITCHETT, V. S. The Living Novel. New York: Reynal and
      Hitchcock.
        Reprint of 1946.B9.

4   RENDALL, VERNON: "George Eliot and the Classics." Notes and
      Queries, 192: 544-546, 564-565.
        George Eliot told R. C. Jebb that Sophocles had influ-
      enced her in the "delineations of the great primitive emo-
      tions." The article includes instances from George Eliot's
      fiction in which she quotes Sophocles.

1948 A BOOKS

1   BENNETT, JOAN. George Eliot: Her Mind and Her Art. Cam-
      bridge, England: University Press.
        The first three chapters are biography. Eight others
      discuss the novels individually. Professor Bennett feels
      that George Eliot concentrated on discovering all the bear-
      ings of the situation she invented. Her novels have or-
      ganic form. They are more entertaining and persuasive than
      those of any other Victorian novelist. Reprinted in
      1962.A1. Pp. 77-101 reprinted as "Visions and Design" in
      1960.A7. Also in 1965.A2.

2   BULLETT, GERALD. George Eliot: Her Life and Books. New
      Haven: Yale University Press.
        Reprint of 1947.A1.

1948 B SHORTER WRITINGS

1   BRIGGS, ASA. "Middlemarch and the Doctors." Cambridge Jour-
      nal, 1: 749-762.
        The historian of public health in the nineteenth century
      must go back to Middlemarch. Lydgate's scheme for the new
      hospital is a symbol of the meeting of his and Dorothea's
      minds. The climax of the novel hangs around an experimen-
      tal prescription given by Lydgate to Bulstrode. The rival-
      ry of his fellow doctors and the ignorance of the public
      both played a part in Lydgate's downfall. The historian
      will find George Eliot's novels of more value than many
      well-established sources in analyzing these vital forces in
      the making of Victorian society.

1948

2 CARTER, JOHN. "Reflections on Rarity." New Colophon, 1, Part 2: 134-150.
   Some mention of George Eliot bibliography. Tells the number of copies printed in the first edition of each novel and comments on the relative availability and conditions of copies of the first editions.

3 CHEW, SAMUEL C. "The Nineteenth Century and After." A Literary History of England. Edited by Albert C. Baugh. New York: Appleton-Century-Crofts, pp. 1378-1381.
   George Eliot exhibits men and women in relation to an ideal based on principles of truth and goodness. Her humane feeling for her characters is futile. Moral choice is everything. Moral degeneration follows acts committed from selfish motives, and moral regeneration is accomplished by acts of love unregardful of self. She constantly intersperses philosophic remarks to serve her didactic purpose. Reprinted in 1967.B3.

4 COOLIDGE, T. "George Eliot in Defense of George Lewes." More Books, 23: 269-270.
   Prints the text of a letter.

5 GREENHUT, MORRIS. "George Henry Lewes and the Classical Tradition in English Criticism." Review of English Studies, 24: 126-137.
   Proclaims Lewes to be a literary critic of a high order of excellence. His views are basically humanistic and classical. He is alert to the intellectual currents of his time, possessing a fine command of language and an extensive knowledge of Continental literature.

6 _____. "George Henry Lewes as a Critic of the Novel." Studies in Philology, 45: 491-511.
   At a time when English literary critics paid little attention to the novel as a literary form, Lewes identifies it with the classical tradition. A novel is good or great to the extent that it is true to the aspect of experience which it represents.

7 HOUGH, GRAHAM. "Novelist-Philosophers--XII--George Eliot." Horizon, 17: 50-62.
   The immediate effect of the novels is of a massive realism which never outweighs the structure of morality and emotional regeneration which is her real theme.

8 HOUSE, HUMPHREY. "Qualities of George Eliot's Unbelief." Listener, 25 (March 25). [BBC Third Programme, March 15].

1949

Outlines the way Christianity lost its traditional meaning for George Eliot, but it remained for her the most
relevant and moving symbolism for the mysteries of life.
Reprinted in 1955.B7.

9   NAUMANN, WALTER. "The Architecture of George Eliot's Novels."
    Modern Language Quarterly, 9: 35-50.
        George Eliot's talent does not lie in plot. She does not
    depict an action but a situation. The dialogues, both the
    single and the group, form the nucleus of her narrative
    art. The mainspring of her novels is sympathy with one's
    fellowman. Gwendolen's initial egoistic pride is broken by
    the awakening of her own subconscious being. Deronda pro-
    vides sympathy and supports Gwendolen in her renunciation.
    He is dependent on no one. By making her hero an ideal,
    George Eliot oversteps and falsifies the circumstances and
    the relationships.

10 RENDALL, VERNON. "George Eliot and the Classics." Notes and
    Queries, 193: 148-149, 272-274.
        The first selection records George Eliot's Latin quota-
    tions. The second continues the list. She uses Horace in
    numerous places, Cicero, Persius, Quintilian, and Plautus
    as well as others.

1949 A BOOKS - NONE

1949 B SHORTER WRITINGS

1   COOKE, JOHN D. and LIONEL STEVENSON. English Literature of
        the Victorian Period. New York: Appleton-Century-Crofts.
        Contains something on George Eliot bibliography along
    with a traditional summary of her attempt to "offer a seri-
    ous interpretation of life."

2   HAIGHT, GORDON S. "George Eliot and Bedford College." London
        Times Literary Supplement, June 3, p. 365.
        Haight comments on an earlier note by Kathleen Tillotson
    which indicated three ladies named Evans were registered
    at Bedford College. In a letter to the Brays, January 28,
    1851, George Eliot said that she was attending Professor
    Newman's course in geometry and that it was expensive.

3   SACKVILLE-WEST, EDWARD. "Middlemarch." Inclinations. London:
        Secker and Warburg, pp. 27-32.
        The tone of the novel is immensely serious. Her theme
    concerns the problems of fidelity.

1949

4   SCHORER, MARK. "Fiction and the Matrix of Analogy." Kenyon
      Review, 11: 539-559.
        George Eliot's metaphors tend always to be, or to become,
      explicit symbols of psychological or moral conditions.
      They actually function to give symbolic value to much of
      the action in the novels. He discusses metaphors of unifi-
      cation, of antithesis, of shaping and making, and of a
      "muted apocalypse." Reprinted in 1952.B1 and 1965.A2.

*5   SIMON, IRÈNE. Formes du Roman Anglais de Dickens à Joyce.
      Liège: Bibliothèque de la Faculté de Philosophie et
      Lettres de l'Université de Liège, pp. 128-153.
        Cited in 1969.B23.

6   TILLOTSON, KATHLEEN. "George Eliot and Bedford College."
      Times Literary Supplement, April 30, p. 281.
        A note which indicates that three ladies named Evans were
      registered for classes at Bedford College.

7   WILLEY, BASIL. Nineteenth Century Studies: Coleridge to Mat-
      thew Arnold. London: Chatto and Windus.
        George Eliot deserves a central place in the main cur-
      rents of thought and belief in nineteenth century England.
      "Probably no English writer of the time, and certainly no
      novelist, more fully epitomizes the century; her develop-
      ment is a paradigm, her intellectual biography a graph of
      its most decided trend." He discusses Hennell, Strauss,
      and Feuerbach as the formative influences on her thinking
      as she turns to a religion of humanity. Reprinted in
      1966.B25. The section on George Eliot is reprinted in
      1960.A7 and 1965.A2.

1950 A BOOKS

1   FOULDS, ELFRIDA VIPONT. Toward a High Attic: The Early Life
      of George Eliot, 1819-1880. London: Hamish Hamilton.
        Classified as juvenile literature. Reprinted in 1971.A3.

2   KITCHEL, ANNA THERESA ed. Quarry for Middlemarch. Berkeley:
      University of California Press. Supplement to Nineteenth
      Century Fiction, 1950.
        This notebook contains detailed notes on medical and
      political information, on the time-schemes and character
      relationships for the novel. The first half of the note-
      book is called "Quarry I" and contains notes on scientific
      and medical matters for the chapters, and political dates
      from the Annual Register. "Quarry II" is written on the

backs of the pages of the first half. It is used for working out the structure of the novel.

1950 B SHORTER WRITINGS

1   ALTICK, RICHARD D. The Scholar Adventurers. New York: Macmillan.
        The letters of George Eliot and Lewes were found in curious places; it seems that a special providence attends the labors of George Eliot scholars.

2   HAIGHT, GORDON S. "Cross's Biography of George Eliot." Yale University Library Gazette, 25: 1-9.
        When Cross's volume (1885.A3) was published, many readers were disappointed. It was unthinkable that a bereaved husband should have done anything but embalm the image of the Ideal George Eliot. To a scholar the destruction of the materials relating to her life seems a crime. Critics today ought to be grateful for what his pious hand has spared. Haight announces his intention to make an edition of the letters.

3   RUST, JAMES D. "George Eliot's Reviews of Three Victorian Poets." Papers of the Michigan Academy of Science, Arts, and Letters, 36: 293-303.
        In 1855 George Eliot reviewed Arnold's Poems, Second Series, Tennyson's Maud, and Browning's Men and Women. For her the most important characteristic of great poetry is its lyrical, melodic quality. Rust finds her first application of the teachings of Feuerbach in her analysis of In Memoriam, which sees sanctification of human love as a religion. She admired Tennyson's exaltation of love.

4   WILLEY, BASIL. "The English Novel--VI. A Nineteenth Century Intellectual Novelist." Listener, February 23, pp. 352-353.
        George Eliot gave the novel a new intellectual standing. She had first-class intellectual equipment: a breadth of scope which could include knowledge of other cultures and languages and a keen awareness of her own age. Her books embody her own life story, and they have become documents of social history.

1951 A BOOKS

1   COOPER, LETTICE ULPHA. George Eliot: Writers and Their Works. London: Published for the British Council by

1951

Longmans, Green, and Co. 46 pp.
Gives a short summary of "standard" estimates of the
novels. A short selected bibliography appears at the end.
Says moral concern for her characters was the very essence
of George Eliot. She left the English novel aware of character on a much deeper level.

*2   DEL GUERCIO, TOSELLI. "Ethics in the Private Letters, Essays,
and Fiction of George Eliot." Doctoral Dissertations Accepted by American Universities, no. 18, p. 228.
Cited in 1967.B31.

1951 B SHORTER WRITINGS

1   BISSELL, CLAUDE T. "Social Analysis in the Novels of George
Eliot." English Literary History, 8: 221-239.
George Eliot's vision of society and her vision of the
individual never split asunder. Her role was recorder and
reflective observer of man in society. Tells how this role
was performed in each novel. Reprinted in 1961.B19.

2   BUCKLEY, JEROME. The Victorian Temper: A Study in Literary
Culture. Harvard University Press. New York: Random
House.
Discusses the way in which George Eliot has integrated
the water symbol into several intellectualized character
studies. Her realism he finds "tedious and unproductive."

*3   JOSIPOVIČ, S. "Povedom Eliotova "Sajlez Marnera.'" Knize-
nost, 13: 109-113.
Cited in ELL (1950-52).

4   KETTLE, ARNOLD. "George Eliot: Middlemarch." An Introduction to the English Novel: From Defoe to George Eliot,
Vol. I. London: Hutchinson and Company.
Compares George Eliot's spacious scope to the world of
Jane Austen. George Eliot's urbanity gives a wonderful
breadth and depth to her criticism. The novel works
through the presentation of very real, rounded characters
in a very real, solidly constructed social situation. Her
view of society is mechanistic and deterministic. Like all
mechanistic thinkers George Eliot ends by escaping into
idealism. Reprinted in 1960.B7.

5   LIPTZIN, SOL. "Daniel Deronda." Jewish Book Annual, 10: 43-
46.
The publication of Daniel Deronda was one important

landmark in the growth of Zionist ideology and in the de-
velopment of the English legend of the Jew. He describes
George Eliot as a "mid-Victorian seeress" and as "a non-
Jewish pioneer of Jewish rebirth."

6   TROUGHTON, MARION. "Elections in English Fiction." Contem-
porary Review, 180: 280-284.
    Discusses Pickwick Papers; John Halifax, Gentleman;
Thackeray's The Adventures of Philip; Trollope's Phineas
Finn; Meredith's Beauchamp's Career; along with Felix Holt.
Describes the vivid but serious account of the election in
Felix Holt under the drawn-out poll system.

1952 A BOOKS

*1   CASEY, FLOYD WELDON. "George Eliot's Practice as a Novelist
in Relation to Her Critical Theory." University of Wisconsin Abstracts of Doctoral Dissertations, 12: 441-443.
    Cited in 1969.B23.

2   DODDS, DOROTHY. The George Eliot Country. Edited by F. J.
Cross. Nuneaton: The George Eliot Fellowship.
    This is an illustrated guide to the places in and around
the parish of Chilvers Coton, Nuneaton, with which George
Eliot was associated. Reprinted in 1966.A3.

3   HANSON, LAWRENCE and ELIZABETH HANSON. Marian Evans and
George Eliot. New York and London: Oxford University
Press.
    Lawrence Hanson sets forth his purpose as "to discover
and set down the whole George Eliot, not simply one aspect
of her. Her life, seen thus, is one of particular interest; and, of course, an understanding of the woman leads
directly to a deeper appreciation of her work." Harvey, in
Victorian Fiction: A Guide to Research (1964.B11), says it
"hovers, a little uneasily between the popular and the
scholarly."

1952 B SHORTER WRITINGS

1   ALDRIDGE, JOHN W. ed. Critiques and Essays in Modern Fiction,
1920-1951. New York: Ronald Press.
    Contains a reprint of 1949.B4.

*2   ARTHOS, JOHN. "George Eliot: 'The Art of Vision.'" Rivista
di Letterature Moderne e Comparate, 3: 260-270.
    Cited in 1969.B23.

GEORGE ELIOT: A REFERENCE GUIDE

3   LEHMANN, ROSAMUND. "Three Giants: Charlotte Brontë, Mrs.
    Gaskell, and George Eliot." New York Times Book Review,
    December 21, p. 5.
        This is a personal tribute to these "thoroughly feminine"
    writers who endured a rigorous moral climate and remained
    high-minded, hypersensitive, conscientious, disciplined,
    and fastidious.

1953 A BOOKS - NONE

1953 B SHORTER WRITINGS

1   ALLOTT, MIRIAM and GEOFFREY TILLOTSON. "Romola and The Golden
    Bowl." Notes and Queries, 198: 124-125, 223.
        In Romola one finds a character similar in moral fiber to
    Maggie Verver. The characters are at a similar stage of
    disillusionment in marriage; both find themselves unable to
    trust their husbands.

2   CASEY, FLOYD WELDON. "George Eliot's Theory of Fiction."
    West Virginia University Bulletin: Philological Papers,
    9: 20-32.
        Her intellectual approach, her method of building a novel
    around ideas, and her detailed psychological analysis of
    character point to the modern novel. Her stories picture
    man in relation to his external world but also reveal his
    inner consciousness. She thought of her novels as a con-
    tribution to the social and moral development of man as
    they revealed her own moral sensibility.

3   COOMBES, HENRY. Literature and Criticism. London: Chatto
    and Windus.
        Refers to George Eliot as an example of expressing the
    power of her characters' thought through the vivid truth of
    concrete detail.

4   DEWAR, ALFRED C., J. P. HULIN, and MARIO PRAZ. "George Eliot
    and Proust." Times Literary Supplement, February 27, p.
    137; March 13, p. 169.
        The first letter points out that the relationship between
    Proust and George Eliot has been known for some time. Praz
    answers that a careful reading of his book would have
    clarified the whole issue.

5   HARRIS, R. J. "Emilia Francis Strong: Portraits of a Lady."
    Nineteenth Century Fiction, 8: 81-98.
        Emilia Francis Strong (1840-1904), the art historian and

critic, was successively the wife of the scholar, the Rev.
Mark Pattison, and the statesman, Sir Charles Wentworth
Dilke, Bart. Suggests that Dorothea Brooke was formed upon
the correspondence between Miss Strong and George Eliot.
Pattison, a great scholar, was changed into a pedant by
George Eliot. "The devoutness and idealism of Dorothea and
Emilia Strong were identical."

6   HOLLOWAY, JOHN. The Victorian Sage: Studies in Argument.
      New York: St. Martin's Press.
         She is quite plainly a novelist who is also a sage. Her
      didactic intention is clear in her characteristic setting
      in the recent past, her habit of linking a particular story
      to known historical conditions, her meticulous charting of
      social and economic patterns, her interest in slow changes
      and events that have remote consequences, her pervasive
      sense of the tie of kinship, and her being rigorously con-
      fined to characters and happenings of a quite distinctive
      kind. Reprinted in 1962.B9 and 1965.B14. The section on
      George Eliot is reprinted in 1965.A2.

*7 HULIN, J. P. "Du Moulin sur la Floss à Jean Santeuil."
      Études Anglaises, 6: 54-55.
         Finds two echoes of George Eliot's work in Proust's.
      Cited in ELL(1953-54).

8   JAMES, HENRY. "George Eliot's Middlemarch." Nineteenth Cen-
      tury Fiction, 8: 161-170.
         Reprint of 1873.B12. Reprinted in 1957.B16, 1965.A2,
      1966.A5, and 1971.A2.

9   PENTIN, HERBERT. "George Eliot's Monastic Bent." Times Lit-
      erary Supplement, May 15, p. 317.
         George Eliot grew up in an old monastic neighborhood, and
      she was always interested in monks, nuns, friars, and the
      Conventional Houses. She made an extensive study of the
      history and legends of the Monastic orders before she began
      to write Romola.

10 RACE, SIDNEY. "Dr. John Chapman, Editor of the Westminster
      Review." Notes and Queries, 198: 211-213.
         Contains several references to George Eliot and Lewes.

11 VAN GHENT, DOROTHY. "Adam Bede." The English Novel: Form
      and Function. New York: Rinehart, pp. 171-181.
         Deals with George Eliot's concern with time and with
      imagery in Adam Bede. The scenes present themselves with
      the patient rhythms of day and night, of the seasons, of

1953

planting and harvest, of the generations of men, and of the thoughts of simple people who are bound by deep tradition to soil and to community. Reprinted in 1965.A2.

1954 A BOOKS

1   HAIGHT, GORDON S. ed. The George Eliot Letters. 7 vols. New Haven: Yale University Press, Vols. 1-3.
    Contains a detailed chronology. This is followed by short biographical sketches of George Eliot and of her correspondents. The letters follow. The last volume contains a summary of her earnings. Vol. I: 1836-1851; Vol. II: 1852-1858; Vol. III: 1859-1861; Vol. IV: 1862-1868; Vol. V: 1869-1873; Vol. VI: 1874-1877; Vol. VII: 1878-1880. Vols. IV-VII, 1955.A2.

*2   SCHNEIDER, ROBERT L. "George Eliot: Her Search for Order." DA, 14: 2073. (Cornell University).
    George Eliot's moral attitudes changed significantly as she lived and wrote. Her fiction reflects the changes.

3   SPEAIGHT, ROBERT. George Eliot. London: Arthur Barker, Ltd. European Novelists Series.
    He says, "For my part, I am concerned to find her new friends, and in so doing I must try to make clear what kind of novelist she was. I shall not attempt to write her biography; she is there, manifestly, in page after page of the novels. But I shall turn, where necessary, to illustrate her books from her biography." Reprinted in 1968.A15.

1954 B SHORTER WRITINGS

1   ALLEN, WALTER. The English Novel: A Short Critical History. New York: E. P. Dutton and Company, pp. 253-274.
    By placing the responsibility for a man's life and fate firmly on the individual and his moral choices, she changed the nature of the English novel. Character becomes plot. Every action of her characters is important. She was that common English type, the radical Tory. Her radicalism, at once cautious and courageous, lay in the spheres of theology and ethics. "It is not altogether pleasant to be lectured by George Eliot" in her novels.

2   FYFE, ALBERT J. "The Interpretation of Adam Bede." Nineteenth Century Fiction, 9: 134-139.
    George Eliot's ethics are primarily naturalistic, and

1954

Adam Bede exemplifies the utilitarian system of her friend Charles Bray as expressed in his The Philosophy of Necessity. She simply translated her rationalistic beliefs into terms familiar to her church or chapel-going readers.

3   HAIGHT, GORDON S.   "George Eliot's Royalties." Publishers Weekly, August 7, pp. 522-523.
      George Eliot regularly commanded 30 to 40 per cent of the list price of her books and still retained the copyright. In twenty years she earned more than £41,000.

4   HARDY, BARBARA.   "The Moment of Disenchantment in George Eliot's Novels."   Review of English Studies, n.s. 5, 19:   256-264.
      In almost all George Eliot's novels there is a crisis of disenchantment described in images which echo a passage in a letter of June 4, 1848. It is of the disenchanted day-lit room. It is in "Janet's Repentance," Adam Bede, "The Lifted Veil," The Mill on the Floss, Romola, Felix Holt, Middlemarch, and Daniel Deronda. The disenchantment marks a stage in metamorphosis. Reprinted in 1970.A4. A revised version appears in 1959.A3.

5   KETCHAM, CARL H.   "A Woman's Arm: George Eliot and Rhoda Broughton." Notes and Queries, 1: 117-118.
      Finds a direct verbal influence in The Mill on the Floss from Rhoda's Cometh Up As A Flower.

6   LEAVIS, F. R.   The Great Tradition: George Eliot, Henry James, and Joseph Conrad. New York: Doubleday and Company, pp. 28-125 on George Eliot.
      Her attitude toward life is characterized by a profound seriousness of the kind that is a first condition of any real intelligence and an interest in human nature that made her a great psychologist. Her best work has a Tolstoyan depth and reality. Reprinted in 1960.A7 and 1965.A2.

7   PAUNCZ, ARPAD.   "The Lear Complex in World Literature." American Imago, 11: 50-83.
      This is on Silas's love for Eppie.

8   PIKE, ROYSTON.   "In Search of George Eliot." Fortnightly, 181 (April), 264-269.
      Begins with a description of George Eliot's Sunday afternoon receptions. There is a George Eliot country and a George Eliot Society, but the "Real" George Eliot is in the pages of her novels.

1954

9   PROUST, MARCEL. "Notes on George Eliot." Contre Sainte-Beuve.
    Translated by S. Townsend Warner. Paris: Librairies Gul-
    limard.
        Comments on the things that strike him about Adam Bede.
    He mentions the careful, detailed, respectful, poetic, and
    sympathetic portrayal of the humblest and most hardworking
    walk of life and notes that suffering is greater in a per-
    son who has no spiritual life, no moral solidarity with
    others. Reprinted in 1957.B18, 1958.B13, and 1960.A7.

10 SVAGLIC, MARTIN J. "Religion in the Novels of George Eliot."
    Journal of English and German Philology, 53: 145-159.
        Christianity was the basic inspiration which gave direc-
    tion to all George Eliot's works and led her to make the
    novels a plea for human solidarity. Yet her good charac-
    ters have no devotional lives and do not pray. Middlemarch
    is a deeply skeptical novel for no Providence guides human
    destinies. Dinah Morris is her most exquisite tribute to
    the value of the religion she could not accept. Reprinted
    in 1965.A2.

11 THALE, JEROME. "River Imagery in Daniel Deronda." Nineteenth
    Century Fiction, 7: 300-306.
        Life as a river is a recurrent image in the novel and
    suggests all states of life. The moral man must take up
    oars and row; the drifting without a set course indicates
    Deronda's lack of a goal. He finally finds a course in
    life. Meetings at bridges are important metaphorically.

12 WEST, ANTHONY. "The Higher Humbug." New Yorker, October 2,
    pp. 132-141.
        West follows the tortuous path of George Eliot's reli-
    gious doubt through her letters. Decides that her novels
    were popular because they were entirely serious and could
    be read on Sunday without raising any suspicion of Sabbath-
    breaking. The George Eliot dialectic of self-justification
    transferred to the field of fiction proves to be one of the
    most effective devices for flattering mediocrity ever in-
    vented.

1955 A BOOKS

*1 BARRY, JAMES D. "The Literary Reputation of George Eliot."
    DA, 15: 1851. (Northwestern University).
        This is a survey of the criticism of the novels since the
    1920 "return" of Middlemarch. When George Eliot died, she
    was the most highly esteemed novelist in England.

2   HAIGHT, GORDON S. ed. The George Eliot Letters. 7 vols.
      New Haven: Yale University Press, Vols. 4-7.
      Vols. 1-3, 1954.A1.

*3   MOLDSTAD, DAVID FRANKLYN. "Evangelical Influences on George
      Eliot." University of Wisconsin Abstracts of Doctoral Dis-
      sertations, 15: 620-21.
          Cited in 1967.B31.

*4   PANTUČKOVÁ, LIDMILA. George Eliotová o uměni a její tvurčí
      methoda. Sborník prací Filosofické fakulty Brněnske Uni-
      versity, 4: 41-55.
          Cited in ELL (1955-56).

1955 B SHORTER WRITINGS

1   BEEBE, MAURICE. "Visions are Creators: The Unity of Daniel
      Deronda." Boston University Studies in English, 1: 166-
      177.
          The two stories in the novel are variations on a theme.
      Both Gwendolen and Daniel are apprentices to life who seek
      a mission which will bring self-fulfillment in society.
      Each story lends depth to the other through parallel de-
      velopment by accidents and coincidences. Thus the inner
      visions of the characters are dramatized by external
      events. The main theme of the novel is the need to lose
      one's life to find it. Gwendolen is in a state of "pre-
      redemption" and reaches renunciation of self; Daniel is in
      the state of "post-redemption" and ends in submission to a
      higher purpose.

2   BLOTNER, JOSEPH L. The Political Novel. Garden City, New
      York: Doubleday and Company.
          This contains a short section on Felix Holt as a study
      from which emerges the political complexion of Loamshire
      in the English midlands in 1832.

3   HAIGHT, GORDON S. "Dickens and Lewes on Spontaneous Combus-
      tion." Nineteenth Century Fiction, 10: 53-63.
          In Part 10 of Bleak House Dickens describes the death of
      Krook by spontaneous combustion. December 11, 1852, Lewes
      objected to the episode as overstepping the limits of fic-
      tion and giving currency to vulgar error; they continued to
      exchange comments on the subject. Haight cites it as giv-
      ing a striking example of the intellectual limitations
      which made Dickens indifferent or hostile to the scientific
      developments of his age.

George Eliot: A Reference Guide

1955

4   HAIGHT, GORDON S. "The Tinker Collection of George Eliot
       Manuscripts." Yale University Library Gazette, 29: 148-
       150.
         Except for the 1879 diary, now in the Berg Collection,
       and the Spanish journal of 1867, which has dropped out of
       sight, all the known George Eliot journals and diaries are
       now brought together in the Yale Library. Other notebooks
       and individual letters are described.

5   HARDWICK, ELIZABETH. "George Eliot's Husband." Partisan Re-
       view, 22: 260-264.
         As a husband Lewes discovered his wife's genius, or rath-
       er he "uncovered" it as one may, peeling off the surface
       inch by inch, uncover a splendid painting beneath. All
       this he did with excitement and delight as if it were his
       own greatness he had come upon.

6   HARDY, BARBARA. "Imagery in George Eliot's Last Novels."
       Modern Language Review, 50: 6-14.
         In Middlemarch and Daniel Deronda the unifying images
       have also the function of thematic emphasis. She is clear-
       ly working away from a full use of omniscient commentary
       towards the indirect method of hinting images. The imagery
       gradually creates a private ironical understanding between
       author and reader. Reprinted in 1960.A7.

7   HOUSE, HUMPHREY. "Qualities of George Eliot's Unbelief." All
       in Due Time. London: Rupert Hart-Davis, pp. 109-115.
         Reprint of 1948.B8.

8   HUSSEY, MAURICE. "Structure and Imagery in Adam Bede." Nine-
       teenth Century Fiction, 10: 115-129.
         The novel is a study of psychology in contrasting envir-
       onments and of the perpetual cycle of the seasons. The
       explicit time scheme runs from June, 1799, to June, 1807.
       The weather and the characteristics of the seasons are used
       symbolically. The sense of continuity is much deeper than
       the passage of time.

9   JONES, WILLIAM M. "From Abstract to Concrete in Adam Bede."
       College English, 17: 88-89.
         George Eliot builds the plot of the novel from the sermon
       in the second chapter which contains the major moral ideas
       with which the novel deals. The novel becomes a lengthy
       example proving the general statements of the sermon.

10   KAMINSKY, ALICE R. "George Eliot, George Henry Lewes, and the
       Novel." Publications of the Modern Language Association,
       70: 997-1013.

Lewes's naturalism formed the basis of his literary aesthetics. His theory of art had long recognized the novel
as a serious art form. He advocated a realism which is a
kind of idealism. His ideas about fiction are clearly set
forth in his reviews. A footnote contains a list of these
reviews. George Eliot knew him as a critic before she met
him. When she came to know him, she valued and depended on
his criticism; she accepted his theory of the novel and
made it the basis of her own.

11   LEAVIS, Q. D. "A Note on Literary Indebtedness; Dickens,
     George Eliot, Henry James." Hudson Review, 8: 423-428.
         Finds similarities in the use of Rome as background,
     symbolism, and to precipitate experience for the heroine in
     Little Dorrit, 1857; Middlemarch, 1872; and Portrait of a
     Lady, 1881. George Eliot's use of Dickens is highly crea-
     tive; James simply read with admiration and envy and con-
     sciously or unconsciously had used the idea by imitation.

*12 MILNER, IAN. "Felix Holt, the Radical and Realism in George
     Eliot." Casopis pro moderní filologii, 37: 96-104.
         Cited in 1969.B23.

13   MURPHY, HOWARD R. "The Ethical Revolt Against Christian Or-
     thodoxy in Early Victorian England." American Historical
     Review, 60 (July), 800-817.
         Outlines her rejection of traditional Christianity as
     being typical of her age. She was relieved to discover the
     Bible could be convincingly interpreted in a quite unortho-
     dox sense. She was alienated from orthodoxy by a variety
     of factors unrelated to the question of the literal veraci-
     ty of Holy Writ.

*14 O'BRIEN, KATE. "George Eliot: A Moralizing Fabulist." Es-
     says by Divers Hands, Being the Transactions of the Royal
     Society of Literature, 27: 34-46.
         In Victorian Fiction: A Guide to Research (1964.B11),
     Harvey says this essay is "very slight and rambling."

15   RUST, JAMES D. "George Eliot on the Blithedale Romance."
     Boston Public Library Quarterly, 7: 207-215.
         The review of Hawthorne's Blithedale Romance in the West-
     minster Review of October, 1852, was probably by George
     Eliot. She feels that the emphasis on character analysis
     impedes the development of a good plot. This failure is
     not linking the people of Blithedale together with strong
     enough bonds. She also objects to Hawthorne's use of
     Brook Farm as being purely aesthetic and imaginary, without

1955

any effort to inculcate the moral lessons to be drawn from
the socialistic experiment.

16   STEINER, F. GEORGE. "A Preface to Middlemarch." Nineteenth
     Century Fiction, 9: 262-279.
        Says that beyond questions of technique Middlemarch suf-
     fers from lack of structural unity. He points out four
     plots which are unequal in emphasis. There is no center of
     gravity, no real mark of penetration into the tangle of in-
     cident. George Eliot fails to differentiate individual
     styles of expression; she raises or lowers her storytelling
     voice but cannot disguise it.

17   STEINHOFF, WILLIAM R. "Intent and Fulfillment in the Ending
     of The Mill on the Floss." The Image of the Work: Essays
     in Criticism. Edited by Bertrand Evans, Josephine Miles,
     and William R. Steinhoff. Berkeley and Los Angeles: Uni-
     versity of California Press, pp. 231-251.
        Gives evidence that George Eliot did careful planning for
     the ending and shows the symbolic relation between the
     river and the theme of the work. Tom and Maggie are caught
     up by the forces of change, and both feel that their secur-
     ity lies in what they can salvage from the past. They can-
     not press forward to the things which are before them.

18   THALE, JEROME. "Adam Bede: Arthur Donnithorne and Zeluco."
     Modern Language Notes, 70: 263-265.
        In 1799 Dr. John Moore's Zeluco was a popular novel.
     Arthur has the book under his arm as he meets Hetty and
     kisses her. He hurries home and pitches it into the most
     distant corner. This is a symbolic prophecy of Arthur's
     conduct. The hero of Zeluco is an arch-seducer, and the
     novel tells of his downfall. The novel becomes a symbol
     of seduction for George Eliot.

1956 A BOOKS

*1   BEATY, JEROME. "Middlemarch: From Notebook to Novel: A
     Study of George Eliot's Creative Method." DA, 16: 1138.
     (University of Illinois).
        Chapter one presents a detailed chronological account of
     the writing of Middlemarch, 1869-1872. The other chapters
     discuss her use of historical details, the chronology of
     the novel, the fusion of two separate stories, the publica-
     tion, the progress from notebook to novel, and a discussion
     of the nature of her inspiration. See 1960.A1.

1956

*2 BRITZ, JOHN PETER. "French Criticism of George Eliot's Nov-
      els." DA, 17: 846. (University of Minnesota).
          French criticism tends to be personal and impressionistic.
      The French critics hail her as a novelist of ideas rather
      than as a technician.

*3 HUZZARD, JOHN AMOS. "George Eliot and Italy: A Comprehensive
      Study of Romola." DA, 16: 1454-55. (The Pennsylvania
      State University).
          Examines the origins of George Eliot's interest in Italy,
      the methods of her research, her theory of the historical
      novel, and her handling of Italian characters. The effect
      of the novel on George Eliot's later novels is also con-
      sidered.

*4 O'CLAIR, ROBERT MATHESON. "A Critical Study of George Eliot's
      Middlemarch." (Harvard University).
          Cited in ELL(1955-56).

1956 B SHORTER WRITINGS

1   COLBY, ROBERT A. "'How It Strikes a Contemporary': The Spec-
      tator as Critic." Nineteenth Century Fiction, 11: 182-
      206.
          Reviews R. H. Hutton's attitudes to Victorian writers as
      Hutton expresses them in his Spectator reviews. His dis-
      trust of "self-consciousness" as opposed to spontaneity
      made him impatient with the disquisitive tendency of George
      Eliot's novels. He considered her preeminent in sympathy
      and in her exhaustive psychological analysis.

2   CREEGER, GEORGE R. "An Interpretation of Adam Bede." English
      Literary History, 23: 218-238.
          Finds the novel in two major divisions: one in Loamshire
      and one in Stonyshire. The two stand in complete antithe-
      sis suggested by the quasi-symbolic names. Most of the ac-
      tion takes place in Loamshire around Hayslope, a kind of
      later-day Eden, a land of Goshen. Adam leaves the Loam-
      shire world and enters Stonyshire when he possesses a sense
      of enlarged being which is the consequence of a fuller life
      brought about by suffering. He comes to see Stonyshire
      through Dinah's eyes when love overcomes his fears. Re-
      printed in 1970.A4.

3   HAIGHT, GORDON S. "George Eliot's Theory of Fiction." Vic-
      torian Newsletter, No. 10, pp. 1-3.
          Discusses George Eliot's contributions to the Westminster

Review, Lewes's influence on her writing, and her theories of fiction in terms of James D. Rust's two articles "George Eliot and the Blithedale Romance"(1955.B15) and "The Art of Fiction in George.Eliot's Reviews" (1956. B11) and Alice R. Kaminsky's "George Eliot, George Henry Lewes, and the Novel" (1955.B10).

4   HAIGHT, GORDON S. "Introduction." Middlemarch. (Riverside Edition.) Boston: Houghton Mifflin.
    Few English novelists have attempted so broad a canvas. She undertook to study every phase of provincial life on the eve of the Reform Bill, to show the effect of actions and opinions on individuals widely separated in rank. There are many images of weaving, binding, and linking. The images grow out of fundamental conceptions of the characters and are applied consistently. "Not many novels in the world will bear so close a scrutiny."

5   HARDY, BARBARA. "Mr. Browning and George Eliot." Essays in Criticism (Oxford), 6: 121-123.
    This is an answer to his review of Letters (1954.A1 and 1955.A2). She says that he goes too far in saying that George Eliot's encounter with Chapman is the seed for all her fiction. The characters are exempla of woman's lot.

6   HOUGHTON, WALTER E. ed. The Wellesley Index to Victorian Periodicals: 1824-1900. London: Routledge and Kegan Paul.
    Covers the period of George Eliot's contributions to periodicals and of Lewes's work.

*7 MÜLLER-SCHWEFE, GERHARD. "George Eliot als Übersetzerin." Die Neueren Sprachen, n.s. 1: 1-11.
    Cited in ELL(1955-56).

8   PARIS, BERNARD J. "Toward a Revaluation of George Eliot's The Mill on the Floss." Nineteenth Century Fiction, 11: 18-31.
    The central action of the novel arises out of the mutual incompatibility of Maggie Tulliver and her environment. She must adapt or abide the consequences. She ultimately discovers a philosophy of life which resolves her inner struggle and thus reconciles her to her environment. Her death is her triumph. In death Maggie and Tom become part of the long river of tradition.

9   PRAZ, MARIO. The Hero in Eclipse in Victorian Fiction. Translated from the Italian by Angus Davidson. London:

Oxford University Press, pp. 319-383.
Like Wordsworth George Eliot wants to stir sympathy with
commonplace troubles. Tells how she does this in her various works.

10 RUBIN, LARRY. "River Imagery As a Means of Foreshadowing in
The Mill on the Floss." Modern Language Notes, 71: 18-22.
Rather than being a melodramatic contrivance, the ending
is so heavily foreshadowed that it seems impossible that
the novel would end any other way.

11 RUST, JAMES D. "The Art of Fiction in George Eliot's Reviews."
Review of English Studies, 7: 164-172.
Refers to the period from January, 1852, to January, 1857,
as her critical apprenticeship. Almost all of George Eliot's characteristics as a novelist appeared in her early
reviews. Rust states her artistic credo in four points and
relates them to the reviews. First, art's greatest benefit
to men is to widen their sympathies. Second, art has a
moral mission. Third, art must minister morality through
pleasure, not pain. And fourth, art can fulfill its moral
and aesthetic purpose only if it presents life realistic-
ally.

12 STONE, W. H. "Hale White and George Eliot." University of
Toronto Quarterly, 25: 437-451.
Hale White came in October, 1852, to Chapman's establishment. In his writings Hale White reveals much of his acquaintance with George Eliot. He goes through White's
works and quotes details. George Eliot appears not only as
a potent intellectual and moral force but, in a curiously
English and Puritan way, as a femme fatale. She existed
for Hale White more as a symbol than as a woman.

13 TOSELLO, MARIA. Le Fonte Italiane della "Romola" di George
Eliot. Turin: Giappichelli.
Concentrates on George Eliot's debt to Italian histori-
ans.

1957 A BOOKS

*1 STUMP, REVA JUANITA. "Vision as Imagery, Theme, and Structure
in George Eliot's Novels." DA, 17: 2018. (University of
Washington).
In George Eliot's novels the artistically unifying element is her concept of moral vision. The major image
patterns and the major themes all derive their symbolic
meaning from the concept of moral vision.

1 BEATY, JEROME. "George Eliot's Notebook for an Unwritten Novel." Princeton University Library Chronicle, 18: 175-182.
In the Morris L. Parrish Collection of the Princeton University Library is a notebook containing George Eliot's preliminary plans for a novel she never wrote. Cyril Ambrose has a yearning to complete the development of his own philosophic system. In the meantime he is trying to sell a destructive military weapon to the government. Birth and death dates of a list of characters are given. She seems to plan two plots or perhaps three. The dating is uncertain; the only clue as to the possible date is that she began to use purple ink in 1872. It was probably written in her later years, possibly after 1877.

2 _____. "History by Indirection: The Era of Reform in Middlemarch." Victorian Studies, 1: 173-179.
The events of the novel take place between September 30, 1829, and the end of May, 1832. George Eliot introduces political history through references to historical personages; she mentions but never explains current issues. She presents history dramatically as part of the lives of the characters. She uses the details from the political history accurately and extensively, yet few readers realize they are reading a novel full of documented, accurate historical information because of her skillful indirection. Reprinted in 1965.A2.

3 _____. "Visions and Revisions: Chapter 81 of Middlemarch." Publications of the Modern Language Association, 72: 662-679.
George Eliot told John Cross that the scene between Dorothea and Rosamond was written, without preparation, during a moment of vision and passed without change into print. Beaty says that her notebook and MS in the British Museum show this to be untrue. She made changes in writing, in rereading, in reading proof; for her vision and revision were one.

4 CARTER, JOHN. "George Eliot's Agatha, 1869-and After." Book Collector, 6: 244-252.
The poem "Agatha" was published in the August, 1869, number of The Atlantic. Then the poem was printed in pamphlet form. The first issue was twenty copies; fifty more were then ordered. There are three pamphlet editions dated 1869. B was not very carefully copied from A, and C was very carelessly copied indeed. They were marketed by Wise as fraudulent imitations.

5   COLBY, ROBERT A. "An American Sequel to Daniel Deronda."
    Nineteenth Century Fiction, 12: 231-235.
        There was an anonymous novel Gwendolen published in Bos-
    ton in 1878 by the firm of Ira Bradley with the intention
    of remedying the chief defect of Daniel Deronda. There is
    no evidence that George Eliot ever learned of it.

6   COVENEY, PETER. "George Eliot and Maggie Tulliver." Poor
    Monkey: The Child in Literature. London: Rockliff, pp.
    120-135.
        Once George Eliot was able to rid herself artistically of
    the need to write of children, she left them alone. In the
    children George Eliot does portray, Coveney finds personal
    responses to her own situations as a child. He mentions
    the children in Scenes of Clerical Life and Adam Bede and
    in the other novels. The presentation of her children went
    exactly, and significantly, pari passu with the whole pre-
    sentation of her genius as she revealed it. She bestowed
    on the child her subjective weakness and also her abiding
    strength.

7   DENEAU, DANIEL P. "Notes on the Image and the Novel." Vic-
    torian Newsletter, No. 12, pp. 27-29.
        Discusses the approaches which have been employed in dis-
    cussing the image in the novel genre. He discusses Barbara
    Hardy's approach in "The Moment of Disenchantment in George
    Eliot's Novels" (1954.B4) and "Imagery in George Eliot's
    Last Novels" (1955.B6). She offers valuable comments on
    George Eliot's development, her technique and her themes.
    Her conclusions are open to question, but her methods are
    excellent.

8   DICKSON, SARAH AUGUSTA. "The Arents Collection of Books in
    Parts and Associated Literature." Bulletin New York Public
    Library, 61: 267-280.
        Discusses the novels which appeared piecemeal, each part
    having a separate cover. Daniel Deronda and Middlemarch
    appeared in such parts.

9   GOLDBERG, HANNAH. "George Henry Lewes and Daniel Deronda."
    Notes and Queries, 4: 356-358.
        The youthful Lewes of the 1830's, an intense, restless
    young man in search of a creed, has obviously provided
    George Eliot with the basis of her creation of Deronda.

10 HARDY, BARBARA. "The Image of the Opiate in George Eliot's
    Novels." Notes and Queries, 4: 487-490.
        Opiates are used by various characters seeking consolation

and escape. The idea always appears in the context of pain, escape, and illusion. There is no glamour to this weak and futile escape. A drugged existence is a necessary step in the human progress from egoism.

11 HARVEY, W. J. "The Treatment of Time in Adam Bede." Anglia, 75: 429-440.
   An accurate chronological chart can be made of the actions in Adam Bede to the hour and minute. Each of the ways time manifests itself has some particular function or some bearing upon the structure and themes of the novel. The emphasis is placed on consequences rather than motives. The interlocking parallels are intimately connected to ever-widening perspectives. The effect is a sense of other lives and other stories impinging on those of the major characters. Partially reprinted in 1965.A2.

12 HEILMAN, ROBERT B. "Return to Raveloe: Thirty Five Years After." English Journal, 46: 1-10.
   In each of her books George Eliot treats the problem of opening up, thawing out, and unhardening the self-walled, the blockaded personality. This change comes in a regular though quiet movement of contrasts and resemblances. Silas attains full consciousness through knowing and feeling, opening his heart, and re-entering the community.

13 HOUGHTON, WALTER E. The Victorian Frame of Mind. 1830-1870. New Haven: Yale University Press.
   Makes the promotion of benevolence based on understanding the central aim of her fiction. Her purpose is to call forth sympathy. Perhaps the best revelation of the commercial spirit in Victorian society is in her novels. She felt that patriotism could be utilized for a moral purpose as long as it aroused heroic attitudes of devotion and self-sacrifice.

14 HUZZARD, JOHN A. "The Treatment of Florence and Florentine Characters in George Eliot's Romola." Italica, 34: 158-165.
   This is the first novel by a major British novelist that deals sincerely and exclusively with Italian people living in their native habitat. Tito is the most fully developed character. In using Savonarola, George Eliot wanted her readers to feel the impact that a great moral force exerts on the conscience of succeeding ages. She wanted to enlighten man's concept of his moral duty toward himself and his fellows.

15 HYDE, WILLIAM J. "George Eliot and the Climate of Realism."
    Publications of the Modern Language Association, 72: 147-
    164.
        She turned the doctrine of realism from a common assump-
    tion to a working creed. For her realism must concentrate
    on searching for the good without concealing the truth.
    Plot is unified by her own moral certainty as she unravels
    the web of circumstances to strengthen her moralistic plots.
    Character, not events, lies at the center of her novels.
    Partially reprinted in 1965.A2.

16 JAMES, HENRY. "George Eliot's Middlemarch." House of Fic-
    tion. Edited by Leon Edel.
        Reprint of 1873.B12. Reprinted in 1953.B8, 1965.A2,
    1966.A5, and 1971.A2.

17 NIEBUHR, H. RICHARD. "Introduction." Feuerbach's The Essence
    of Christianity. New York: Harper and Row.
        George Eliot sought to retain the ethos of Christianity
    without its faith, its humanism without its theism, and
    its hope for man without its hope for the sovereignty of
    God.

18 PROUST, MARCEL. "Notes on George Eliot." Marcel Proust on
    Art and Literature. Translated by Chatto and Windus, Ltd.
        Reprint of 1954.B9. Reprinted in 1958.B13. The section
    on George Eliot is reprinted in 1960.A7.

19 STANG, RICHARD. "The Literary Criticism of George Eliot."
    Publications of the Modern Language Association, 72: 952-
    961.
        Feels that George Eliot had formulated her ideas about
    life and art before she started to write her first novel.
    Finds in her essays and reviews almost all her important
    ideas about art, and they are thus stated explicitly. He
    takes essay by essay and shows this to be true.

20 THALE, JEROME. "'Daniel Deronda': The Darkened World."
    Modern Fiction Studies, 3: 119-126.
        In Daniel Deronda a radically new tone comes into George
    Eliot's fiction: a concern with the sinister and malign.
    There is a new and direct confrontation of certain kinds of
    evil, of perversity, hitherto unacknowledged. Grandcourt
    is the most striking manifestation of the new development
    in Daniel Deronda. The imagery used to describe him shows
    his moral perversity, and about him is an atmosphere of
    cruelty. Gwendolen shows the same new and sinister quali-
    ty. Her suffering does not ennoble; it makes the sufferer

1957

more miserable and increases her self-hatred. Deronda simply conducts her through the dark night of the superego,
urging her to self-reproach, to fear of self and of consequences. Reprinted in 1959.A6 and 1960.A7.

21   THALE, JEROME. "Image and Theme: The Mill on the Floss."
     University of Kansas City Review, 23: 227-234.
          For the Tullivers the river is life, literally and meta-
     phorically. The river as symbol is fully and thoroughly
     developed and reinforces all the major themes of the novel.
     Maggie's existence, like the Floss, is constricted into a
     narrow channel. Finally the river as life overwhelms and
     drowns Maggie; it becomes a fitting symbol for her incom-
     patibility with life at St. Ogg's.

22   WATT, IAN. The Rise of the Novel: Studies in Defoe, Richard-
     son, and Fielding. Berkeley: University of California
     Press.
          George Eliot inherited everything of Puritanism except
     its religious faith. Her characters seek by introspection
     and observation to build their own personal scheme of
     moral certainty.

1958 A BOOKS

*1   MAHEU, PLACIDE-GUSTAVE. La pensée religieuse et morale de
     George Eliot: Essai d'Interpretation. Paris: Didier.
          Harvey says in Victorian Fiction: A Guide to Research
     (1964.B11) that the title is misleading, and the work is
     mainly concerned with tracing parallels between George
     Eliot's thought and Defoe's History of the Devil.

*2   WOLFF, MICHAEL. "Marian Evans to George Eliot: The Moral and
     Intellectual Foundations of Her Career." DA, 19: 2350.
     (Princeton University).
          This is a detailed study of George Eliot's intellectual
     background and an account of her moral and intellectual
     habits. In the book reviews which she wrote 1855-1857,
     she conducts her readers from her most basic assumptions
     up to the threshold of her artistic career.

1958 B SHORTER WRITINGS

1   ANDERSON, QUENTIN. "George Eliot in Middlemarch." From
     Dickens to Hardy. Edited by Boris Ford. Baltimore:
     Penguin Books.

George Eliot is incapable of suggesting the tone of a given period or historical moment. Middlemarch is carefully plotted. She uses the landscape of opinion as the scene of action. It informs and gives depth to the conventional motifs and attitudes of character. The scene of the novel is wholly dominated by the finely tempered mind which envisions it. She cannot make the novel an instrument which can register the fate of a society in the perspective of history and heroic achievement. Reprinted in 1960.A7 and 1970.A4.

2 BEATY, JEROME. "The Forgotten Past of Will Ladislaw." Nineteenth Century Fiction, 13: 159-163.
     Suggests that George Eliot may have intended to show her interest in the Jewish people before Daniel Deronda. He points out three indications that in the early, abandoned "Miss Brooke" conception of the story Will may have been Jewish. First is the mystery attached to his heritage; second is the similarity to the next novel, Daniel Deronda, in which a young man discovers he is a Jew; and third, Will is referred to twice in Middlemarch as the grandson of a Jewish pawnbroker.

3 _____. "'Into the Irrevocable': A New George Eliot Letter." Journal of English and Germanic Philology, 57: 704-707.
     Prints the letter in which she says a portion of her manuscript has passed "into the irrevocable," November 11, 1874. The letter does not suggest her writing in a moment of inspiration words never to be revised. Beaty recognizes that in one case at least George Eliot makes no claim of inspired composition.

4 BELL, INGLIS F. and DONALD BAIRD. The English Novel, 1578-1956: A Checklist of Twentieth-Century Criticisms. Denver: Alan Swallow.
     Contains selected criticism on each novel.

*5 BĪCANIC, SONIA. "The Effect of Magazine Serialization on Romola." Studia Romanica et Anglica Zagrabiensia, 6: 15-23.
     Cited in 1967.B31.

6 CLARK, ALEXANDER P. "The Manuscript Collection of the Princeton University Library." Princeton University Library Chronicle, 19: 159-190.
     In the Morris L. Parrish Collection of Victorian Novelists, there are more than forty letters of George Eliot as well as other MS material by and relating to her. The

1958

Collection contains G. H. Lewes's <u>Problems of Life and Mind</u> with corrections and additions in the hand of George Eliot.

7   CURREY, R. N. "Joseph Liggins: A Slight Case of Literary Identity." <u>Times Literary Supplement</u>, December 26, p. 753.
     The story of a man who deliberately let it be thought that he was George Eliot is revealed in Haight's letters (1954.A1 and 1955.A2). This article outlines the references to him in letters and newspapers.

8   FERRIS, SUMNER J. "<u>Middlemarch</u>, George Eliot's Masterpiece." <u>From Jane Austen to Joseph Conrad</u>. Edited by Robert C. Rathburn and Martin Steinmann, Jr. Minneapolis: University of Minnesota Press, pp. 194-207.
     Says George Eliot portrays men best by means of a technique approaching that of the caricaturist; she lets one prominent characteristic represent the man. Each character is given his own psychological development. Each man's fate is of little concern to his fellows in a society shaped by the individual characters.

9   HAIGHT, GORDON S. "George Eliot." <u>Victorian Newsletter</u>, No. 13, p. 23.
     This guide to research materials gives the location of the manuscripts of the novels, the letters, the journals and diaries, and the notebooks.

10   _____. "George Eliot's Originals." <u>From Jane Austen to Joseph Conrad</u>. Edited by Robert C. Rathburn and Martin Steinmann, Jr. Minneapolis: University of Minnesota Press, pp. 177-193.
     Discusses the sources of her characters; he suggests that the novels are based on actual objects and events and people.

11   HARVEY, W. J. "George Eliot and the Omniscient Author Convention." <u>Nineteenth Century Fiction</u>, 13: 81-108.
     The omniscient author is for George Eliot the bridge between the real macrocosm and the fictional microcosm and has a necessary function in establishing the kind of reality being portrayed. The individual is related to a wider social context through intrusive comments. These comments are the sober, unemphatic, and mature statements of those great commonplaces of human nature which underlie all human situations, real or imaginary.

12 OWENS, R. J. "The Effect of George Eliot's Linguistic Inter-
      ests on Her Art." Notes and Queries, 5: 311-313.
        She wanted her characters to speak the idiom of their own
      class. Her artist's perception of the self-revelatory na-
      ture of a speaker's words lends to her humorous irony and
      serves to express her moral judgments.

13 PROUST, MARCEL. "Notes on George Eliot." Marcel Proust on
      Art and Literature. Meridian Books, Inc.
        Reprint of 1954.B9. Reprinted in 1957.B18. The section
      on George Eliot is reprinted in 1960.A7.

14 RALEIGH, JOHN HENRY. "Victorian Morals and the Modern Novel."
      Partisan Review, 25: 241-264.
        The subjective line of stream of consciousness novelists
      began with George Eliot in her minute, internalized treat-
      ment of the middle-class consciousness. Joyce and Lawrence
      follow her. Her own extra-legal sexual union and the sex-
      ual unions of her characters are typical of the complex
      Victorian moral "code." Her treatment of them looks toward
      modern fiction.

*15 STANG, RICHARD. "The Theory of the Novel in England, 1850-
      1870." DA, 19: 330. (Columbia University).
        George Eliot as a novelist and George Henry Lewes as an
      important critic began to work out important concepts for
      the criticism of fiction as a distinct branch of imagina-
      tive literature. See 1959.B15.

16 THALE, JEROME. "George Eliot's Fable for Her Times." College
      English, 19: 141-146.
        This calls Silas Marner a perfect book, a serious and
      intelligent treatment of human life and conduct. The sym-
      bols are the familiar ones of Christianity. The Godfrey
      half is realistic while the Silas half is pastoral and
      fairytale-like. The conversion of Silas is a kind of alle-
      gory of the intellectual movement of the age. He moves
      from earnest belief through disbelief to a new, secular
      faith. The fortunes of Silas and Godfrey alternate through
      a series of pairings in character and situation. The two
      visions of the world become an artistic piece. Reprinted
      in 1959.A6 and 1960.A7.

17 WALTERS, GERALD. "A Memory of George Eliot." Listener, Janu-
      ary 2, p. 20.
        She and Lewes were both tired of poverty, so she searched
      her memory and used the places she knew to create fictional
      settings: Spring Farm in Kirk Hallam where Robert Evans

1958

made his reputation, Daniel Knott's farm in "Gilfil," and others are mentioned.

18 WILLIAMS, RAYMOND. <u>Culture and Society, 1780-1950</u>. New York: Columbia University Press, pp. 102-109 on <u>Felix Holt</u>.
    Suggests that George Eliot follows the general feelings of her generation in a novel in which the formal plot turns on the complications of the inheritance of property. Reprinted in 1971.B24.

19 WOOLF, VIRGINIA. <u>Granite and Rainbow: Essays</u>. London: Hogarth Press.
    Refers to George Eliot throughout.

1959 A BOOKS

*1 DENEAU, DANIEL PIERRE. "From 'Amos Barton' to <u>Daniel Deronda</u>: Studies in the Imagery of George Eliot's Fiction." DA, 20: 1783. (University of Notre Dame).
    Points out the river and the web as the two central images of George Eliot's fiction. Throughout her career she showed an increasing interest in enlarging the dimensions of her literal fictionalized world through the use of imagery.

*2 DIAMOND, NAOMI JUNE. "Vision and the Role of the Past in the Novels of George Eliot." DA, 20: 2782-83. (University of Washington).
    Clear vision is a significant key to structure and theme in George Eliot's novels. The measure of truth of a vision depends on the degree of imaginative sympathy involved.

3 HARDY, BARBARA. <u>The Novels of George Eliot: A Study in Form</u>. London: Athlone Press; New York: Oxford University Press.
    Chiefly concerned with George Eliot's power of form, Professor Hardy finds that the novels are social tragedy. The formal relations of the characters are presented unassertively. Similarly her images echo much more quietly than one might expect. It is the quiet, normal appearance of the world which is perhaps responsible for the kind of tragedy which emerges from her human delineation. Pp. 135-154 reprinted in 1965.A2.

*4 LEVINE, GEORGE L. "Determinism in the Novels of George Eliot." DA, 20: 4112. (University of Minnesota).
    George Eliot was one of the first novelists to see every event as determined by a causal antecedent. Her determinism

118

did not entail powerlessness of the will. She emphasizes
the difficulty of making choices and the crucial moment of
choice.

5   STUMP, REVA. Movement and Vision in George Eliot's Novels.
     Seattle: University of Washington Press.
         Finds the key to the artistic meaning of George Eliot's
     novels to be "vision." Gives a very detailed study of the
     imagery involving vision in Adam Bede, The Mill on the
     Floss, and Middlemarch.

6   THALE, JEROME. The Novels of George Eliot. New York: Colum-
     bia University Press.
         Declares that there has scarcely been a more learned
     writer in English since Milton. While she read Schiller
     and Tasso, she was also making damson cheese; and she could
     bake mince pies and put up currant jelly. Discusses each
     of the novels.

1959 B SHORTER WRITINGS

1   APPLEMAN, PHILIP, WILLIAM A. MADDEN, and MICHAEL WOLFF. eds.
     1859: Entering An Age of Crisis. Bloomington, Indiana:
     Indiana University Press, pp. 31-50, 229-246, 269-289.
         Discusses Strauss and his purpose to expose the shallow-
     ness of the old-fashioned rationalist attack on the Bible,
     and considers George Eliot's loss of faith. Includes three
     essays which deal with George Eliot. They are: Noel
     Annan, "Science, Religion, and the Critical Mind"; G.
     Armour Craig, "Victims and Spokesmen: The Image of Society
     in the Novel"; Michael Wolff, "Victorian Reviewers and
     Cultural Responsibility."

2   BARRY, JAMES D. "The Literary Reputation of George Eliot's
     Fiction: A Supplementary Bibliography." Bulletin of Bib-
     liography, 22: 176-182.
         A checklist to supplement the bibliographies in Browning,
     Cooke, and the "new edition" of Blind.

3   BEATY, JEROME. "Daniel Deronda and the Question of Unity in
     Fiction." Victorian Newsletter, No. 15, pp. 16-20.
         Outlines the various critical studies which have been
     made of Daniel Deronda to call attention to a discrepancy
     between the definition of "unity" and the demonstration of
     "unity" in current critical practices. It is easy to mis-
     take the cogency of the outline for the achieved unity of
     the work. The existence of unity cannot be proved through
     the examination of theme and image alone.

1959

*4   BELL, VEREEN M. "Character and Point of View in Representa-
       tive Victorian Novels." DA, 20: 3740-41. (Duke Univer-
       sity).
         Studies Dickens, Thackeray, Emily Brontë, George Eliot,
       Meredith, and James. This is an examination of changing
       concepts of character and the corresponding adjustments of
       fictional method. The introspective method of presenting
       character is the most significant development.

5   CARROLL, DAVID R. "The Unity of Daniel Deronda." Essays in
       Criticism, 9: 369-380.
         The visions of Gwendolen and Mordecai, one of fear and
       one of hope, crystallize the essential function of each
       half of the novel in the education of Daniel Deronda. He
       is fulfiller and redeemer for both. The whole of the novel
       is couched in the political and religious terms of the Jew-
       ish nation. The balance of separateness with communication
       defines on a national level the meaning of the personal
       relations. Deronda's intense emotional involvement with
       Gwendolen acts as a catalyst to plunge him into his public
       role.

6   _____. "Unity Through Analogy: An Interpretation of Middle-
       march." Victorian Studies, 2: 305-316.
         Carroll finds the subtle finish of a poem in the prose
       narrative and analyzes the undertones of thought and har-
       mony of the lines; an awareness of the undertones of
       thought leads to a realization of unity through analogy.
       An analysis of Dorothea's quest shows her finding out about
       the nature of her relations with her fellow human beings
       and finds her characterization to be the unifying element
       of the novel.

7   CASSON, ALLAN. "'Thee' and 'You' in Adam Bede." Notes and
       Queries, 6: 451.
         George Eliot's use of pronouns is careful and consistent.
       Adam uses "thee" for his mother and brother. But even when
       he asked Hetty to marry him, he uses "you." But he calls
       Hetty "thee" as she leaves for the scaffold. This under-
       lines the pathos of a new intimacy achieved only when it is
       too late.

8   DENEAU, DANIEL PIERRE. "Inconsistencies and Inaccuracies in
       Adam Bede." Nineteenth Century Fiction, 14: 71-75.
         Points out a slip in the speech of Mr. Poyser and several
       chronological errors. He uses these to argue a distinction
       between this novel and George Eliot's later, more painfully
       composed works.

_____. "A Note on George Eliot's 'Amos Barton'--Reticence and Chronology." Notes and Queries, 6: 450-451.
Finds George Eliot in a minor example of Victorian reticence; a seventh child is expected in February. The expectant mother is "ill," but the word miscarriage never appears. A child finally appears the next December.

10 FOAKES, R. A. "Adam Bede Reconsidered." English, 12: 173-176.
The pastoral Hayslope community is set against the harsher world of Stonyshire. The pattern is pseudo-pastoral as a harmonious way of life is broken and made whole again.

11 HUZZARD, JOHN A. Review of Maria Tosello's Le Fonti Italiane de la "Romola" di George Eliot. Modern Language Quarterly, 20: 289-291.
This volume covers the researches pursued by George Eliot in Florence and in London. She compares the respective influences of Nardi and Villari on George Eliot. Includes a discussion of George Eliot's Italian sources.

*12 MONOD, SYLVÈRE. "George Eliot et les personnages de Middlemarch." Études Anglaises, 12: 306-314.
Cited in ELL(1959).

13 PARIS, BERNARD J. "George Eliot's Unpublished Poetry." Studies in Philology, 56: 539-558.
Prints and analyzes poems from an autographed MS notebook from the Yale University Library Collection of George Eliot MS material. The poems are "In a London Drawingroom," 1865; "Ex Oriente Lux," 1866; and "In the South," 1867; and five fragments, 1867-1874.

14 PETERSON, VIRGIL A. "Forgotten Bastards: A Note on Daniel Deronda." Victorian Newsletter, No. 15, p. 29.
Gerald Bullett claims that Grandcourt has fathered three bastards. Joan Bennett claims two. Actually there are four. In chapter 13 Lydia Glasher states the fact clearly. This is an indication of Grandcourt's passionate nature and an illustration of the tangential manner in which sex was handled by a perceptive but discreet Victorian.

15 STANG, RICHARD. The Theory of the Novel in England, 1850-1870. London: Routledge and Kegan Paul; New York: Columbia University Press.
Discusses George Eliot in chapter 1, "The Sacred Office." Her intentions in writing and her notion of the novelist's position as a sacred office are held up as typical of the

period. In chapter 2, "The Craft of Fiction," he discusses her ideas on form. And in chapter 3 he discusses her emphasis on fiction as a picture of real life in "Mid-Victorian Realism."

16 STEVENSON, LIONEL. "1859: Year of Fulfillment." The Centennial Review, 3: 337-356.
It is quite remarkable that this plain, sickly, self-educated provincial woman was accepted on equal footing by some of the most eminent thinkers of the day. Adam Bede is a sort of fictional counterpart of Mill's essay On Liberty in its scrupulous respect for individuality and its corollary that every individual must accept the responsibility for his actions.

17 THOMSON, FRED C. "The Genesis of Felix Holt." Publications of the Modern Language Association, 124: 576-584.
Suggests that Felix Holt is not a political novel. She used a political setting to afford topical appeal and lend her theme a public scope. Yet she committed herself to subjects that her creative imagination could not quite assimilate and shape even though her intelligence could master them.

18 WELSH, ALEXANDER. "George Eliot and the Romance." Nineteenth Century Fiction, 14: 241-254.
The Mill on the Floss adheres closely to the typical plot and typical dark-haired heroine of the romance, predominately that of Sir Walter Scott. It even ends with a triangular love affair and the death of Maggie. The intentions of the novel are clearly anti-romantic, but the anti-romance is superimposed on the typical solution and plot of romance.

19 WOLFF, MICHAEL. "Critic's Poll--Eighteen Fifty-Nine." Saturday Review, 42 (October 10), 19-20.
Among the books of 1859, Idylls of the King by the Laureate and Adam Bede by an unknown novice were among the bestsellers. Summarizes the compliments paid to the novel by its reviewers.

1960 A BOOKS

1 BEATY, JEROME. Middlemarch from Notebook to Novel: A Study of George Eliot's Creative Method. Illinois Studies in Language and Literature, Vol. 47. Urbana: University of Illinois Press.

Outlines the progress of the writing of the novel. Gives a detailed account of the many changes and additions which George Eliot made during the actual writing of the chapters. Tries to disprove the image of her as a "spontaneous" or "inspired" writer.

2   CROMPTON, MARGARET. George Eliot: The Woman. London: Cassell.
     A straight biographical survey from the day of her birth through her funeral. Contends that "although her brain was masculine, her soul was feminine."

*3   LYONS, RICHARD SMILIE. "A Study of Middlemarch." DA, 21: 2276-77. (Princeton University).
     Lyons attempts a full critical analysis of Middlemarch with an examination of its composition and critical reception. He discovers that the themes are unselfish love and perfect harmony.

*4   PETERSON, VIRGIL ALLISON. "Moral Growth in the Heroines of George Eliot." (University of California, Los Angeles).
     Cited in ELL(1961).

*5   PINNEY, THOMAS CLIVE. "Wordsworth's Influence on George Eliot." (Yale University).
     Cited in ELL(1961).

*6   SCHUTZ, FRED CHRISTMAN. "Sense and Sensibility: A Study of Reason and Emotion as Elements of Character and Conduct in the Novels of George Eliot." (University of California, Berkeley).
     Cited in ELL(1961).

7   STANG, RICHARD ed. Discussions of George Eliot. Boston: D. C. Heath.
     Presents thirteen critics in selections designed to give a rather complete history of the critical reputation of George Eliot's novels. He has tried to include the most interesting treatments of as many significant aspects of her work as possible. All thirteen selections are listed and annotated separately.

*8   TUCKER, HOUSTON CLAY. "George Eliot's Ideal Self: A Study of Subjective Influences on Her Prose Fiction." DA, 21: 2723. (Vanderbilt University).
     George Eliot's art evolves out of her own experience. Plot is a device for carrying her moral ideas. Sympathy is the basis of her purpose in writing fiction. Her characters

1960

relive her life as they resign themselves to their environment and seek sympathy with humanity.

*9   WHEATLEY, JAMES HOLBROOK. "George Eliot and the Art of
       Thought: Studies in the Early Novels." (Harvard Univer-
       sity).
            Cited in ELL(1961).

1960 B SHORTER WRITINGS

1   CARROLL, DAVID R. "An Image of Disenchantment in the Novels
       of George Eliot." Review of English Studies, 11: 29-41.
            Sets forth the archetypal pattern for all the novels.
       The main character, usually the heroine, through lack of
       self-knowledge embraces an illusory way of life. The il-
       lusions are stripped away by means of successive disen-
       chantments which lead finally through a realistic knowledge
       of self to regeneration. She creates her own symbols for
       this process. For example, ruins are used throughout the
       novels in increasingly significant ways. This use of ruins
       is delineated.

*2   CASSON, ALLAN PENHAM. "The Early Novels of George Eliot."
            Cited in ELL(1961).

3   _____. "'The Mill on the Floss' and Keller's 'Romeo und Julia
       auf dem Dorfe.'" Modern Language Notes, 75: 20-22.
            Finds the Keller story (1856) a striking analogue to The
       Mill on the Floss. There do not seem to be references to
       Keller in George Eliot's letters or journals, but George
       Henry Lewes's article "Realism in Art: Modern German Fic-
       tion," written while he and George Eliot were in Germany in
       the summer of 1858, includes a four-page account of Kel-
       ler's collection Die Leute von Seldwyla, dealing almost
       entirely with Romeo und Julia.

4   DAICHES, DAVID. A Critical History of English Literature,
       Vol. 2. New York: Ronald Press Company, pp. 1066-1072.
            George Eliot was the first English novelist to move in
       the vanguard of the thought and learning of her day, and in
       doing so added new scope and dignity to the English novel.

5   HAIGHT, GORDON S. "George Eliot: The Moralist as Artist."
       Victorian Newsletter, No. 16, pp. 25-27.
            In this review of Thale's The Novels of George Eliot
       (1959.A6), Haight points out several aspects of the novels
       which Thale has overlooked in his attempt to identify the

central moral process. He has failed to account for the excellence of the novels.

6   HANDLEY, GRAHAM. "A Note on Daniel Deronda." Notes and Queries, 7: 147-148.
    A mistake in referring to the Quallons at the archery meet before she has introduced them provides some clue as to George Eliot's methods of revising and rewriting.

7   KETTLE, ARNOLD. "George Eliot: Middlemarch." An Introduction to the English Novel: From Defoe to George Eliot, Vol. 1. New York: Harper and Row.
    Reprint of 1951.B4.

8   LEAVIS, F. R. "George Eliot's Zionist Novel." Commentary, 30: 317-325.
    He explains the "failure" of the Daniel Deronda part of the novel as being the result of George Eliot's expending herself on the Jewish question because of a personal emotional need and working in an area which she does not sufficiently understand. Deronda is very positively a feminine expression. Reprinted in 1961.B12.

9   LERNER, LAURENCE. "The Cool Gaze and the Warm Heart." Listener, 64: 518-519, 522.
    Suggests that George Eliot tries to end Middlemarch by revealing her "warm heart" with three pages on wedded bliss and happiness, but her "terrible cool gaze" is fixed on the reader as he closes the book.

10 PREST, JOHN M. "The Historical Value of Middlemarch." The Industrial Revolution in Coventry. Oxford: Oxford University Press. Appendix pp. 143-145.
    She has laid a large part of Coventry society bare to the roots, but her accuracy is not great enough for the historian to accept it as literal truth.

11 PREYER, ROBERT. "Beyond the Liberal Imagination: Vision and Unreality in Daniel Deronda." Victorian Studies, 4: 33-54.
    The novel dramatizes George Eliot's deepest conviction about the human situation in the conflict between sympathy and selfishness. Her only safeguard against the vast, tangled spectacle of society is the human heart and its ability to respond to those higher minds which have in every generation created works of enduring beauty capable of educating the feelings and firming the will. She wants to persuade readers of the need for moral awareness and of

the significance of individual endeavor for general good. She wants to break through the usual accounts of the way we are psychologically determined. George Eliot was struck by the frequency of significant, unexpected communications wafting in from surprising quarters.

12   ROSENBERG, EDGAR. "The Jew As Hero and Isaiah Reborn: Eliot." From Shylock to Svengali: Jewish Stereotypes in English Fiction. Stanford, California: Stanford University Press, pp. 161-184.
      All the Jewish characters tend to polemicize "the Jewish problem" blatantly and deteriorate into talking puppets. George Eliot puts her own humanitarian dogmas into the mouths of her characters. Yet, Daniel Deronda, translated into Hebrew, became a Zionist Bible. In 1948 George Eliot received the monumental tribute of having a street named after her in Tel-Aviv.

*13   SIMON, IRÈNE. "George Eliot and Hendrik Conscience." Revue des Langues Vivantes, 26: 386-389.
      Cited in 1967.B31.

14   STALLKNECHT, NEWTON P. "Resolution and Independence: A Reading of Middlemarch." Twelve Original Essays on Great English Novels. Edited by Charles Shapiro. Detroit: Wayne State University Press, pp. 125-152.
      Never has a novelist gone further in defense of a character than George Eliot in the Prelude as she shows the resolution and independence of Dorothea when she puts Middlemarch behind her. The novel is an exhaustive study of human motivation, of interdependence of people, and their mutual influence upon one another. Only Caleb and Mary Garth are mature from the beginning. He is a touchstone. Dorothea and Ladislaw do well to leave Middlemarch. Their simple honesty and good sense are out of place in that world of deception.

15   STEVENSON, LIONEL. The English Novel: A Panorama. Boston: Houghton Mifflin Company.
      Contains a short summary of George Eliot's life and of the works.

1961 A BOOKS

*1   COLLINS, ROWLAND LEE. "The Present Past: The Origin and Exposition of Theme in the Prose Fiction of George Eliot." DA, 22: 3657. (Stanford University).

George Eliot uses man's past to influence his present in terms of the inseparability of man and his environment, the irrevocability of man's deeds, and the need for sympathy for other human beings. She delineates the vital effect of every man on his present and future.

2   HARVEY, W. J. The Art of George Eliot. London: Chatto and Windus.
    Defends George Eliot against the modern critics' misconceptions of the nature of her achievement and makes an attempt to put her in an historical context and to adapt critical methods to her achievement.

*3 HESTER, WAVERLY ERWIN. "George Eliot's Technique As a Novelist." DA, 22: 2396-97. (University of North Carolina).
    Analyzes George Eliot's fiction in terms of point of view, structure, imagery, and pattern as one character develops sympathetic ties to his community.

*4 LAING, ROBERT CUTTER, JR. "Humor in George Eliot's Novels." DA, 22: 3666. (University of Pittsburgh).
    George Eliot's fiction is never devoid of humor; her humor changed as she progressed. She moved from spontaneous, expansive humor to more subtle, more satirical, better-controlled humor, which was more closely integrated into themes and plots.

5   McKENZIE, KEITH ALEXANDER. Edith Simcox and George Eliot. London: Oxford University Press.
    Edith Simcox was a remarkable Victorian spinster, who told her own story in "Autobiography of a Shirt Maker." She wrote extensively for periodicals and published several books. She was for women's liberation; her interest in the shirt-makers led her to take an active part in the trades union movement. Her inner life centered for more than a decade around her secret love for George Eliot. This is recorded in minute detail in her writings. She was one of many disciples turning for guidance to George Eliot. This book follows the story of Miss Simcox's life.

*6 McMAHON, CATHERINE ROSE. "George Eliot and the Feminist Movement in Nineteenth-Century England." DA, 22: 3649-50. (Stanford University).
    George Eliot made a definite contribution to the feminist movement through her novels, but she never committed herself to the "movement" as such. She was firmly convinced of unique qualities of women that could make the world better or worse. She did not approve of career women or of

1961

equality in a man's world. Yet her own role was and is one of the best arguments for the feminist cause.

1961 B SHORTER WRITINGS

1   ALLOTT, MIRIAM. "George Eliot in the 1860's." Victorian
    Studies, 5: 93-108.
        In the 1860's it was herself as much as her readers she
    needed to convince of the truth of her meliorist beliefs.
    She toiled on trying to ennoble her readers while the hor-
    rible skepticism about all things paralyzed her mind and
    imagination. In Middlemarch she "finds her way out" of her
    depression, but it is still a profoundly melancholy book.

2   AUCHINCLOSS, LOUIS. "Is George Eliot Salvageable?" Reflec-
    tions of a Jacobite. Boston: Houghton Mifflin, pp. 43-59.
        A rather general treatment of the novels.

3   BUCKLER, WILLIAM E. ed. Novels in the Making. Boston:
    Houghton Mifflin.
        Reprints "Quarry Two" from Anna T. Kitchel's Quarry for
    Middlemarch (1950.A2).

4   CASSON, ALLAN. "The Scarlet Letter and Adam Bede." Victorian
    Newsletter, No. 20, pp. 18-19.
        Seven months before George Eliot began Adam Bede, she and
    Lewes reread The Scarlet Letter. There are many specific
    similarities in theme, in chapter topics and organization,
    in imagery, and in the names of the characters.

5   GREENBERG, ROBERT A. "The Heritage of Will Ladislaw." Nine-
    teenth Century Fiction, 15: 355-358.
        Answers the accusation that George Eliot has made a mis-
    take in connection with Will's past. The "mistake" occurs
    when the town makes the mistake of repeating gossip and
    Farebrother believes it.

6   HAGAN, JOHN. "Middlemarch: Narrative Unity in the Story of
    Dorothea Brooke." Nineteenth Century Fiction, 16: 17-32.
        Outlines in detail the process of initiation, growth, and
    education of Dorothea as she makes decisive discoveries
    about her own nature and the reality around her. Isolating
    the story of Dorothea from the incredibly intricate design
    of the whole novel shows George Eliot as a highly conscious
    craftsman in full control of her narrative art.

7   HAIGHT, GORDON S. "The George Eliot and George Henry Lewes
    Collection." Yale University Library Gazette, 35: 170–
    171.
        An account of the important collection of diaries, let-
    ters, and manuscripts of George Eliot at Yale. This col-
    lection, assembled by Chauncey Brewster Tinker, has long
    been known as the most important of its kind. The manu-
    scripts of her published works are at the British Museum
    and at Yale. There are several groups of letters. One
    section of the manuscripts relates to George Eliot's estab-
    lishment at Cambridge of the George Henry Lewes Studentship
    in Physiology. There are many other miscellaneous materi-
    als such as deeds, contracts, accounts of sales and royal-
    ties, and articles by and about George Eliot and Lewes.

8   _____. "Introduction." The Mill on the Floss. (Riverside
    Edition.) Boston: Houghton Mifflin Co.
        Suggests that Maggie's extraordinary susceptibility to
    music is a recurrent trait. George Eliot saw that moral
    factors play a part in evolution. The flood which ends the
    novel is not an afterthought but was the part planned
    first. Reprinted in 1965.A2.

9   HANDLEY, GRAHAM. "A Missing Month in Daniel Deronda." Times
    Literary Supplement, February 3, p. 73.
        Gives evidence to show that the month from September 20
    to October 20 is omitted, a singular oversight in view of
    the otherwise meticulous attention to chronological detail.

10 KNOEPFLMACHER, U. C. "Daniel Deronda and William Shakespeare."
    Victorian Newsletter, No. 19, pp. 27–28.
        After the publication of Daniel Deronda George Eliot be-
    came to many nothing less than a "modern" Shakespeare.
    There is evidence of a deliberate process of imitation on
    the part of the novelist. Daniel Deronda is the most con-
    sciously "Shakespearean" of all her novels. Outlines sim-
    ilarities between the novel and several of Shakespeare's
    plays.

*11 _____. "The Victorian Novel of Religious Humanism: A Study
    of George Eliot, Walter Pater, and Samuel Butler." DA, 22:
    2794–95. (Princeton University).
        Treats Middlemarch, Daniel Deronda, Marius the Epicurean,
    The Way of All Flesh. Sees George Eliot's religious human-
    ism as a fusion of science, morality, and historicism. She
    continues to feel religious yearnings even when she has no
    religious object for those yearnings. See 1965.B19.

1961

12 LEAVIS, F. R. "Introduction." Daniel Deronda. New York:
    Harper Brothers (Torch Books edition). Reprint of 1960.B8.

13 MAISON, MARGARET M. The Victorian Vision: Studies in the
    Religious Novel. New York: Sheeh and Ward.
        Includes as "religious novels" Scenes of Clerical Life,
    Adam Bede, and Romola. George Eliot clearly exemplifies
    the "Nonconformist conscience" at work, tracing in her nov-
    els the grim, inexorable consequence of sin, with all the
    Puritan emphasis on punishment for evil.

*14 PRICE, LAWRENCE M. "Otto Ludwig's Zwischen Himmel und Erde
    und George Eliot's Adam Bede." Dichtung und Deutung, Ge-
    dächtnisschift für Hans M. Wolff. Berne: Trancke, pp. 113-
    116.
        Cited in ELL(1961).

15 SELIG, ROBERT L. "The Red Haired Lady Orator: Parallel Pas-
    sages in The Bostonians and Adam Bede." Nineteenth Century
    Fiction, 16: 164-169.
        In The Bostonians, 1886, Verena Tarrant delivers a lec-
    ture on women's rights. Dinah Morris seems to have given
    Henry James a lot of ideas for her appearance and her atti-
    tude. The two women have the same air of girlish simplici-
    ty, and James even uses the same metaphors. He intends to
    supply in Verena the "dramatic progression" he misses in
    Dinah.

16 SIMON, IRÈNE. "Innocence in the Novels of George Eliot."
    English Studies Today, Second Series. Lectures and papers
    read at the Fourth Conference of the International Associa-
    tion of University Professors of English held at Lausanne
    and Berne, August, 1959, edited by G. Bonnard. Berne:
    Trancke, pp. 197-215.
        She explores the implications of innocence and experi-
    ence. The sympathies and imaginations of the characters
    are enlarged by their experience with life. Self-centered-
    ness is evil. This evil may be overcome through an exten-
    sion of the sensibilities and of imaginative perception.

17 STEINHOFF, WILLIAM R. "The Metaphorical Texture of Daniel
    Deronda." Books Abroad, 35: 220-224.
        The characters are at first isolated by a mental barrier,
    preoccupation with self. They break the walls and move
    out into the larger world of common human sympathy. They
    attain a larger capacity to attain the good. This good is
    expressed figuratively as that which is wide, enlarged,
    growing and developing. Metaphors of brightness, vision,

130

and deliverance characterize the culmination of this growth.
Metaphors of water, thirst, drought, currents and streams,
fruit and seed, and sight indicate movement of the individual toward a state of heightened consciousness and wid-
ened perception.

18   THOMSON, FRED C. "Felix Holt as Classic Tragedy." Nineteenth
      Century Fiction, 16: 47-58.
          Points out evidence that George Eliot meant Felix Holt to
      conform in some way to the example of Greek drama. But the
      effect is that of Elizabethan luxuriance with an injection
      of grand opera. He examines the elaborate underpinning of
      antecedent history, the prominent plot, the themes of neme-
      sis and the collision of the individual with the general,
      and the heightened rhetoric.

19   WRIGHT, AUSTIN ed. Victorian Literature: Modern Essays in
      Criticism. New York: Oxford University Press, pp. 231-
      236.
          Contains a reprint of 1951.B1.

1962 A BOOKS

  1   BENNETT, JOAN. George Eliot: Her Mind and Her Art. Cam-
      bridge, England: University Press.
          Reprint of 1948.A1.

 *2   CATE, HOLLIS LANIER. "The Literary Reception of George Eli-
      ot's Novels in America (1858-1882)." DA, 23: 3885-86.
      (University of Georgia).
          George Eliot's realistic techniques had a definite in-
      fluence in America on the writing of fiction as well as on
      critical theory. The simplicity and genuineness of the
      early novels was attractive to the Americans, but the ab-
      sence of the characters' dependence on a higher power was
      not. The later novels were more influential in America
      with the emphasis placed on morality and the clinical
      treatment of many of the characters.

 *3   COOLEY, E. MASON. "The Uses of Melodrama in George Eliot's
      Fiction." (University of California).
          Cited in ELL(1964).

 *4   SANTANGELO, GENNARO ANTHONY. "The Background of George Eli-
      ot's Romola." DA, 24: 2485-86. (University of North
      Carolina).
          Romola is based on the idea that basic sympathy with

1962

altruistic feeling constitutes the true moral and intellectual values which derive from compassion rather than divine
revelation. Romola grows beyond Savonarola's other-wordly
values to universal compassion.

*5   WILLEY, FREDERICK WILLIAM. "George Eliot and the Conventions
      of the Novel: Studies of a Writer in the Traditions of
      Fiction." (Harvard University).
          Cited in ELL(1963).

1962 B SHORTER WRITINGS

1   ADAM, I. W. "Restoration Through Feeling in George Eliot's
     Fiction: A New Look at Hetty Sorrel." Victorian Newslet-
     ter, No. 22, pp. 9-12.
         Hetty, like Silas and Romola, is restored by the appeal
     of a child as she emerges from her egoism. She redeems
     herself from the hardness and lack of human feeling charac-
     teristic of her before the birth of her child. The story
     of her night with the child is given in Hetty's simple,
     faltering vocabulary.

*2   AITKEN, DAVID JARED. "The Victorian Idea of Realism: A Study
      of the Aims and Methods of the English Novel Between 1860
      and 1875." DA, 23: 2910. (Princeton University).
          Anthony Trollope and George Eliot are two important nine-
      teenth century novelists who called themselves realists.
      George Eliot was regarded by her contemporaries as the
      greatest realist as well as the greatest writer of fiction
      of her time. Gives special attention to Middlemarch.

*3   BILLINGSLEY, BRUCE A. "Take Her Up Tenderly: A Study of the
      Fallen Woman in the Nineteenth-Century Novel." DA, 23:
      1681-82. (University of Texas).
          Treats Adam Bede and places it in the tradition of the
      seduction novels. In every case the seducer is a man of
      upper class, and he is almost always treated sympathetical-
      ly. George Eliot wanted a single standard of purity for
      both sexes.

4   CARROLL, DAVID R. "Felix Holt: Society as Protagonist."
     Nineteenth Century Fiction, 17: 237-252.
         At the center of the novel Felix is engaged in a private
     and public struggle; he tries to reform both Esther Lyon
     and the working class. The interdependence of his two
     roles is suggested structurally in a parallel series of
     events which contradicts his assertion of their incompati-

bility. He learns that any attempt to reform or modify the
social organism without due regard for and commitment to
the individual is bound to fail from lack of reality, just
as an egoistic assertion of the claims of the individual
will fail by its very exclusiveness. Reprinted in 1970.A4.

5   DAICHES, DAVID. "The Return of George Eliot." Nation, June 9,
    pp. 518-519.
        In the last fifteen years George Eliot has been estab-
    lished as one of the very greatest of English novelists and
    Middlemarch as one of the supreme classics of fiction. She
    finds an appropriate fictional form to give imaginative em-
    bodiment to her moral insights.

*6 GREENE, PHILIP LEON. "Henry James and George Eliot." DA, 24:
    4188-89. (New York University).
        The most important influence George Eliot had on James
    was her development of feminine sensibility as the heroine
    seeks social and moral emancipation. George Eliot develops
    toward the subjective penetration of consciousness.

7   GREGOR, IAN and BRIAN NICHOLAS. The Moral and the Story.
    London: Faber and Faber.
        Deals with novels written in the last century which em-
    ploy the theme of the innocent or guilty woman in society.
    Included among Mme. Bovary, Lady Chatterley's Lover, and
    others is Adam Bede.

8   HOGGART, RICHARD. "A Victorian Masterpiece." Listener, 67
    (March 8), 407-408.
        Middlemarch explains concretely how people face their
    perennial problems in moral frameworks within a rapidly
    changing society and deals subtlely with perennial problems
    in moral relationships.

9   HOLLOWAY, JOHN. The Victorian Sage: Studies in Argument.
    Hamden, Connecticut: Archon Books.
        Reprint of 1953.B6. Reprinted in 1965.B14. The section
    on George Eliot is reprinted in 1965.A2.

10 JERMAN, B. R. "Nineteenth Century Holdings at the Folger."
    Victorian Newsletter, No. 20, p. 23.
        Reports the recent discovery of two new Middlemarch note-
    books in the Folger Shakespeare Library. One is dated
    1868-70. In the latter are interesting notes on Lydgate,
    Casaubon, Harvey, Vesalius, apothecaries, fever hospitals,
    medical school qualifications, the influence of personal
    character on destiny, and several chapter mottoes.

1962

11   KREISEL, HENRY. "Recent Criticism of the Novel." <u>Toronto</u>
       <u>Quarterly</u>, 31: 246-250.
          He uses various of George Eliot's novels in a discussion
       of David Daiches' changing views of literary criticism.
       He shows how George Eliot's moral and social concepts are
       translated into significant forms. She uses coincidence as
       a means to force her characters to demonstrate their moral
       direction.

12   LAINOFF, SEYMOUR. "James and Eliot: The Two Gwendolens."
       <u>Victorian Newsletter</u>, No. 21, pp. 23-24.
          A minor but interesting specimen of James' indebtedness
       to George Eliot is in the description of Gwendolen Erme in
       the story, "The Figure in the Carpet," 1896.

13   LASKI, MARGHANITA. "Some Words from George Eliot's <u>Scenes of</u>
       <u>Clerical Life</u>." <u>Notes and Queries</u>, 9: 304-305.
          Finds many words which ante-date the listings in the OED.
       The words, such as balloon-sleeve, fancy-work, thumb-suck-
       ing, and washing-up, suggest that the former reader for the
       OED must have been a man.

14   LEVINE, GEORGE. "Determinism and Responsibility in the Works
       of George Eliot." <u>Publications of the Modern Language</u>
       <u>Association</u>, 77: 268-279.
          George Eliot was a consistent determinist. This is in no
       way incongruous with her conscious emphasis on moral re-
       sponsibility and duty. Every man's life is at the center
       of a vast and complex web of causes, and each man remains
       responsible for his choices and actions. A man is good to
       the extent that he has trained himself to exercise his will
       for what past experience has taught him is good. Her ma-
       ture characters understand that their lives are irrevocably
       dependent on the lives of others. Reprinted in 1965.A2.

15   MASTERS, DONALD C. "George Eliot and the Evangelicals."
       <u>Dalhousie Review</u>, 41: 505-511.
          While George Eliot disliked the Evangelical viewpoint,
       her treatment of the Evangelicals is much more sympathetic
       than that of other Victorian novelists. She attended two
       Evangelical schools and had an accurate understanding of
       the doctrine. She criticizes them for laying insufficient
       stress upon emotions and too much on ideas and doctrines.
       Examples are Janet's description of her conversion and
       Dinah's sermon.

16   NEILL, DIANA. <u>A Short History of the English Novel</u>. New
       York: Collier Books; London: Collier-Macmillan, Ltd.

Gives an interesting introduction to George Eliot's life
and to each novel. Says, "Her novels reveal an exceptional
sense of the pathos of human life, and a deep conviction
that human nature can be tried and purified only in the
fires of suffering." Suggests that her concept of suffering is based on her own experiences.

17 PARIS, BERNARD J. "George Eliot's Religion of Humanity."
    English Literary History, 29: 418-443.
        George Eliot felt that it was impossible to satisfy man's
    need for a sense of moral relation to the world without the
    illusion of God. She sees a human moral order responsive
    to consciousness and which is a source and sanction of
    moral values. It is manifested in love and fellow-feeling
    between individuals, in the products and traditions of hu-
    man culture. The individual's duties and his identity are
    defined in his relations to society, hereditary and as-
    sumed. She felt Christianity was important because it had
    grown out of human experience. As a realist she recognized
    that men are not morally responsible for their actions, but
    as a moralist she felt that moral judgment of past actions
    can have a potent influence upon future behavior. Reprint-
    ed in 1970.A4.

18 PINNEY, THOMAS. "Another Note on the Forgotten Past of Will
    Ladislaw." Nineteenth Century Fiction, 17: 69-73.
        Pinney says that Will's Jewish heritage pointed out by
    Beaty, 1958, is not important. But there is a crucial
    resemblance between Will and Daniel Deronda and with Esther
    in Felix Holt. All of these are cut off from their right-
    ful inheritances. All search for a past, an identity, and
    a binding duty. This search takes the folk tale form of
    the search for a father or the psychological equivalent
    thereof.

19 ROBINSON, CAROLE. "Romola: A Reading of the Novel." Victo-
    rian Studies, 6: 29-42.
        Defines the theme as the contrast or conflict between
    unscrupulous egoism and self-sacrificing devotion to duty.
    Tito's choices are simple, and he consistently chooses
    evil. Romola's choices are difficult; each decision in-
    volves a crisis, and she has to determine anew the value of
    established sanctions. Philosophic uncertainty is the
    keynote of the novel.

20 RUBINSTEIN, ELLIOT L. "A Forgotten Tale by George Eliot."
    Nineteenth Century Fiction, 17: 175-183.
        Cyril Connolly includes "The Lifted Veil" in his anthol-
    ogy of Great English Short Novels, New York, 1953. The

story is in first person, and the scene is the waste land
of a diseased mind. She describes Latimer's childhood with
the attention of a modern psychiatric worker preparing a
case history. In his early years he is deprived of intel-
ligent sympathy and an encompassing society. He is George
Eliot's most extreme treatment of unfulfillment. His mind
is beyond saving by any means but death. The experiment at
resuscitation, which dominates the end of the tale and
which provides Latimer with his final revelation, bears at
best a very uneasy connection with the preceding matter.

21 RYALS, CLYDE DE L. "The Thorn Imagery in Adam Bede." Victorian Newsletter, No. 22, pp. 12-13.
The "thorn" appears in many important passages to empha-
size the disparity between outward appearances and inner
character. Arthur inflicts misery like a thorn. Dinah's
fears for Arthur and Hetty are expressed in terms of
thorns. Sorrel is an attractive color, but also is a flow-
ering tree with needlelike leaves. Both thorn and sorrel
trees bear flowers, but also bear nettles.

22 WORTH, GEORGE J. "The Intruder Motif in George Eliot's Fiction." Six Studies in Nineteenth-Century English Literature and Thought. Edited by Harold Orel and George J.
Worth. Lawrence: University of Kansas Press, pp. 55-68.
Most of George Eliot's characters are seriously at odds
with their social environments and even seem to be intrud-
ers in the worlds they inhabit. At times the intrusion is
physical: the character enters a circumscribed area from
the outside, and his values and beliefs clash with the
dominant values and beliefs of his new associates. In
other cases there is no physical intrusion, but the character's sense of alienation from his world is very strong.
Discusses various characters in each of these groups.

23 YOUNG, G. M. "The Mercian Sibyl." Victorian Essays. London:
Oxford University Press.
To many of George Eliot's contemporaries, she was the
Sibyl who had restated the moral law, and the process of
soul-making, in terms acceptable to the rationalist, ag-
nostic conscience.

24 YWILL, W. E. "Character is Fate: A Note on Thomas Hardy,
George Eliot and Novalis." Modern Language Review, 57:
401-402.
Hardy's quotation from Novalis in The Mayor of Caster-
bridge, "Character is fate," comes from The Mill on the
Floss where George Eliot probably quoted from memory,
"Character is destiny."

1963 A BOOKS

*1   ANDERSON, ROLAND FRANK. "Formative Influences on George Eli-
      ot, With Special Reference to George Henry Lewes." DA, 25:
      1205-06. (University of Toronto).
         George Eliot acted on ungovernable impulse rather than
      reasoned motives. Lewes persuaded her to write fiction.
      He shared his literary and philosophical insights with her.
      He protected her from opposition and encouraged her to con-
      tinue writing.

*2   CHANDER, JAGDISH. "Religious and Moral Ideas in the Novels
      of George Eliot." DA, 24: 2905. (University of Wiscon-
      sin).
         Man determines his deeds, according to George Eliot, as
      much as his deeds determine him. All of her characters
      must discover some unifying principle to reconcile their
      inward promptings with outward facts. Each person adopts
      his religion in moments of passionate inwardness and in
      moments of disenchantment.

3   DAICHES, DAVID. George Eliot: Middlemarch. Great Neck, New
      York: Barron's Educational Series, Inc.; London: E. Ar-
      nold. 69 pp.
         Daiches says his emphasis is on clarification and evalua-
      tion, not biography. "Illumination" is the key word; the
      novel illuminates human experience through the interweaving
      of the fates of the characters and her use of imagery.

4   PINNEY, THOMAS. "Introduction." Essays of George Eliot. New
      York: Columbia University Press; London: Routledge and
      Kegan Paul.
         Feels that the belief that art teaches not by preaching
      but by a sympathetic and imaginative presentation is re-
      peatedly affirmed in her articles and becomes one of the
      vital principles of her own novels. The conception of ir-
      reversible but ultimately beneficent law as the unifying
      basis of morality, politics, and science underlies George
      Eliot's frequently misunderstood doctrine of consequence,
      her conservative view of society, and her meliorism.

1963 B SHORTER WRITINGS

1   BUCHEN, IRVING H. "Arthur Donnithorne and Zeluco: Charac-
      terization via Literary Allusion in Adam Bede." Victorian
      Newsletter, No. 23, pp. 18-19.
         When Arthur fails to identify himself with the hero of the
      novel and does not take Moore's warning seriously, he

discards the opportunity to overcome temptation. This allusion suggests George Eliot's affirmation of free will and
her related belief that moral self-knowledge is the only
antidote to deterministic despair. Arthur threw away the
opportunity given to all men to exercise his free will and
see the unforeseen.

2 COX, C. B. "George Eliot: The Conservative-Reformer." The
Free Spirit: A Study of Liberal Humanism in the Novels of
George Eliot, Henry James, E. M. Forster, Virginia Woolf,
Angus Wilson. London: Oxford University Press, pp. 13-37.
George Eliot is most acute when she demonstrates that the
humanistic desire for individual self-development can easi-
ly lead to loneliness and futility. Her answer is that her
characters should make new relationships with society
through the traditional service of family and community.
Her answers are simple Christian truisms.

3 DREW, ELIZABETH. "The Tragic Vision." The Novel: A Modern
Guide to Fifteen English Masterpieces. New York: Dell
Publishing Company, pp. 127-140.
As a sociological novelist she establishes a close, organic relationship between the nature of the individual and
society. Maggie is plunged into the hardest of all conflicts, not that between good and evil but between one good
and another good. The end of the novel lapses into moral
melodrama, but even so the creative achievement of the
whole stands firm. Reprinted in 1965.B8.

*4 ELSBREE, LANGDON. "The Breaking Chain: A Study of the Dance
in the Novels of Jane Austen, George Eliot, Thomas Hardy,
and D. H. Lawrence." DA, 24: 2476. (Claremont Graduate
School).
For George Eliot the dance signifies the kinds of love
and marriage a community permits and objectifies a character's inner life. The dance becomes one means of separat-
ing the past from the present, of showing relationships in
a society and the degree and kind of freedom the individual
has.

5 FERGUSON, SUZANNE C. "Mme. Laure and Operative Irony in
Middlemarch: A Structural Analogy." Studies in English
Literature, 3: 509-516.
Suggests that Lydgate's affair with actress Laure pre-
pares the reader for his otherwise barely credible bad
judgment about his involvement with Rosamond Vincy and ini-
tiates important structural elements. Analyzes Lydgate's
role in the novel and concludes that Rosamond's very

rejection of Lydgate's love and ambition forces him to a clearer perception of the world as it is.

6   FERNANDO, LLOYD. "George Eliot, Feminism and Dorothea Brooke." Review of English Literature, 4: i, 76-90.
     Analyzes George Eliot's attitude toward women. Says George Eliot did not consider men and women as having the same inherent capabilities. Women are more capable of a higher proportion of feeling with a greater capacity for love, pity, and sympathy. Yet a woman's place is in the home. Dorothea is a type of an emancipated woman.

7   HASTINGS, ROBERT. "Dorothea Brooke: The Struggle for Existence in Middlemarch." Thoth (Department of English, Syracuse University), 4: 61-66.
     Dorothea is portrayed in terms of the St. Theresa allusion. One of the salient characteristics of mysticism is the renunciation of self, the abandonment and purgation of ego. Dorothea can find no better way to relinquish herself to an ideal than in marriage to Casaubon. The story of her interest in Will parallels in its development the story of her interest in Casaubon. Marriage remains an unsatisfactory outlet for Dorothea's idealism. The world will not let her become another Theresa.

8   ISAACS, NEIL D. "Middlemarch: Crescendo of Obligatory Drama." Nineteenth Century Fiction, 18: 21-34.
     Isaacs sees the dramatic form of the novel as being governed by two principles: the philosophical and the structural. A perceptible pattern may be observed in the manner in which George Eliot reveals her attitude of ultimate sympathy and benevolence for all the characters in Middlemarch. In the first stage she takes a cold and objective external view of her characters; in the second stage she moves into the consciousness of the character; in the third stage the reader is told why he is to sympathize with the characters as she looks down upon them with sympathy. The dramatic pattern alternates the conglomerate scene with the obligatory scene. Isaacs finds eight group scenes, one in each book except for two in book seven; these are the conglomerate scenes. An obligatory scene is the inevitable coming together of two characters in dramatic conflict. Every major character has part in at least one obligatory scene; these scenes form a structure of their own and build toward a climax of climaxes.

*9   KATONA, ANNA. "Problems of Adjustment in George Eliot's Early Novels." Acta Litteraria Academiae Scientiarum Hungaricae

1963

(Budapest), 6: i-ii, 149-162.
Cited in 1969.B23.

10 LEVINE, GEORGE. "Isabel, Gwendolen, and Dorothea." English
    Literary History, 30: 244-257.
        Compares Gwendolen and Dorothea to Isabel of Portrait of
    a Lady. All three make discoveries about the limited pos-
    sibility of the "larger life." Their dignity lies in their
    ability to accept their limitations and fulfill the obliga-
    tions imposed by their own choice. He feels that Dorothea
    was the hardest thing that George Eliot attempted and she
    failed because she falls in love with Dorothea as a noble
    woman suffering from her own difficulties.

*11 McAULEY, JAMES PHILLIP. Edmund Spenser and George Eliot: A
     Critical Excursion. Hobart: University of Tasmania. 21
     pp.
        Cited in 1969.B23.

*12 MANSELL, DARREL LEE, JR. "George Eliot's Theory of Fiction."
     (Yale University).
        Cited in ELL(1964).

*13 MILNER, IAN. "The Genesis of George Eliot's Address to Work-
     ing Men and Its Relation to Felix Holt, the Radical."
     Prague Studies in English, 10: 49-51.
        Cited in ELL(1963).

*14 _____. "George Eliot and the Limits of Victorian Realism."
     Philologica Pragensia, 6: 48-59.
        Cited in 1969.B23.

15 PINNEY, THOMAS: "George Eliot's Reading of Wordsworth: The
    Record." Victorian Newsletter, No. 24, pp. 20-22.
        Gives a record of her knowledge of Wordsworth. Her in-
    terest in him was sustained throughout her adult life. Her
    emphasis on the moral value of spontaneous feeling owes
    much to him. There is much that is Wordsworthian in the
    psychology of her characters, her analysis of duty, her
    conception of the historical process, her view of child-
    hood, her use of setting, and her theory of literary real-
    ism.

16 SAMBROOK, A. J. "The Natural Historian of Our Social Classes."
    English, 14: 130-134.
        George Eliot's distinctive success in characterization
    and her effectiveness as a moralist are in no small part
    due to her ability in placing a character in its social
    setting.

17   SMITH, GROVER. "A Source for Hopkins' 'Spring and Fall' in
     The Mill on the Floss." English Language Notes, 1 (Sep-
     tember), 43-46.
          Suggests that the poem by Hopkins may be founded on the
     hair-cropping episode of Maggie Tulliver's childhood (Book
     1, Chapter 7). In any case the comparison of the poem to
     the novel throws into relief the psychological implication
     of "Spring and Fall" as an address "to a young child."

18   THOMSON, PATRICIA. "The Three Georges." Nineteenth Century
     Fiction, 18: 137-150.
          Both George Eliot and George Henry Lewes recognized
     George Sand as the most distinguished woman novelist of her
     country. Outlines their references to her. Then compares
     her work to George Eliot's.

*19 TOMLINSON, T. B. "Middlemarch and Modern Society." Melbourne
     Critical Review, 6: 44-55.
          Cited in 1969.B23.

20   WADE, ROSALIND. "George Eliot and Her Poetry." Contemporary
     Review, 204: 38-42.
          Considers several of the poems individually and finds
     many passages smoothly regal; yet the overall effect bor-
     ders on the ponderous. The childhood sonnets seem to be
     the only group in which her emotions were engaged.

21   WILSON, ANGUS. "Evil in the English Novel." Listener, 69
     (January 3), 15-16.
          The first of this series is called "From George Eliot to
     Virginia Woolf," and it is the only one of the series which
     deals with George Eliot. Wilson discusses various images
     of evil; to represent George Eliot he chooses Daniel Deron-
     da. In this novel George Eliot tries to portray an evil
     which transcends psychological or social analysis.

1964 A BOOKS

1   ALLEN, WALTER. George Eliot. New York: Macmillan Company;
     London: Weidenfeld and Nicolson.
          Divided into two parts: the life and the novels. Allen
     feels that George Eliot had little love for pretty girls.
     She saw prettiness and sexual attractiveness as qualities
     dangerous to the moral nature of those who possess them.

*2   BURNS, JOHN SANDIDGE. "The Wider Life: A Study of the Writ-
     ings of George Eliot." DA, 25: 1903-04. (Rice Univer-
     sity).

1964

The moral progress of society depends on individual moral growth which begins with personal fellowship, and all of life is a spiritual pilgrimage toward sanctification with many struggles to live up to the new self. The influence of spiritual masters opens to their followers a wider life.

*3   TEMPLIN, LAWRENCE HOWARD. "George Eliot: A Study of the Omniscient Point of View in Her Fiction." DA, 25: 2967-68. (Indiana University).

George Eliot's omniscient author is not identical with the historical person of the author herself. It is a narrative persona which is designed to be an essential part of her artistic intention. Her sympathetic realism requires such a persona to bridge the gaps of understanding of the points of view of the reader, the author, and the characters.

1964 B SHORTER WRITINGS

1   ADAM, IAN. "A Huxley Echo in Middlemarch." Notes and Queries, 11: 227.

Suggests that George Eliot uses as illustration rather than end the physiological reality of Huxley as defined in his essay "The Physical Basis of Life," Fortnightly Review, February, 1869, and in Lay Sermons, 1870. An example is the way in which the noise of growing grass becomes an image of Dorothea's inaudible suffering.

*2   BEDIENT, CALVIN BERNARD. "The Fate of the Self: Self and Society in the Novels of George Eliot, D. H. Lawrence, and E. M. Forster." DA, 25: 1187. (University of Washington).

George Eliot devotes her heart and fiction to the self on the social side, preferring for the self the paradoxical fate of a self within a secular context. In the conflict between the individual and society, she chooses society. Her central theme is the sacrifice of the sensuous private fate of the human being to a rigorous ideal.

3   BROWN, KEITH. "The Ending of The Mill on the Floss." Notes and Queries, 11: 226.

Says the final catastrophe is a physical impossibility because of the handling of the description of the pieces of wreckage propelled by the current.

4   BURN, W. L. The Age of Equipoise: A Study of the Mid-Victorian Generation. New York: W. W. Norton and Company.

Contains several comments on George Eliot.

5   COCKSHUT, A. O. J. The Unbelievers: English Agnostic Thought, 1840-1890. London: Collins, pp. 44-58.
       Without George Eliot readers would be inclined to say that the tradition of agnostic seriousness encouraged talent and inhibited genius. She attained her great works by an unexpected refinement and development of the virtues of conventional agnostic discourse. Adam Bede himself could link the new agnostics and the English country tradition. Her clergymen are also well-suited to develop into high-minded agnostics. Daniel Deronda deals with the idea of the religious pilgrimage or quest. When she wished to show the new agnostic religion of humanity at work, she had to fall back on a very old religion. She leans heavily on Divine Providence to arrange the events.

6   FELTES, N. N. "George Eliot and the Unified Sensibility." Publications of the Modern Language Association, 79: 130-136.
       She gives emphasis to the "whole souls" of her characters as they are converted. Religious experience is both intellectual and emotional. Lewes's ideas of wholeness expressed in Problems of Life and Mind illuminate this aspect of her novels. His insistence is invariably on the "felt" quality of an experience. Her characters move toward "felt" knowledge. She was as intellectual as John Donne in being able to feel thought as immediately as the odor of a rose.

7   GILLESPIE, HAROLD R., JR. "George Eliot's Tertius Lydgate and Charles Kingsley's Tom Thurnall." Notes and Queries, 11: 226-227.
       This Tom of Kingsley appeared fourteen years before Middlemarch in Two Years Ago. He has many of the characteristics of Lydgate noted by Haight in his introduction to the Riverside edition; he is a physician-hero who is ahead of his time professionally.

8   GOLDFARB, RUSSELL M. "Caleb Garth of Middlemarch." Victorian Newsletter, No. 26, pp. 14-19.
       Caleb Garth figures importantly in the philosophy and plot of Middlemarch and with his own bedrock philosophy and uncompromising integrity aids in character development and thematic unity. He also provides an easy access to different areas in the novel.

9   HARDY, BARBARA. "Implication and Incompleteness: George Eliot's Middlemarch." The Appropriate Form: An Essay on the Novel. London: Athlone Press, pp. 105-131.

1964

The form, with its structural features—antithesis and parallelism, anticipation and echo, and scenic condensation, is the means to the ends of good story, moral argument, and the imitation of life. Middlemarch is only restricted but truthful in its treatment of sexuality. Casaubon's impotence is part of a larger incapacity for life. The novel shows the unhappy consequences of restricted treatment of sex in Dorothea's relationship with Will Ladislaw. Sensibility acts as a surrogate for sensuality. Reprinted in 1971.B24.

*10   HARRIS, STEPHEN LeROY. "The Mask of Morality: A Study of the Unconscious Hypocrite in Representative Novels of Jane Austen, Charles Dickens, and George Eliot." DA, 25: 4699. (Cornell University).
George Eliot examines the morally disastrous effects of an unexamined allegiance to some humanly inadequate ideal. Lydgate struggles against his wife's maddening "insensibility," her self-satisfaction. He is made to feel as if he belonged to a "different species."

11   HARVEY, W. J. "George Eliot." Victorian Fiction: A Guide to Research. Edited by Lionel Stevenson. Cambridge: Harvard University Press.
Finds two biographical extremes. One is the sibyl or oracle; the other wants George Eliot to be a shy, diffident girl. The more recent concerns in criticism have been with imagery and symbolism as related to her typical moral concerns.

*12   HEAGARTY, MARY ALICE. "Aesthetic Distance in the Techniques of the Novel." DA, 25: 4687-88. (University of Illinois).
George Eliot's imagery is investigated to determine how it works to inspire the reader's sympathetic perception of the characters. She uses the fine arts as a major source of imagery for the heroic characters. This fails because Victorian aestheticism repels the modern reader.

13   KARL, FREDERICK R. "George Eliot: The Sacred Nature of Duty." A Reader's Guide to the Nineteenth Century British Novel. New York: Noonday Press, pp. 253-293.
A man's faith raises him to a higher order of experience through the self-mastery of impressions, desires, and impulses. Sympathy enlarges the spirits of George Eliot's characters. She probes into human motivation and analyzes the causes and effects in lives filled with adversity and directed by duty.

14 KNOEPFLMACHER, U. C. "George Eliot, Feuerbach, and the Question of Criticism." Victorian Studies, 7: 306-309.
    Critics must learn to deal with George Eliot simultaneously as artist and philosopher. She successfully transmuted ideas into the form and structure of her novels. In Adam Bede she adopted Feuerbach's unorthodox explication of the Christian sacraments. The symbol of water is important as Adam builds the coffin and takes sips of water as his father dies. At the young squire's birthday feast he learns to rise above nature. The third communion scene sees him converted to the awe and pity at the core of the religion of humanity. The fourth such use of the sacrament is at the supper scene of the harvest festival. Reprinted in 1970.A4.

15 LEDGER, MARSHALL A. "George Eliot and Nathaniel Hawthorne." Notes and Queries, 11: 225-226.
    Finds an early comparison in a review of Adam Bede in Edinburgh Review, 110 (July, 1859), 114-125. Finds resemblances in the minute description of the two and in their wit and charm. Also points out two punning conceits on Hawthorne's name.

16 LEE, R. H. "The Unity of The Mill on the Floss." English Studies in Africa, 7: 34-53.
    Seeks to dispel the views that the early scenes are simply recreations of George Eliot's own childhood and family and that the problem with Maggie and Stephen's love is brevity or its not being autobiographical. Then shows that the problem in the novel is its two-part structure. Her inadequate view of tragedy betrays the thematic cohesion and intricate structure.

17 LUECKE, SISTER JANE MARIE: "Ladislaw and the Middlemarch Vision." Nineteenth Century Fiction, 19: 55-64.
    Ladislaw is not a mistake in the artistic whole of Middlemarch but a consistent and revealing achievement as his sensitivity, quick perception, and glibness of speech counterbalance Dorothea's ascetic bent and active sense of duty. It is only after Dorothea is absorbed into Ladislaw that he becomes notably successful.

*18 McKENZIE, K. A. "George Eliot and George Sand." Austa-lasian Universities Language and Literature Proceedings, pp. 61-62.
    Cited in ELL(1964).

1964

19   MERTON, STEPHEN. "George Eliot and William Hale White." Vic-
      torian Newsletter, No. 25, pp. 13-15.
        White was George Eliot's fellow lodger in the Chapman
      household. He refers to her in two letters in Athenaeum,
      No. 3502 (December 8, 1894), p. 790 and No. 3031 (November
      28, 1885), p. 702.

*20   MILNER, IAN. "George Eliot's Realist Art." Zeitschrift für
      Anglistik und Amerikanistik (Berlin), 12: 387-394.
        Cited in ELL(1964).

*21   _____. "Herr Klesmer: George Eliot's Portrait of the Artist."
      Philologica Pragensia, 7: 353-358.
        Cited in ELL(1964).

22   _____. "Writing in Bohemia." Times Literary Supplement,
      June 18, p. 538.
        George Eliot and George Henry Lewes were favorably im-
      pressed by their visit of July, 1858, to Prague. The Bo-
      hemian influences are clear in Daniel Deronda. Mirah makes
      her escape from Prague to England.

23   PARIS, BERNARD J. "George Eliot, Science Fiction, and Fan-
      tasy." Extrapolation (College of Woucester, Ohio), 5:
      26-30.
        At the heart of George Eliot's view of the human condi-
      tion is a strong sense of the disparity between the inward
      and outward, between desire and reality, consciousness and
      the world. Science is present in her fiction not so much
      in its specific findings and technological consequences as
      in its basic principles, its fundamental philosophy. Sci-
      ence fiction is separated from the fairy tales and allied
      to fiction by its attempt to do justice to the laws of
      nature.

24   POSTON, LAWRENCE SANFORD, III. "Romola and Thomas Trollope's
      Filippo Strozzi." Victorian Newsletter, No. 25, pp. 20-22.
        Trollope's work may have influenced George Eliot's treat-
      ment of Tito. Strozzi's devious course is analogous to
      Tito's.

*25   _____. "Five Victorians on Italian Renaissance Culture: A
      Problem in Historical Perspectives." DA, 25: 484.
      (Princeton University).
        Treats Ruskin, Browning, Eliot, Pater, and Symonds in an
      attempt to show the relation of the Renaissance culture to
      the theme of Romola. Emphasis is placed on her evocation
      of Florence in the fifteenth century and not on those

purely Victorian overtones which are stressed by most critics.

26   ROBINSON, CAROLE. "The Severe Angel: A Study of <u>Daniel Deron-</u>
     <u>da</u>." <u>English Literary History</u>, 31: 278-300.
     Says the whole novel is curiously distorted, for its
     moral judgment is contradicted by its aesthetic judgment.
     The splendid Gwendolen and the spurious Daniel make the
     ethical distinction an absurdity. The labored creation of
     Daniel shows him as he embarks on his odyssey of social
     dedication, the secular immortality of the positivist. But
     it is to Gwendolen that the true vitality, and thus the
     literary immortality, belongs. Deronda remains a helpless
     savior; his role is neither sexual nor sisterly; it is
     pseudo-religious.

1965 A BOOKS

*1   DUNCAN, CHARLES FREEMAN, JR. "Time-Levels and Value-Struc-
     tures in George Eliot's Novels." DA, 26: 1039. (Emory
     University).
     Finds an unresolved duality in the conflict between
     George Eliot's representational and moral motives. She at-
     tempts to affirm the worth of the individual's aspirations
     without committing him to an autonomous existence. The
     flaws related to her levels of time are related to her
     developing ideas of the role of the individual in society.

2   HAIGHT, GORDON S. ed. <u>A Century of George Eliot Criticism.</u>
     Boston: Houghton Mifflin Company; London: Methuen.
     An "Introduction" reviews the critical reception of
     George Eliot's work. The selections are representative,
     not "the best." Each selection contained in this volume is
     listed and annotated separately.

*3   KATONA, ANNA. <u>A regényiró George Eliot és XX. századi átér-</u>
     <u>tekelésenek problémái.</u> Budapest: Akadémiai nyomda. 11
     pp. Theses of a dissertation.
     Cited in ELL(1965).

4   NOBLE, THOMAS A. <u>George Eliot's Scenes of Clerical Life.</u>
     New Haven and London: Yale University Press.
     In George Eliot's first work of fiction it is possible to
     see emerging the literary and philosophical principles that
     make her work a significant departure in the history of
     English fiction. The first chapter gives an account of the
     composition, publication, and reception of the work. The

1965

second chapter outlines her theory of fiction; the third considers the world as an expression of her moral philosophy. Chapter 4 deals with various aspects of her narrative technique. The last part suggests ways in which this early fiction foreshadows the later work.

5   PARIS, BERNARD J. Experiments in Life: George Eliot's Quest for Values. Detroit: Wayne State University Press.
     This is a study of George Eliot's intellectual development and of the ways in which she employed her novels in her quest for values in a Godless universe. Chapters 1-5 define her ideas as shaped by her intellectual milieu. Chapter 6 tells how she used art as a means of discovery, verification, and expression of enduring truths. Chapters 7-11 examine the novels. Chapter 12 provides a synthesis of her quest for values.

*6   PRATT, JOHN CLARK. "A Middlemarch Miscellany: An Edition with Introduction and Notes on George Eliot's 1886-1871 Notebook." DA, 26: 6050. (Princeton University).
     Examines the one-hundred-seventy-one page notebook which George Eliot used 1868-1871 for notes of her readings from prose and poetry. It serves as a guide to backgrounds, influences, and sources for Middlemarch. From the study a more complete picture of her as a meliorist emerges.

*7   ROBINSON, CAROLE L. "The Idealogy of Sympathy: A Study of George Eliot's Later Phase." DA, 27: 1383A. (Brandeis University).
     Romola, Felix Holt, The Spanish Gypsy, and Daniel Deronda contain aspects which give rise to the "less satisfactory" products of her art. They result in part from a philosophy of fellowfeeling derived from the Comtist religion of humanity and from conscientious agnosticism. The distinctions are too rigid between altruism and egoism.

*8   RUST, JAMES DARIUS. "George Eliot's Periodical Contributions." DA, 27: 186A. (Yale University).
     This is a complete bibliography of George Eliot's contributions to periodicals. Most of them are reviews. They have been analyzed to set forth her opinions and to make clear her position among reviewers of her time.

*9   WILSON, JACK HAMILTON. "George Eliot in America: Her Vogue and Influence, 1858-1900." DA, 27: 190A. (University of North Carolina, Chapel Hill).
     In her realism George Eliot was always a step ahead of the American literary movements. Wilson lists specific works which she influenced.

1965 B SHORTER WRITINGS

1 ADAM, IAN. "Character and Destiny in George Eliot's Fiction."
    Nineteenth Century Fiction, 20: 127-143.
        In George Eliot's novels the characters demonstrate an
    anti-deterministic spirit and show the Evangelical view of
    the possibilities of human conversion and salvation. The
    basic action in each novel is a conversion in which the
    central character emerges from egoism through successive
    disenchantments. She sees a latent principle of goodness
    developing through experience and choices. She stresses
    the heredity of her characters.

*2 BLONDEL, JACQUES. "Morale, psychologie, destinée dans La
    moulin sur la Floss." Les Langues Modernes, 59: 342-348.
        Cited in ELL(1965).

*3 BOLTON, F. "Le Manuscript du Mill on the Floss." Études An-
    glaises, 18: 53-58.
        Cited in ELL(1965).

4 CARROLL, DAVID R. "Mansfield Park, Daniel Deronda, and Ordi-
    nation." Modern Philology, 62: 217-226.
        The Gwendolen Harleth part of the novel is similar to the
    world of Jane Austen's novel. In each novel the central
    dilemma is related to the inability to reconcile the de-
    mands of vocation with those of the heart. Gwendolen is
    shocked therapeutically into an awareness of self by a
    glimpse of Deronda's cosmic role; his own conflict is be-
    tween his daily discerned ordination and his personal prob-
    lems.

5 CATE, HOLLIS L. "George Eliot's Middlemarch: Its Initial
    American Publication and Reception, 1871-1874." Xavier
    University Studies, 4: 177-187.
        Harper gave George Eliot £1200 for the rights to Middle-
    march in Canada and in the United States. The article
    traces the manner in which Harper came into possession of
    the rights. Then outlines the responses of American crit-
    ics to her use of irony, her emphasis on reaction to ac-
    tion, and her strong stress on the psychological approach.

6 COLBY, ROBERT A. "Miss Evans, Miss Mulock, and Hetty Sorrel."
    English Language Notes, 2: 206-211.
        Early in 1860 a Paris literary review insulted George
    Eliot by comparing her to Dinah Mulock, author of John
    Halifax, Gentleman. Colby suggests more similarities than
    have been noticed. Her attitude toward the straying woman
    was much that of George Eliot toward Hetty.

1965

7 DENEAU, DANIEL P. "Imagery in the Scenes of Clerical Life."
   Victorian Newsletter, No. 28, pp. 18-22.
      All of the stories are apprentice work but show the grow-
   ing desire to employ the figurative. "Amos Barton" has no
   meaningful image patterns; the few images are awkward and
   overly ingenious and at best colorful decorations. In "Mr.
   Gilfil's Love Story" there is an array of images in distinct
   groups with an obvious attempt to gain strength through
   incremental repetition. In "Janet's Repentance" the images
   intensify the surface drama and externalize the escape
   Janet seeks. She is locked out from a communion with the
   world, and images outline the way Janet travels out of her
   torturing enclosure.

8 DREW, ELIZABETH. "The Tragic Vision." The Novel: A Modern
   Guide to Fifteen English Masterpieces. New York: Norton.
      Reprint of 1963.B3.

9 DUERKSEN, ROLAND A. "Shelley in Middlemarch." Keats-Shelley
   Journal, 14: 23-31.
      George Eliot's two direct references to Shelley in her
   presentation of Will Ladislaw are more than incidental.
   She seems to have intended him as a strongly Shelleyan
   character. It is most probable that she relied greatly on
   the ideas of Lewes for this. Lewes is known to have helped
   W. M. Rossetti in 1869 with the preparation of his Memoir
   of Shelley, and during his many years of association with
   Leigh Hunt, Lewes had ample opportunity to learn about
   Shelley.

10 FISCH, HAROLD. "Daniel Deronda or Gwendolen Harleth?" Nine-
    teenth Century Fiction, 19: 345-356.
       Suggests that the main difficulty in Daniel Deronda may
    be George Eliot's use of epic rather than dramatic tech-
    nique. Deronda provides Gwendolen's concerns an ironical
    perspective whereby their relative diminutiveness might be
    properly assessed. He fails to assimilate to Gwendolen's
    world where time is a dimension of ordinary life. In his
    world epic time measures his experiences in a Jewish world.
    The very difference between the two halves is the central
    theme of the novel.

*11 GELLEY, ALEXANDER. "Symbolic Setting in the Novel: Studies
     in Goethe, Stendhal, and George Eliot." DA, 26: 2210-11.
     (Yale University).
        George Eliot's art is deeply rooted in her vision of the
     English countryside. This is shown through an analysis of
     the description of the landscape and the nature imagery in
     Adam Bede and The Mill on the Floss.

*12   GOTTHEIM, LAWRENCE ROBERT. "The Ideal Hero in the Realistic Novel." DA, 26: 4627. (Yale University).

One of the tenets of realism has generally been a rejection of the ideal, especially of the ideal character. In Daniel Deronda the conflict between Deronda's idealization and Gwendolen's psychological realism is not a flaw; it is part of a developed theme involving the nature of reality.

13   HARVEY, W. J. ed. "Introduction." Middlemarch. Baltimore: Penguin.

The moral vision embodied in Middlemarch creates a corresponding response in the reader. This is achieved through a wide variety of viewpoints and of changing perspectives. George Eliot's use of metaphor and the setting of comedy and wit against pathos and moral seriousness help to achieve this effect. But above all the poise of the omniscient author acts as guide and unobtrusive chorus throughout the novel.

14   HOLLOWAY, JOHN. The Victorian Sage: Studies in Argument. New York: W. W. Norton and Company.

Reprint of 1953.B6. Reprinted in 1962.B9. The section on George Eliot is reprinted in 1965.A2.

15   KARL, FREDERICK R. An Age of Fiction: The Nineteenth Century British Novel. New York: Farrar, Straus, & Geroux.

Refers to George Eliot several times but has no specific treatment of her or her works.

*16   KATONA, ANNA: "A változó világ George Eliot regényeiben." Kulonvenyom at a Filologiai Közlöng (Budapest), 11: 140-154.

Cited in ELL(1965).

17   _____. "The Changing Image of George Eliot." Hungarian Studies in English, 2: 47-59.

Madame Bodichon, one of George Eliot's best friends, commented on finding in her fiction "her great big head and heart and her wise views." In spite of the profound alteration in views toward her writings, this is still a valid observation. Professor Katona reviews the changing attitudes toward the fiction. A summary of the article written in Hungarian follows it.

18   KILLHAM, JOHN. "The Use of 'Concreteness' as an Evaluative Term in F. R. Leavis' The Great Tradition." British Journal of Aesthetics, 5: 14-24.

Criticizes Leavis for repeatedly using the term "con-

creteness" to indicate a whole variety of possible responses. "Concreteness" should not be used as a critical
term to refer to a particular feature of a work.

19   KNOEPFLMACHER, U. C. Religious Humanism and the Victorian
     Novel: George Eliot, Walter Pater, and Samuel Butler.
     Princeton: Princeton University Press.
        George Eliot's adoption of a Feuerbachian creed of sym-
     pathy allowed her to retain an "essence" of Christianity
     amidst the evolutionary world of Darwin and Huxley. Her
     humanism contended that the "essential" ethos of Christi-
     anity could live on in the "idea of humanity as a whole,"
     but it failed to present her with an actual vehicle for
     this positive, and positivist, morality. She was fully
     aware of this dilemma. Transplanted to the realm of pure
     imagination and handled by a moralist craftsman of George
     Eliot's stature, these ideas of her humanism are given the
     ultimate permanence of art. Discusses her scientific posi-
     tivism, her humanization of Christianity, and her Arnold-
     like belief in the force of tradition.

20   LERNER, LAURENCE. "The Education of Gwendolen Harleth."
     Critical Quarterly, 7: 355-364.
        Gwendolen's awakening is George Eliot's greatest study in
     conversion. The psychological process which interested her
     most was that by which a limited personality, whose emo-
     tional life was constricted by egoism, learns under the
     influence of a nobler nature to yield to more generous
     impulses and transcend the bounds of self.

21   LEVINE, GEORGE. "Intelligence as Deception: The Mill on the
     Floss." Publications of the Modern Language Association,
     80: 402-409.
        Finds a weakness in the novels which results from a com-
     plex mode of self-deceit, a combination of high intelli-
     gence with powerful moral revulsion from that which intel-
     ligence tended to reveal. She uses the empirical and
     rationalist determinism of Comte and Feuerbach to escape
     the implications of her own most deeply felt insights.
     Reprinted in 1970.A4.

22   MANSELL, DARREL, JR. "George Eliot's Conception of 'Form.'"
     Studies in English Literature, 5: 651-662.
        Argues that George Eliot intended for analogies like
     those which are recognized in Middlemarch to be a unifying
     principle in her fiction. Her theory of art is expressed
     in her "Notes on Form in Art (1868)." The form she strives
     for attempts to show as many relationships as possible of

the relations which in her universe connect everything to everything else. Such a form must of necessity seem incomplete; the more relations the novel establishes, the more must be severed where they do not end. Thus the higher the form of her novels, the more incomplete they seem. Reprinted in 1970.A4.

23 _____. "A Note on Hegel and George Eliot." Victorian Newsletter, No. 27, pp. 12-15.
George Eliot conceives of her novels as tragedy and seems to be influenced by Hegel's ideas. Tragedy is the "downfall of individuality" as an individual protagonist is set against life. One person cannot divorce himself from the general.

24 _____. "Ruskin and George Eliot's 'Realism.'" Criticism, 7: 203-216.
George Eliot understands Ruskin's idea that the artist should begin by humbly and faithfully studying nature and then produce art which is distinctly different from nature in that the artist's imagination is evident in his treatment of his subject. She regards the novel as being the language of men in Wordsworth's "State of Vivid Sensation." Emotion for her is the core of the novel. Her opinions, often regarded as digressions, mirror her own emotions as she interprets nature.

25 PRITCHETT, V. S. "The Pains of Others." New Statesman, 70 (November 12), 737-738.
Says George Eliot was really a frustrated prude, incapable of understanding her own expressions, jealous of girls prettier than herself, and sadistic in the treatment of them. Only melodrama relieves the preaching in her novels.

26 SCHNEEWIND, JEROME B. "Moral Problems and Moral Philosophy in The Victorian Period." Victorian Studies, 9, suppl., 29-46.
Daniel Deronda is the novel in which freedom is closest to being George Eliot's theme. Deronda's will is so impartial and impersonal it is in danger of becoming incapable of seeking any ends or making any moral distinctions. Gwendolen's aim is to do what she likes. She discovers herself in a slavery brought on herself. Through the novel George Eliot attempts to bring together her intuitional morality and her determinist sense of the world.

27 SMITH, DAVID. "Incest Patterns in Two Victorian Novels." Literature and Psychology, 15: 135-162.

1965

Jane Eyre and The Mill on the Floss are the two novels.
The organizing principle of The Mill on the Floss is an
unconscious incestuous passion between Maggie and Tom. The
passion is mutual, but it is more intense for Maggie; it is
an "erotic" passion: physical, sexual, and desperately
intense. George Eliot was probably not fully aware of this
relationship. In the end gratification and self-annihila-
tion are merged in a single moment of ecstasy.

28   THOMSON, FRED C. "The Theme of Alienation in Silas Marner."
      Nineteenth Century Fiction, 20: 69-84.
          In the sense of discontinuity or of disconnectedness of
      Silas' life George Eliot finds a common experience with
      tragic possibilities on a level of actuality surpassing the
      comprehension of the unenlightened country folk. His trade
      combines the familiar and the strange; his way of life is
      both continuous and discontinuous with established society.
      George Eliot thus combines the theme of social and spiri-
      tual discontinuity with the double plot. Tragedy occurs
      when the well-intentioned individual acts in ignorance or
      defiance of the intricate web that binds his moral behavior
      to that of collective society. The resultant tragic experi-
      ence consists in the feeling of disconnection from the
      roots of one's beliefs and assumptions about what the world
      is like.

29   TILLOTSON, GEOFFREY and KATHLEEN. "The George Eliot Letters."
      Mid-Victorian Studies. London: The Athlone Press, pp.
      62-79.
          Quotes from the letters (1954.A1) to give an overall im-
      pression of George Eliot such as comes from reading
      Haight's letters. The letters tell the story of a life
      "serenely heretical, constantly aspiring, deliberately
      emotional."

30   WELSH, D. J. "Two Talkative Authors: Orzeszkowa and George
      Eliot." Polish Review, 10: i, 53-60.
          Both Eliza Orzeszkowa and her English contemporary were
      excessively serious; both expounded moral ideas; and both
      portrayed human life in terms of certain principles and
      truths. The essential difference derives from the very
      different conditions under which they wrote.

31   WOLFF, MICHAEL. "The Uses of Context: Aspects of the
      1860's." Victorian Studies, 9, suppl., 47-63.
          Felix himself in Felix Holt, though a self-styled Radi-
      cal, shares Arnold's and Carlyle's disgust with the machin-
      ery of liberty. Like J. S. Mill, P. A. Taylor, and Lewes,

GEORGE ELIOT: A REFERENCE GUIDE

George Eliot was committed to Reform, and her solution to the political agitation of 1867 lay in the revival of some sort of authority similar in its inescapability to religion. She wanted to revive the old hierarchic values of reverence, obedience, and perfection.

1966 A BOOKS

*1   CHEN, ALICE W. W. "The Mind of George Eliot." DA, 28: 225A-6A. (University of Pennsylvania).
    George Eliot did not turn away from Christianity but removed herself from a mental state in which Christianity was considered the way to human perfection. Her God became moral perfection in man. The essence of morality consisted of an intense concern for the feelings and needs of others.

2   COCKSHUT, A. O. J. Middlemarch. Notes on English Literature. New York: Barnes and Noble, Inc.
    Describes Middlemarch as "Portrait of a Society," considers the characters, and "some moments of the story," and gives an analysis of chapter 18. Each section is followed by questions over that section.

3   DODDS, DOROTHY. The George Eliot Country. Edited by F. J. Cross. Nuneaton: The George Eliot Fellowship.
    Reprint of 1952.A2.

*4   FURUYA, SENZO. A Study of George Eliot. Tokyo: Azuma-Shobo. Cited in ELL(1966).

5   HOLMSTROM, JOHN and LAURENCE LERNER eds. George Eliot and Her Readers: A Selection of Contemporary Reviews. New York: Barnes and Noble; London: Bodley Head.
    Contains a linking commentary by Laurence Lerner. The purpose of this anthology of criticism is to show what contemporaries thought of the novels of George Eliot. The Mill on the Floss, Middlemarch, and Daniel Deronda have been selected for really thorough coverage. The main source of material is the daily, weekly, and quarterly papers published in England. Each section contains a short note on the publishing history of the novel, the reviews, then an editorial commentary. Each review is annotated separately in this bibliography.

*6   HURLEY, EDWARD T. "The Family as an Instrument for Theme and Structure in the Fiction of George Eliot." DA, 28: 677A. (University of Michigan).

The plots in George Eliot's novels are built around the formation of a family. The family becomes an instrument for the expression of realism and idealism, romantic love, freedom and determinism, emancipation of women, transvaluation of religion, and examination of individual and collective pasts.

*7 KRIEFALL, LUTHER HARRY. "A Victorian Apocalypse: A Study of George Eliot's Daniel Deronda and Its Relation to David F. Strauss' Das Leben Jesu." DA, 28: 234A. (University of Michigan).

The prophetic-religious theme of the novel is a version of the Messianism George Eliot came to know through translating Strauss' Das Leben Jesu. The character of Deronda embodies Strauss' idea of Christ.

*8 SZIROTNY, JUNE MARJORIE SKYE. "The Religious Background of George Eliot's Novels." DA, 27: 2547A. (Stanford University).

George Eliot's emphasis on sacrifice lies in her inability to free herself from Evangelical religion. She illogically insists on equating the demands of charity with renunciation.

*9 WACHI, SEINOSUKE. The Novels of George Eliot. Tokyo: Nanundo.

Cited in ELL(1966).

1966 B SHORTER WRITINGS

1 BEETON, D. R. "George Eliot's Greatest and Poorest Novel: An Appraisal of Daniel Deronda." English Studies in Africa, 9: 8-27.

Daniel Deronda is a prime example of how power and ineptness can exist side by side in an indisputably great mind. Daniel and Mirah, the bad part, is perhaps the poorest piece of fiction George Eliot ever wrote. It is melodramatic and wantonly emotive. Sometimes it is even hysterical. The achievement is all to be found in the Gwendolen Harleth part. The article has some interesting observations on the Arrowpoint family.

2 BELLRINGER, A. W. "Education in The Mill on the Floss." Review of English Literature, 6: iii, 52-61.

Finds criticism of contemporary educational theory and practice in the novel. The novel is about personality development, and the inadequacy of the Tulliver children's education is clear. The absence of proper educational facilities for Maggie forces her to rely on self-help but without success. The only really well-educated character is Dr. Kenn, the High Church Rector.

3   BROWN, HUNTINGTON. Prose Styles: Five Primary Types. Minneapolis: University of Minnesota Press.
     In a chapter called "The Deliberative Style: The Style of Persuasion," Brown illustrates his points with three quotations: Demosthenes's oration supporting the city of Olynthus, one from Thucydides, and one from Middlemarch. George Eliot argues and moralizes as she explains that Bulstrode acted from understandable, if unpraiseworthy, motives in preparing to leave Middlemarch.

4   BURTON, THOMAS G. "Hetty Sorrel, the Forlorn Maiden." Victorian Newsletter, No. 30, pp. 24-26.
     Hetty's plight as she confesses to Dinah is that of the Forlorn Maiden common to English and Scottish ballads.

5   DeLAURA, DAVID J. "Romola and the Origin of the Paterian View of Life." Nineteenth Century Fiction, 21: 225-233.
     Reading Romola may have been the impetus that set Pater on the road to Studies in the Renaissance. Evidence is given from Pater's essays. Perhaps the influence of Pater is most marked in Marius the Epicurean, 1885. Both are agnostic conversion novels.

6   DUNCAN-JONES, E. E. "Hazlitt's Mistake." Times Literary Supplement, January 27, p. 68.
     In Middlemarch, chapter 19, there is a reference to "the most brilliant critic of the day." W. J. Harvey guesses Hazlitt. What Hazlitt calls a vase is indubitably a tomb, and his ignorance clearly makes George Eliot's point. He is writing of a picture in the Vatican, Raphael's "Coronation of the Virgin" in Notes of a Journey Through France and Italy (1826).

7   HARVEY, W. J. "Ideas in George Eliot." Modern Language Quarterly, 27: 86-92.
     This review of 1965.B19 and 1965.A5 compares and contrasts the two within the larger context of a discussion of the content and quality of George Eliot's humanism. Paris sets up a picture of George Eliot's moral universe. There seems to be a kind of struggle between the perception of the quality of her thought and his effort to measure that thought against some externally applied philosophy. Knoepflmacher's stress is on the Higher Criticism and on

contemporary science. His best chapter is on Middlemarch; his most challenging is on Daniel Deronda. He argues that George Eliot is cautiously groping her way back to some notion of supernatural agency.

8   HESTER, ERWIN. "George Eliot's Use of Historical Events in Daniel Deronda." English Language Notes, 4: 115-118.
        George Eliot in this novel uses historical events almost like images to define the situations of her characters and selects historical events which accord with one of the significant image patterns in the novel, that of rule and rebellion. Historical fact acquires a metaphorical signi-ficance to illuminate the moral situation of the characters.

9   HORNBACK, BERT G. "The Organization of Middlemarch." Papers on Language and Literature, 2: 169-175.
        George Eliot creates the structure as she weaves charac-ters and events together to make the social world of Mid-dlemarch. Dorothea is trapped by her idealism outside the world of Middlemarch; she finally achieves a real social perspective and becomes a part of the social pattern. Dorothea can join the common fate of common men when she sees Middlemarch as the place in which real life can be lived in the most significant way possible.

10   JONES, W. GARETH. "George Eliot's 'Adam Bede' and Tolstoy's Conception of 'Anna Karenina.'" Modern Language Review, 61: 473-481.
        Adam Bede must have profoundly influenced Tolstoy in the initial stages of the creation of Anna Karenina. Points out specific characters, situations, and stylistic devices. The prototype for Anna is Hetty. Even the expansion of the novel into a panorama of contemporary Russian society could have been prompted by the social documentation of George Eliot's England.

11   LYONS, RICHARD S. "The Method of Middlemarch." Nineteenth Century Fiction, 21: 35-48.
        Lyons discusses chapter 39, Book 4, to show how the events described there further the plot of the novel and are even representative of the way the action proceeds throughout Middlemarch. George Eliot traces the gradual action of ordinary causes, and individual lives are illus-trative of the subtle movement in society in which munici-pal town and rural parish make fresh threads of connection. Plot becomes the growth in consciousness by which character is defined. The three main themes are the problem of re-form in its multiple aspects, the question of the nature of

true religion, and the issue of the proper ends of art. The three themes are related by recurring light and dark imagery and associated with the varied uses of contrast elsewhere.

*12 MILLS, NICOLAUS C. "Romance and Society: A Re-Examination of Nineteenth Century American and British Fiction." DA, 28: 687A. (Brown University).
     Treats Adam Bede, Hard Times, Jude the Obscure, Heart of Darkness, and Great Expectations. The primary differences in American and British fiction can be observed in structural terms.

13 MILNER, IAN. "Structure and Quality in Silas Marner." Studies in English Literature, 6: 717-729.
     The full meaning of the novel lies in the tension between the legendary and the realistic. Silas is at the center of the legendary element. He is dehumanized, reduced to the world of objects; then he finds the child by chance. The drama of his rehumanization is expressed in a more realistic vein as he gradually acquires a voice and gestures of his own.

14 _____. "The Structure of Values in Adam Bede." Philogia Pragensia, 9: 281-291.
     Deals with the historical validity of the circumstances and activities of Adam Bede as a cut above the ordinary workman. His dialect is examined and other specific details to show that "truthfulness" of representation is a cardinal principle of George Eliot's aesthetics.

15 MYERS, W. F. T. "Politics and Personality in Felix Holt." Renaissance and Modern Studies (University of Nottingham), 10: 5-33.
     The novel illustrates George Eliot's use of the thought of Comte, Spencer, and Feuerbach. Felix Holt's central lesson in life and message is that a man's religion is an unconscious projection of his ideas about and hopes for humanity. To be a truly effective Positivist teacher and social reformer, Felix becomes less artistic as a literary creation. He is the incarnation of Positivist political and social aspirations.

16 PARIS, BERNARD J. "George Eliot and the Higher Criticism." Anglia, 74: 59-73.
     Even after her rejection of traditional Christianity, George Eliot could not discard the past as obsolete or irrelevant. She needed to discover a continuity between past

and present in order to escape a sense of psychic fragmen-
tation and rootlessness. Hennell helped her to see that
the records, beliefs, and institutions of former ages become available intellectually and emotionally when they are
accepted as expressions of subjective realities.

17   PINNEY, THOMAS. "The Authority of the Past in George Eliot's
     Novels." Nineteenth Century Fiction, 21: 131-147.
        All except one of George Eliot's novels are set in a past
     at least one generation removed from the time of their com-
     position. The basis of her morality is strength of feeling.
     Old things are cherished because they have drawn to them-
     selves those affections which supply all the meaning of
     life. To describe these things of the past she uses Words-
     worth's phrase, "familiar with forgotten years," The Excur-
     sion, 1, 276. Reprinted in 1970.A4.

18   _____. "More Leaves from George Eliot's Notebook." Hunting-
     ton Library Quarterly, 29: 353-376.
        Lewes's son published "Leaves from a Notebook," but he
     passed over seventeen MS pages. The notebook is now in
     Huntington Library, MS. HM 12993. The items are published
     in their entirety. There are thirty-three separate pas-
     sages from one sentence to seven and a half pages in length.
     Lewes dates them between 1872 and 1879. Pinney observes
     that the notes "exhibit all the vices of her moralizing
     mode."

19   POSTON, LAWRENCE, III. "Setting and Theme in Romola." Nine-
     teenth Century Fiction, 20: 355-366.
        This careful analysis of the novel shows how the destiny
     of the characters is prepared for by judicious use of his-
     torical setting. The process by which Romola is drawn from
     the isolation of her father's house into the stir of Flor-
     entine life is central to the novel. Tito's lack of politi-
     cal roots is identified with his lack of spiritual direc-
     tion.

*20 RIMER, A. P. "Ariadne and Cleopatra: The Treatment of Doro-
     thea in Middlemarch." Southern Review (University of
     Adelaide), 2: 50-58.
        Cited in MLA(1966).

*21 ROBEY, CORA. "Matthew Arnold's Concept of Culture in the Late
     Victorian Novel: The Operation of This Idea in The Novels
     of George Eliot, George Meredith, Thomas Hardy, and George
     Gissing." DA, 27: 3061A-62A. (University of Tennessee).
        Culture is defined to be a pursuit of total perfection:
     inward, general, harmonious, and dynamic. George Eliot
     emphasizes the importance of a practical education, one

suitable for the individual's needs. There is to her something humorous and impractical about the idea of a perfectly harmonized individual.

*22   SMITH, DAVID J. "The Arrested Heart: Familial Love and Psy-
chic Conflict in Five Mid-Victorian Novels." DA, 27:
1839A. (University of Washington).
      The novels are Jane Eyre, The Mill on the Floss, Wuthering
Heights, Pendennis, and Henry Esmond. Principal characters
in each novel are motivated by an unconscious conflict between an incest wish and an incest taboo. The authors were
largely unconscious of depicting this kind of motivation.

*23   TICK, STANLEY. "Forms of the Novel in the Nineteenth Century:
Studies in Dickens, Melville, and George Eliot." DA, 27:
1349A-50A. (University of California, San Diego).
      Examines the psychological realism of Adam Bede and Mid-
dlemarch. Her history of place employs the concepts of
community of family and continuity of experience as parts
of the past which are uniquely and privately ordered.

24   WALKER, R. B. "Religious Changes in Cheshire, 1750-1850."
Journal of Ecclesiastical History, 17: 77-94.
      Quotes George Eliot's statement in Silas Marner that at
Raveloe all who were not household servants or young men
were to take the sacrament at one of the great festivals,
and explains that in Cheshire non-participation was not
restricted to these classes.

25   WILLEY, BASIL. Nineteenth Century Studies: Coleridge to
Matthew Arnold. New York: Harper and Row.
      Reprint of 1949.B7. The section on George Eliot is re-
printed in 1960.A7 and 1965.A2.

1967 A BOOKS

1   COUCH, JOHN PHILIP. George Eliot in France: A French Appraisal of George Eliot's Writings: 1858-1960. Chapel
Hill: University of North Carolina Press.
      Explores the politics of the leading French magazines in
order to place the first French opinions in proper perspective. Then makes a survey of articles appearing in or before 1880. The second chapter is on the articles of Émile
Montégut and Edmond Scherer; the third is "Brunetière,
George Eliot and Literary Cosmopolitanism"; and the fourth
is "George Eliot and Her Modern Readers (1890-1960)." The
three appendices include a list of the French-language
editions of George Eliot, a note on D'Albert-Durade as

translator, and a comment on George Eliot's attitudes toward France.

2 HARDY, BARBARA. "Introduction." Middlemarch: Critical Approaches to the Novel. New York: Oxford University Press.
       The essays suggest ways of reading and thinking about
   Middlemarch but do not claim to be telling the whole truth.
   Because it is a novel of such range and profundity, because
   it is a treasure-house of detail and a remarkable whole,
   because it is a fine and subtle work of art and a creation
   of character and communities, it raises issues which touch
   off responses to most novels. Each of the eight essays is
   listed and annotated separately.

*3 MARTIN, BRUCE KIRK. "Standards of Behavior in George Eliot's
    Fiction." DA, 28: 3191A. (University of Cincinnati).
        The ideological content of each novel forms a broad base
    of values by which the reader is meant to judge the central
    characters. The base represents a standard of behavior.

*4 NORMAN, LIANE. "The Novel as Moral Experiment: George Eliot's
    Novels." DA, 28: 2257A. (Brandeis University).
        The bulk of George Eliot's novels are badly flawed by
    evasive resolutions. Where moral courage and insight
    exist, excellence of creation is likely to ensue. Where
    moral cowardice exists, artistry is always inadequate.

1967 B SHORTER WRITINGS

1 BEATY, JEROME. "The Text of the Novel: A Study of the Proof."
   In 1967.A2.
       Looks at specific revisions which George Eliot made be-
   fore Middlemarch was published and suggests their significance. For example spelling out four contractions in the
   speech of Caleb Garth helps to dignify his role and solidi-
   fy his position as a moral norm. The emphasis of the earlier version seems to be on the individual's duty to try to
   live his life in a noble way and to make things "not so
   ill" for those to follow. The published version gives only
   half the credit for our relative well-being to those who
   struggled but who now rest in "unvisited tombs."

2 CARROLL, DAVID R. "Silas Marner: Reversing the Oracles of
   Religion." Literary Monographs (Wisconsin), 1: 167-200,
   312-314.
       The two stories in Silas Marner are two versions of the
   same theme. The reader watches the parallel degeneration
   of Godfrey and Silas. Each has followed a sequence of
   moral choices which forms his character. Then both take

decisive action, and both are regenerated. Godfrey's regeneration lacks the dramatic suddenness of Silas's. The
final confrontation completes the definition of the central
theme. The characters create and assess various myths and
attempt to make them into a meaningful whole.

3   CHEW, SAMUEL C. "The Nineteenth Century and After." A Liter-
       ary History of England, ed. Albert C. Baugh. London:
       Routledge and Kegan Paul, Ltd.
         Reprint of 1948.B3.

4   CIRILLO, ALBERT R. "Salvation in Daniel Deronda: The For-
       tunate Overthrow of Gwendolen Harleth." Literary Mono-
       graphs (Wisconsin), 1: 203-245, 315-318.
         Daniel's reality lies in his ideality. He helps Gwendo-
       len to overcome her narrow egoism. He is an objectifica-
       tion of the moral life which Gwendolen finally achieves.
       Her psychological progress is bound up with the resolution
       of Daniel's own movement towards a centered purpose. Only
       by Daniel's absence can Gwendolen really be saved.

5   CLARKE, ISABEL C. Six Portraits. Freeport, New York: Books
       for Libraries Press, Inc.
         Reprint of 1935.B2.

6   COLBY, ROBERT A. "Middlemarch: Dorothea Brooke and the Eman-
       cipated Woman; or The Heroine of the Nineteenth Century."
       Fiction With a Purpose: Major and Minor Nineteenth Century
       Novels. Bloomington: Indiana University Press, pp. 256-
       302.
         Discusses the education which Dorothea and Celia have had
       and George Eliot's attitudes toward it. Dorothea's educa-
       tion leads her to a "new consciousness of interdependence."
       For George Eliot's women vocation, courtship, and marriage
       are stages in their moral education. Her more idealistic
       characters seek "a conception of the world, of man and of
       society wrought out with systematic harmonizing of princi-
       ples." Her novels were designed to teach; they were to
       transcend temporal bounds and contribute to an education of
       the race. Her characters are archetypes of the moral ideas
       of their time. Gives a list of characteristic, contempora-
       neous fiction.

7   _____. "The Mill on the Floss: Maggie Tulliver and the Child
       of Nature." Fiction with a Purpose: Major and Minor Nine-
       teenth Century Novels. Bloomington: Indiana University
       Press, pp. 213-255.
         Maggie stays home while her brother is sent off to school.
       George Eliot gives what she calls an "epic breadth" to her

story by an intense rendering of their various environments: nature, home, school, and society. Of all these,
nature is the primal influence on the young seedlings and
the one to which they will eventually return. Her many
allusions to Wordsworth bear this out; The Prelude anticipates the novel in its psychological ideas. She makes her
children realistic as they respond to beauty and things of
the intellect and imagination. A list of characteristic
contemporary fiction is included.

8 COLLITS, T. J. "Middlemarch and Moral Stupidity." Critical
Review, 10: 88-98.
Discusses whether George Eliot's serious-minded somber-
ness limits her greatness. Dorothea is never brought into
active relation with the Middlemarch world. When George
Eliot is trying to discover moral truths about life by using Dorothea, she is most interesting to us. Through Lydgate the Middlemarch world is brought into closest conflict
with the highest human aspirations. She fails to draw the
different strands of the story together into one powerful
element; it is here that the failure of the novel lies.

9 CRAIG, DAVID. "Fiction and the Rising Industrial Classes."
Essays in Criticism (Oxford), 17: 64-73.
Bleak House and Felix Holt, two important literary treat-
ments of nineteenth century history, are examined. Felix
Holt presents in the speeches of the anonymous trade-
unionist and of Felix, two kinds of radicalism. One is
historical, and the other expresses George Eliot's own ardent humanism. She understood the viewpoint, idiom, and
culture of the militant mass-representative, but her sympathy was not with him.

*10 DENEAU, DANIEL P. "The River and the Web in the Works of
George Eliot." Research Studies (Washington State Univer-
sity), 35: 155-166.
Cited in ELL(1967).

11 DEVONSHIRE, MARION G. English Novel in France, 1830-1870.
London: Frank Cass and Company.
Reprint of 1929.B1.

*12 GARRETT, PETER K. "Scene and Symbol: Changing Mode in The
English Novel from George Eliot to Joyce." DA, 27: 4251A.
(Yale University).
Discusses the changing function of the narrator and the
use of imagery and theme. George Eliot's use of the om-
niscient narrator establishes a firm conceptual framework

for meaning. This framework also controls her patterns of imagery.

13 HARDY, BARBARA. "The Surface of the Novel: Chapter 30," in 1967.A2.
    The process of Middlemarch in authorial report and in dramatic scene is a series of vivid moments, alive to sense and feeling, mutable and continuous. In a careful analysis of the details in chapter 30, she shows the sense and feeling, the continuous flow, and the subtle organization within chapters, which characterize the novel and have been neglected in other types of examination of the novel.

14 HARVEY, W. J. "Criticism of the Novel: Contemporary Reception," in 1967.A2.
    The verdict that Middlemarch is George Eliot's masterpiece was slow to form, but the original diversity has gradually resolved into a remarkable unanimity. Surveys the attitudes of the Victorian reviewers.

15 _____. "The Intellectual Background of the Novel: Casaubon and Lydgate," in 1967.A2.
    Casaubon's intellectual life has nothing to do with either his religious life or his position in society. Yet there is no such divorce between Lydgate's idea of social good and his intellectual conquests. Casaubon is ironically too late for the work done by German scholars, and Lydgate is too premature with his research and his medical practice. Reprinted in 1971.B24.

16 HESTER, ERWIN. "George Eliot's Messengers." Studies in English Literature, 7: 679-690.
    A pattern in George Eliot's novels involves a messenger which has the task of converting the protagonist from a purposeless existence to a life of dedicated service to his fellowman. The pattern is always the same. First, the two become acquainted. Second, the protagonist submits himself to the guidance of the messenger and then after his conversion enters a sympathetic relationship with his community. Third, the protagonist can now live a purposeful and sympathetic life by himself. He is then "baptized" into a secular religion of service and sympathy.

17 HIRSHBERG, EDGAR W. "George Eliot and Her Husband." English Journal, 56: 809-817.
    Reminds the reader that with all of her extraordinary intellectual powers George Eliot was still a woman with a woman's need for love and understanding. He feels that she

and Lewes had a desperate and sincere need for one another. He even suggests that George Eliot would have written no novels if it were not for Lewes.

18 HORNBACK, BERT G. "Middlemarch." Times Literary Supplement, December 21, p. 1239.
    This is a note on alleged anachronisms in the novel.

19 HULME, HILDA M. "The Language of the Novel: Imagery," in 1967.A2.
    Analyzes a characteristic "movement" image in Middlemarch. Through three kinds of movement, the abstract is made concrete, and the double unity of body and mind, thinker and thought, is readily established. The second section shows how the diction of everyday is used to establish a tension between generalized and individual expression. The third section is called "Strategies of Indirection" and shows George Eliot's tendency to use imagery to have the reader "conceive with that distinctness which is no longer reflection but feeling." The fourth explains that the full energy of George Eliot's thinking and feeling life is flowing into her novel-language. Spinoza's Ethics, with its rigorously ordered propositions, describes the struggle to "form a clear and distinct idea" which defines Dorothea's progress.

20 HURLEY, EDWARD T. "Piero di Cosimo: An Alternate Analogy for George Eliot's Realism." Victorian Newsletter, No. 31, pp. 54-56.
    Piero di Cosimo, the Renaissance classicist, becomes an alternate to the Dutch realistic painters of chapter 17 of Adam Bede. He is the natural artist, obedient to his inspiration and honestly painting what he "sees."

21 JOHNSON, R. BRIMLEY. The Women Novelists. Freeport, New York: Books for Libraries, Inc.
    Reprint of 1919.B2.

*22 KATONA, ANNA. "George Eliot és Thomas Hardy: Filozofiai és etikai szempontok az angol naturalizmus Kialakulásánál." Kulonvenyom at a Filologiai Közlöny (Budapest), 13: 3-4, 345-354.
    Cited in ELL(1967).

23 KILLHAM, JOHN. "Autonomy Versus Mimesis?" British Journal of Aesthetics, 7: 274-285.
    Discusses Barbara Hardy's idea of "appropriate form." She thinks the appropriate form is inherent in the

"truthfulness" of the novel. The term is ambiguous and depends on the idea that novels are imprisoned people and not collections of words. The abandonment of "characters" considered as moral agents as in nineteenth century fiction may be essential if the territory of the novel is to encompass more of humanity's experiences of life in the twentieth century.

24 KNOEPFLMACHER, U. C. "George Eliot's Anti-Romantic Romance; 'Mr. Gilfil's Love-Story.'" Victorian Newsletter, No. 31, pp. 11-15.
     The tale hinges on a single negation of the "other-worldliness" that George Eliot had rejected; it reaffirms the nature of a world in which happiness is short-lived and romance lies hidden. Her very diction betrays her reservations about the world she wanted to ennoble.

25 _____. "The Post-Romantic Imagination: Adam Bede, Wordsworth and Milton." English Literary History, 34: 518-540.
     Finds in Adam Bede a double indebtedness to the Romantic poets who tried to find the ideal in the factual and to Paradise Lost in the attempted justification of man's banishment to a temporal world. George Eliot created an entire setting in which the emblematic and the naturalistic can coincide.

*26 KONDRAT'EV, YU. M. Glavnye osobennosti esteticheskoi pozitsii Dzhordzh Eliot Kak vyrazhenie obshchiks tendentsii v razvitii realisticheskogo romana v Anglii vtoroi poloviny XIX veka. U.Z.: Moskovskii gosudarstrenngi pedagogicheskii Institut imeni Lenina, Moscow, 245: 285-343.
     Cited in ELL(1967).

*27 _____. Pozdnee tvorchestro Dzhordzh Eliot: Roman Middlemarch. U.Z.: Moskovskii gosudarstrenngi pedagogicheskii Institut imeni Lenina, Moscow, 280: 96-124.
     Cited in ELL(1969).

28 LEAVIS, F. R. "Adam Bede." Anna Karenina and Other Essays. London: Chatto and Windus, pp. 49-58.
     The interest in Arthur Donnithorne and the inner drama of conscience in him is deeply characteristic of George Eliot. This seduction theme is developed in her later studies of Tito, Bulstrode, and Gwendolen. Discusses the influences of Scott, of Hawthorne, of Greek tragedy, of Rasselas, of Shakespeare, and of Wordsworth. She is a novelist who was not in need of instruction from modern psychologists. Adam Bede is annunciatory of her later works.

1967

29   LERNER, LAURENCE. The Truthtellers: Jane Austen, George Eli-
     ot, D. H. Lawrence. London: Chatto; New York: Schocken
     Books.
          Almost all of George Eliot's novels offer a study in con-
     version. In Scenes of Clerical Life and Adam Bede the
     conversions deal with religious experience. The others are
     purely secular. She treats Christianity as a human phenom-
     enon. A noble nature leads the unregenerate out of their
     egoism. The greatest happiness her characters ever attain
     is opening their hearts and letting their feelings flow out
     to other human beings. In The Mill on the Floss Maggie's
     final experience is one of pure self-fulfillment.

30   MANSELL, DARREL, JR. "George Eliot's Conception of Tragedy."
     Nineteenth Century Fiction, 22: 155-171.
          George Eliot consciously, but certainly not systematical-
     ly, applies Aristotle's Poetics to her fiction. Some of
     the protagonists are tragic in the sense that their emo-
     tional nature causes them to struggle in vain against the
     law that every cause has inexorable effects. Their falls
     come at the pinnacle of good fortune. She confronts her
     characters with their duty by requiring them to calculate
     the consequences that will follow if they take certain
     paths. Each makes decisions which allow him to take on
     heroic stature, yet his efforts are doomed to failure be-
     cause of the laws of consequences.

31   MARSHALL, WILLIAM H. "A Selective Bibliography of Writings
     About George Eliot, to 1965. Part I." Bulletin of Bibli-
     ography, 25: 70-72.
          Marshall says, "The fact that the list is called 'selec-
     tive' attests the unlikehood of human attainment of the
     'definitive' in an instance like this; it also reflects
     intention and the inevitable need to make decisions in the
     case of certain minor items."

32   _____. "A Selective Bibliography of Writings About George
     Eliot, to 1965. Part II." Bulletin of Bibliography, 25:
     88-94.
          A continuation of 1967.B31.

33   MASEFIELD, MURIEL. Women Novelists From Fanny Burney to
     George Eliot. Freeport, New York: Books for Libraries
     Press, Inc.
          Reprint of 1934.B2.

34   MAXWELL, J. C. "George Eliot and the Classics." Notes and
     Queries, 14: 388.

168

Adds to the Virgil allusions one from Georgics, 2, 490, in Adam Bede, Chapter 52.

*35 MILNER, IAN. "The Quest for Community in The Mill on the Floss." Prague Studies in English, 12: 77-92.
    Cited in ELL(1967).

36 MOLSTAD, DAVID. "George Eliot: A Higher Critical Sensibility." Victorian Essays, A Symposium: Essays on the Occasion of the Centennial of the College of Wooster in Honor of Emeritus Professor Waldo H. Dunn. Edited by Warren P. Anderson and Thomas D. Clareson. Kent State University Press.
    George Eliot's real contribution to the novel lies in her rational awareness of the mental and emotional landscape. She depicts the characters from a rational perspective. He attempts to show the nature of her rational sensibility and to make clear the connection with the kind of thinking Biblical higher critics did. She saw Biblical figures as limited by ideas usual to their historical period, their class, and their condition in life.

37 OLDFIELD, DEREK. "The Language of the Novel: The Character of Dorothea," in 1967.A2.
    Dorothea's changing style is her changing self throughout Middlemarch. Suggests three different stylistic methods used in presenting Dorothea. First is the narrator's voice; second is the dramatization of Dorothea's own speech; and third is Dorothea's method of communicating her thoughts. Dorothea's tragedy is that life in Middlemarch denies her public expression, either in words or in acts.

*38 PETERSON, VIRGIL A. "Romola: A Victorian Quest for Values." West Virginia University Philological Papers, 16: 49-62.
    Cited in ELL(1967).

*39 PISAPIA, BIANCAMARIA. "George Eliot e Henry James." Studi Americani (Roma), 13: 235-280.
    Cited in MLA(1969).

*40 RINGLER, ELLIN JANE. "The Problem of Evil: A Correlative Study in the Novels of Nathaniel Hawthorne and George Eliot." DA, 28: 5068A. (University of Illinois).
    The moral precepts which George Eliot and Hawthorne hold in common are based on the idea that man is fundamentally an egoist and a sinner. Creeds or doctrines will not provide him with final solutions and are themselves evidence of intellectual egoism. Only a sympathetic relationship with individuals can partially redeem man.

1967

41 ROBBINS, LARRY M. "Mill and Middlemarch: The Progress of
   Public Opinion." Victorian Newsletter, No. 31 (Spring),
   pp. 37-39.
      Like John Stuart Mill in On Liberty, George Eliot under-
   stands the force of public opinion in establishing rules of
   conduct. In chapter seventy-one of Middlemarch she depicts
   a society whose rules of conduct are responsible for the
   accusation, judgment, and condemnation of transgressors.
   This public opinion based on self-interest becomes a powerful but neutral force, capable of being tyrannical as well
   as beneficial.

42 SCHORER, MARK. "The Structure of the Novel: Method, Metaphor and Mind," in 1967.A2.
      Finds five different prominent stories in Middlemarch.
   The work achieves its unity as the introduction of nearly
   every book contains a social scene where representatives
   of most of the five stories are allowed to come together.
   There are other internal devices which unify. One is the
   theme of the book. The third shows the interoperation of
   these as choices are made in social circumstances. Her
   concept of character is of growth, of alteration, of change,
   of progress. Association with noble spirits helps the
   characters to become better.

43 THOMSON, FRED C. "The Legal Plot in Felix Holt." Studies in
   English Literature, 7: 691-704.
      The legalism of the novel has a specific relationship to
   the central theme, a ruling concept of "hereditary, en-
   tailed Nemesis." Her limited adherence to the instruction
   of Frederic Harrison on the laws of entail and limitations
   caused the essentials of her plot to be confused with the
   accidentals and her purpose to be blurred.

44 TOMPKINS, J. M. S. "A Plea for Ancient Lights," in 1967.A2.
      There has been a tendency to treat Middlemarch as a
   Sacred Book. There is a likeness between the medieval
   handling of the Bible and the modern approach to Middlemarch. Celia is presented throughout the novel with a
   creative fulness of delicate and humorous detail. Ladislaw seems to be endowed with attitudes and imagery which
   make him a Christ-image. These are his association with
   light, his love of children, his sympathy, and his devotion
   to the quaint Henrietta Noble.

45 TYE, J. R. "George Eliot's Unascribed Mottoes." Nineteenth
   Century Fiction, 22: 235-249.
      George Eliot followed the tradition of chapter tags only

in Felix Holt, Middlemarch, and Daniel Deronda, although
she used mottoes for the earlier novels as a whole. After
Romola she must have realized the difficulty of using the
words of another to convey the particular aspect of truth
and experience she wished to convey. So she began to write
the mottoes herself. Tye analyzes the prose and poetry of
the mottoes and explains their relations to the chapters.
They form an illuminating adjunct to the text and deserve
more than a cursory glance.

1968 A BOOKS

*1   COMBS, JOHN RICHARD. "George Eliot's Mind and the Clerical
        Characters in Her Fiction." DA, 29: 563A. (University of
        Texas, Austin).
           Traces the development of clerical characters in George
        Eliot's fiction, estimating their significance in light of
        her own philosophical, theological, and ethical understand-
        ing.

*2   DOYLE, SISTER MARY ELLEN. "Distance and Narrative Technique
        in the Novels of George Eliot." DA, 29: 3094A-5A. (Uni-
        versity of Notre Dame).
           George Eliot's stated aim was enlargement of her reader's
        sympathies through understanding characters whose feelings
        he had shared. This is a study of her means of establish-
        ing this sympathetic relationship between reader and char-
        acter.

 3   HAIGHT, GORDON S. George Eliot: A Biography. Oxford and New
        York: Oxford University Press.
           Advertised as the definitive biography. Haight includes
        the opening scene of a historical novel written when George
        Eliot was only fifteen. The biography follows the letters
        very closely.

*4   HIGDON, DAVID LEON. "The Sovereign Fragments: A Study of
        George Eliot's Epigraphs." DA, 30: 725A-6A. (University
        of Kansas).
           The two-hundred-twenty-six epigraphs are so closely re-
        lated to their respective chapters in imagery, scenic
        stance, and idea that they become integral parts of George
        Eliot's novels. They reveal rich veins of irony and ab-
        stractness.

 5   JARMUTH, SYLVIA L. George Eliot--Nineteenth Century Novelist.
        New York: Excelsior Publishing Company.

This study begins with a biographical sketch. Two chapters follow on George Eliot's religious and philosophical concepts and her theory of the novel. Individual studies of the novels follow. A rather complete bibliography is included at the end.

*6   JONES, R. T. A Critical Commentary on George Eliot's "Adam Bede." London: Macmillan.
Cited in ELL(1968).

*7   KEARNEY, JOHN PETERS. "George Eliot's Treatment of Time." DA, 29: 4491A. (University of Wisconsin).
Discusses the historical place of the individual in society, the ways in which the individual handles the changes that assault his very self, and the insight which her obsession with time gives to the reader.

*8   KENNEY, EDWIN JAMES, JR. "George Eliot's Presence in Middlemarch." DA, 29: 570A. (Cornell University).
Examines passages from the novels to see what authorial presence is, how it manifests itself in the narrative, and how it affects the reader's experience of fiction. The narrative voice reveals the complexities of George Eliot's own personality and of her aims as an artist.

*9   KILCULLEN, ELIZABETH ANNE. "George Eliot's Treatment of Marriage." DA, 30: 5447A-8A. (University of Toronto).
George Eliot has three main emphases in her treatment of marriage: the problem of fidelity, the role of woman in marriage and society, and the nature of marriage in comparison with other human relationships. Women contribute indirectly to the public good by supporting men whose calling involves wider and more impersonal goals.

10   KNOEPFLMACHER, U. C. George Eliot's Early Novels: The Limits of Realism. Berkeley: University of California Press.
Says that the primary purpose of the book is to discover a rationale for George Eliot's growth as a philosopher. Examines her works as seven "mental phases" which make up the first stage of her development. Hopes to show how she combined the ordinary and temporal existence she accepted with the extraordinary and ideal realm she yearned for. The last two parts of a four-part chapter entitled "Pastoralism and the Justification of Suffering: Adam Bede" reprinted as "On Adam Bede" in 1971.B24.

11   MILNER, IAN. The Structure of Values in George Eliot. Praha: Universita Karlova. Acta Universitatis Carolinae Philogica Monographia, 23.

1968

George Eliot's moral and social values enter into the living form of the novels as she stresses the importance and actual arrangement of the "social medium" in the novels. The form and pressure of the time, the social framework and its stratification, and the impingement of history and society on the lives of her characters are dynamic elements both in the structure and moral design of her fiction. A constant focus of values is in her heroic figure. The tension between his values and those of "good society" operates on many levels.

*12   PLOURDE, FERDINAND J., JR. "Time Present and Time Past: Autobiography as a Narrative of Duration." DA, 30: 334A-5A. (University of Minnesota).
       George Eliot's The Mill on the Floss becomes more nearly the novel she considered it to be when seen as a broken autobiography. Its central theme is the unsuccessful struggle of the heroine to reach the freedom of full consciousness of duration represented in the "autobiographic" narrator.

*13   QUICK, JONATHAN RICHARD. "A Critical Edition of George Eliot's Silas Marner." DA, 29: 3980A. (Yale University).
       The first part is an annotated text, and the second is a critical introduction with particular emphasis on the religious ideas and formal principles which make it unique.

*14   SIFF, DAVID H. "The Choir Invisible: The Relation of George Eliot's Poetry and Fiction." DA, 30: 293A-4A. (New York University).
       George Eliot was one of the first novelists to employ consciously the techniques of poetry in the writing of fiction. Through her poetry she learned to incorporate into the dramatic fabric of her fiction rich but hardly aesthetically pleasing interests, such as history, philosophy, and medicine.

15   SPEAIGHT, ROBERT. George Eliot. London: Arthur Barker, Ltd. Reprint of 1954.A3

16   SPRAGUE, ROSEMARY. George Eliot: A Biography. Philadelphia: Chilton Book Company.
       Says in her introduction, "I have followed the procedure of using primary sources to the fullest extent possible, and such secondary sources as have received the warrant of sound scholarship or genuine knowledge, or both; but I have not denied myself the privilege of a few surmises and suggestions, based on those sources, plainly labeled as such."

1968

*17 WILSON, LILLIAN. "George Eliot and the Victorian Ideal." DA, 29: 3114A. (Ohio University).
     George Eliot's female characters differ markedly from the ideal Victorian woman just as George Eliot herself did. They are totally frustrated by their attempts to exist in a society which refuses to recognize their potentialities as contributing, instead of dependent, social beings.

1968 B SHORTER WRITINGS

1 ADAMS, KATHLEEN. "George Eliot Week." Times Literary Supplement, September 26, p. 1090.
   1969 will be the 150th anniversary of the birth of George Eliot. The George Eliot Fellowship is planning a week of special events in Nuneaton.

*2 ARNOLD, MARY A. "The Unity of Middlemarch." Husson Review, 1: 137-141.
    Cited in MLA(1970).

*3 BENNETT, JOSEPH T. "The Critical Reception of the English Novel: 1830-1880." DA, 30: 272A. (New York University).
    In the reviews of Middlemarch the critics for the first time began to ask questions of the work itself and, thus, to approach the threshold of modern criticism.

4 CHAPMAN, RAYMOND. The Victorian Debate: English Literature and Society 1832-1901. London: Weidenfeld and Nicolson; New York: Basic Books, pp. 284-296.
   Paradoxically, the masculine and overtly religious Victorian age was lectured by a woman who had rejected orthodox Christianity. She anticipates modern times in the themes of existential choice, the influence of people upon each other independently of desire or liking, the sense of alienation, and the fear of meaninglessness.

5 DENEAU, DANIEL P. "Eliot's Casaubon and Mythology." American Notes and Queries, 6: 125-127.
   George Eliot clearly places Casaubon in the tradition of the syncretic mythographers, such as Jacob Bryant and George Stanley Faber. Casaubon labored at his syncretizing when the approach was on the verge of being superseded.

6 FELTES, N. N. "Phrenology: From Lewes to George Eliot." Studies in the Literary Imagination, 1: i, 13-22.
   Traces Lewes's interests in phrenology and his knowledge of it as revealed in his publications. George Eliot's

friend Charles Bray was also an ardent phrenologist. "Materialism," a belief in the physical basis of mind, rather than any specific system, was phrenology's legacy to George Eliot. Feltes examines the novels to point out the variety of influences of her phrenological habits of thought. The diction of her descriptions of mental processes displays her materialism.

7   GROOT, H. B. de. "Lewes and Fourier." Times Literary Supplement," October 17, p. 1177.
    A letter is published which defends Lewes against extreme radicalism. Lewes's own journalism provides supporting evidence for Haight's denial that Lewes ever lived in a Fourierist community.

8   HAIGHT, GORDON S. "George Eliot's Klesmer." Imagined Worlds: Essays on Some English Novels and Novelists in Honour of John Butt. London: Methuen, pp. 205-214.
    The musician Julius Klesmer is among the two or three finest creations in Daniel Deronda. Reactions to Klesmer's playing help to define the attitudes which several characters have toward music and to describe their personalities. Franz Liszt has been generally accepted as the model for Klesmer. Haight suggests a closer resemblance to Anton Rubinstein who was presented to George Eliot and George Henry Lewes on September 18, 1854, by Liszt.

9   _____. "Mark Pattison and the Idea of a University." Notes and Queries, 15: 191-194.
    Does not agree with John Sparrow's ideas in his book on Mark Pattison that he is the model for Casaubon. Haight says he "twists details to support his case."

10 HALL, ROLAND. "Some Antedatings From George Eliot and Other Nineteenth-Century Authors." Notes and Queries, 15: 410-412.
    George Eliot's translations of German theological works contain several uses of words which antedate their earliest occurrence recorded in the O.E.D.; provides a list.

11 HIGDON, DAVID L. "Scenes of Clerical Life: Idea Through Image." Victorian Newsletter, No. 33, pp. 57-58.
    Finds that the three separate stories have many common aspects. A common setting and the appearance of representatives from different generations of the same family link the "scenes." Even more the metaphoric language is markedly similar with the recurring image of a character as a plant, a flower, vine, or tree. The image reveals George

1968

Eliot's attitude toward the character and his situation.
She suggests a complex process in human life parallel to
that operating in nature through using these images.

12   HILL, DONALD L.   "Pater's Debt to Romola." Nineteenth Century
          Fiction, 22: 361-377.
          Reconsiders the import of Pater's remarks about George
      Eliot's fiction.   Then re-examines the significance of his
      repeated references to Savonarola in the essays written
      between 1864 and 1871.   These references demonstrate the
      characteristic working of Pater's imagination. Savonarola
      becomes in a very small way what the major figures of The
      Renaissance become on their much larger scale. They are
      symbolic rather than historical products of his personal
      mythology.

13   HULME, HILDA. "Middlemarch as Science-Fiction: Notes on Lan-
          guage and Imagery." Novel, 2: 36-45.
          Suggests some of the conscious choices through which the
      developing scientific knowledge of the time finds its
      ordered place within the world of the novel. Lydgate and
      his attitudes show George Eliot's awareness of the inter-
      relations of physiological and psychological knowledge.
      Lydgate is inspired by the works of Bichat, the great
      French anatomist and surgeon (1771-1862). And in its em-
      phasis on ordered development Middlemarch is essentially a
      novel of the time of Spencer and his evolutionary theories
      and of Goethe's ideas. These ideas are shown in George
      Eliot's extensive use of "movement" images. Bichat's the-
      ories have their part even in the smallest units of the
      novel's persuasive language, the verbs of motion and the
      "-ing" form.

14   HURLEY, EDWARD. "'The Lifted Veil': George Eliot as Anti-
          Intellectual." Studies in Short Fiction, 5: 257-262.
          Finds George Eliot saying that if perchance one had
      unlimited mental powers, not even the desire for human
      sympathy and an effort to exercise it could save one. The
      intellect left to itself will not arrive at truth and set
      one free but will betray the intellectual and bind him to
      treachery without restraint. Latimer sees what no other
      of George Eliot's characters sees: the complete triviality
      and depravity of humans and the total horror of human life.
      He sees too accurately and objectively and is therefore cut
      off from the human association he wants so badly.

15   HUTCHISON, B. "George Eliot, 1819-1890." Book Collecting and
          Library Monthly, 3 (July), 17.

Brief note which indicates auction prices for George Eliot titles sold 1960-1961.

*16   JACKSON, ARLENE MARJORIE. "Ideals and Realities in Victorian
       England: A Study of the Idealistic Quest Theme in the
       Novels of George Eliot and Thomas Hardy." DA, 29: 872A.
       (University of Michigan).
            Felix Holt, Middlemarch, and Daniel Deronda present ide-
       alists who seek to know and to exercise their duty to soci-
       ety in order to find psychological fulfillment. The loss
       of historical continuity and the deficiencies of the ideal-
       ists themselves account for the difficulty of their quest.

17   KAMINSKY, ALICE R. George Henry Lewes As Literary Critic.
       Syracuse, New York: Syracuse University Press.
            Although Professor Kaminsky makes this a book about Lewes
       and not about George Eliot, she does make many observations
       concerning his role in the creation of the novels. The
       study is an attempt to give Lewes himself recognition for a
       significant contribution to English criticism.

18   KERMODE, FRANK. "Novel, History, and Type." Novel, 1: 231-
       238.
            The critic should make the narrative of a novel as much
       of an historical narrative as possible and impose on it
       relatedness and coherence of a kind that resembles life and
       depends on plausibility. In Middlemarch Mrs. Cadwallader's
       remark that Ladislaw might be a natural son of Bulstrode
       represents the historisch touched by the geschichtlich.

19   KNOEPFLMACHER, U. C. "Of Time, Rivers, and Tragedy: George
       Eliot and Matthew Arnold." Victorian Newsletter, No. 33,
       pp. 1-5.
            The impulses that led to the composition of Merope and
       The Mill on the Floss are far closer than the very dif-
       ferent end products would suggest. Both works begin with
       the description of a mighty river. In both the river be-
       comes an emblem for the stream of change, the permanence
       of impermanence. Both Arnold and George Eliot come to
       adapt their own tragic vision to the moderation of ordinary
       life; he desisted from writing poetry; she turned to the
       world of Middlemarch.

*20   KOHL, NORBERT. "George Eliot, Middlemarch: 'Prelude'--eine
       Interpretation." Deutsche Vierteljahrsschrift für Litera-
       turwissenschaft und Geistesgeschichte, 42: 182-201.
            Cited in MLA(1968).

1968

21 LIEBMAN, SHELDON. "The Counterpoint of Characters in George
    Eliot's Early Novels." <u>Revue des Langues Vivantes</u>
    (Bruxelles), 34: 9-23.
        The setting in each of George Eliot's first four novels
    is a provincial town which appears to its inhabitants to be
    isolated and protected from intrusions of the outside
    world. But early in the novel it becomes obvious that the
    placidity of the self-contained community is challenged by
    the intrusion of an alien morality. The characters are
    drawn toward the two opposing poles of allegiance: love
    and duty. Both the man-of-duty and the man-of-love may be
    motivated by egoism. This opposition between the two ex-
    tremes has its origins in the evolution of the race. The
    characters are transformed and refined in the process of
    evolution. The terminal point in each novel is an earth-
    shattering event in which Fate passes final judgment.

22 MANSELL, DARREL, JR. "'Possibilities' in George Eliot's Fic-
    tion." <u>English Studies</u>, 49: 193-202.
        Considers George Eliot as a novelist of the anti-heroic.
    Her characters are potential heroines, but they fail to
    live up to the glorious possibilities of human nature which
    they share with the great heroes of the past. Yet striving
    after the possibilities of the past gives her characters
    the sense of the vital connection between past and present.
    When their high possibilities disappear, the humiliated
    protagonists fall back on marriage.

23 MARTIN, HAZEL T. <u>Petticoat Rebels: A Study of the Novels of</u>
    <u>Social Protest of George Eliot, Elizabeth Gaskell, and</u>
    <u>Charlotte Brontë</u>. New York: Helios, pp. 40-53.
        George Eliot's union with Lewes was the one thing that
    gave meaning to her life. It gave proof of her innate
    courage and raised her from the mediocrity of an assistant
    editor to the heights of a great novelist. <u>Adam Bede</u> is a
    protest against the double standards of the day and the
    religion which tolerated them. Arthur and Hetty are the
    victims of circumstance. In <u>The Mill on the Floss</u> sin is
    the main theme of the novel. In it the attack on the ad-
    herents and exponents of the Protestant Ethic is particu-
    larly bitter. In <u>Daniel Deronda</u> she dares to elevate the
    Jew and give him dignity.

*24 MELLEN, JOAN. "Morality in the Novel: A Study of Five Eng-
    lish Novelists: Henry Fielding, Jane Austen, George Eliot,
    Joseph Conrad, and D. H. Lawrence." DA, 29: 1543A. (City
    University of New York).
        George Eliot questions old norms because changes in his-

tory and social circumstances may demand a modification of existing standards of morality. History directly affects the life of every individual.

25 MEYER, S. P. "Middlemarch." Times Literary Supplement, January 25, p. 93.
    Answers Hornback, December 21, who says that a reference in Middlemarch to George Borrow is "obviously too late." Actually Lavengro was the work in question and was early enough. In 1872 when the last part of Middlemarch was published Borrow wrote an introduction to an edition.

26 MILLER, J. HILLIS. The Form of Victorian Fiction: Thackeray, Dickens, Trollope, George Eliot, Meredith, and Hardy. South Bend, Indiana: University of Notre Dame Press.
    George Eliot is discussed throughout Miller's work. One section of "Self and Community" is devoted to her. She is the most explicit example of the Victorian transformation from a view of society based on a transcendent ground to a view of it as generating itself. She herself assumed the mind of all humanity, of a Feuerbachian general consciousness. Her narrator is able to speak for the mind of a local community and for the individual sensibility. Her novels follow individual destinies within the context of an inclusive wisdom.

27 PATERSON, JOHN. "Introduction." Adam Bede. (Riverside Edition.) Boston: Houghton Mifflin Company.
    Gives a background sketch of George Eliot's life and her belief that man must develop a more passionate sense of his sympathy and solidarity with other men. The form and doctrine of Adam Bede are realistic; the actions follow a sequence of cause and effect. Dialogue amounts to a formalization or idealization of experience.

28 SALE, WILLIAM M., JR. "George Eliot's Moral Dilemma." Cornell Library Journal, 4 (Winter), 1-12.
    George Eliot found herself forced to abandon her simple intuitive faith in a divine plan for mankind, but her fiction is itself the continuation of an order to be found in the world. She involves her characters in the dilemmas and contradictions that have always beset mankind. She enlarges the sympathies of the reader to share their humanity.

29 SIZIROTNY, J. S. "A Classical Reference in Hard Times and in Middlemarch." Notes and Queries, 15: 421-422.
    George Eliot uses an image from Agamemnon at least twice;

1968

once in <u>Middlemarch</u> in saying that Rosamond's uneasiness
grew "into that ready, fatal sponge which so cheaply wipes
out the hopes of mortals." The second time is in a letter
to Mrs. Elma Stuart.

*30   SMALLEY, BARBARA MARTIN. "The Pattern of Illusion: A Cor-
relative Study in the Novels of Flaubert and George Eliot."
DA, 30: 340A-1A. (University of Illinois).
Both <u>Madame Bovary</u> and <u>Middlemarch</u> embody in effective
scene and symbol a profound awareness of inhabiting a dark,
dead universe. And both novels present richly meaningful
correlatives for their protagonists' unique worlds of inner
experience.

31   SPARROW, JOHN. "Mark Pattison and the Idea of a University."
<u>Notes and Queries</u>, 15: 432-435, 469.
On the matter of whether Casaubon is patterned after Mark
Pattison.

32   SPIVEY, TED R. "George Eliot: Victorian Romantic and Modern
Realist." <u>Studies in the Literary Imagination</u>, 1: ii,
5-21.
The Victorian side of George Eliot is for the most part
not the most powerful element in her work. The rising tide
of materialism and scientism denied the validity of the
romantic viewpoint. A study of the visionary and mythic
progress of man indicates that the loss and recovery of
unity and the healing emotions are recurring facts of man's
existence. The greatness of a realist like George Eliot
lies in the fact that she affirms the freedom of the individual caught in a tragic society and that she writes with
a clarified viewpoint that helps the individual maintain a
sense of his own identity.

*33   SWANSON, ROGER M. "Guilt in Selected Victorian Novels." DA,
30: 342A. (University of Illinois).
The novels are <u>Adam Bede</u>, <u>Great Expectations</u>, <u>Jane Eyre</u>,
and <u>Tess of the d'Urbervilles</u>. George Eliot's examination
of guilt reflects the tenets of positivism.

1969 A BOOKS

1   ADAM, IAN. <u>Profiles in Literature: George Eliot</u>. New York:
Humanities Press.
Shows how wit, observation, and sympathy, combined with
a lucid and energetic intelligence, enabled George Eliot
to invest the commonplace with complexity and importance.

Extracts from the major novels illustrate her treatment of character, setting, dialogue and narrative.

*2 BENSON, JAMES DIMON. "The Moral-Aesthetic Problem in George Eliot's Fiction." DA, 31: 1789A-90A. (University of Toronto).

The consensus that George Eliot sometimes sacrificed art for morality is grounded in Victorian criticism. This criticism forms a context for her theory of the novel. Her explicit statements about aesthetic theory are found in the essays and reviews, in "Notes on The Spanish Gypsy and Tragedy in General," and in the letters.

*3 CARTWRIGHT, JEROME DAVID. "Authorial Commentary in the Novels of George Eliot as Primarily Exemplified in Adam Bede, The Mill on the Floss, and Middlemarch." DA, 30: 5402A. (University of Wisconsin).

The authorial commentary in George Eliot's novels is deliberately unconventional and attacks the conventional falsehoods purveyed by her contemporaries as she promotes her own moral and aesthetic realism.

*4 CLARK, ROBERT NELSON. "The Idealist, the Missionary, and the Overreacher in the Novels of George Eliot." DA, 30: 3903A. (The Florida State University).

This study traces George Eliot's development as a novelist through three phases of her career, showing that she changed and matured in her understanding and presentation of character action.

*5 DeLOGU, PIETRO. La narrativa di George Eliot. Bari: Adriatica.

Cited in ELL(1969).

*6 FUJITA, SEIJI. Structure and Motif in Middlemarch. Tokyo: Itokuseido.

Cited in MLA(1971).

*7 GEIBEL, JAMES W. "An Annotated Bibliography of British Criticism of George Eliot, 1858-1900." DA, 30: 4450A. (Ohio State University).

The bibliography is set up chronologically and presents an account of George Eliot's public life as well as her critical reception.

8 HAIGHT, GORDON S. George Eliot and John Chapman: With Chapman's Diaries. Archon Books.

Reprint of 1940.A2.

1969

*9   KATONA, ANNA. A valóságábázolás problémai George Eliot regén-
     yeiben. Budapest: Akadémiai Kiado.
          Cited in ELL(1969).

*10 SECOR, CYNTHIA ANN. "The Poems of George Eliot: A Critical
     Edition with Introduction and Notes." DA, 30: 5457A-8A.
     (Cornell University).
          Presents collated texts of poems which exist in a number
     of versions and provides accurate texts of poems which have
     not been accessible. There is an introduction to each
     poem, an introduction to all of the poems, and other help-
     ful information. The original verse mottoes and additional
     fragments are also included.

*11 SPINA, GIORGIO. Poesia e umanità nel "Silas Marner" di George
     Eliot. Genoa: Bozzi. 123 pp.
          Cited in ELL(1970).

12   SUPP, DOROTHEE. Tragik Bei George Eliot. Heidelberg: Carl
     Winter Universitatsverlag. 160 pp.
          After an introductory chapter on the tragic theme, she
     discusses the tragedies of Arthur Donnithorne, Tito Melema,
     Mrs. Transome, Gwendolen Harleth, Hetty, Lydgate, Savonaro-
     la, and Maggie Tulliver.

*13 TURNER, WILLIAM HENRY. "George Eliot's Narrative Technique."
     DA, 31: 1818A-19A. (University of Toronto).
          George Eliot's narrative technique illuminates the moral
     framework of her fiction through her skill in employing
     commentary, narrative summary, and erlebte Rede.

1969 B SHORTER WRITINGS

*1   BAREISS, DIETER. Die Vierpersonenkonstellation im Roman:
     Strukturuntersuchungen zur Personenführung. Bern: Herbert
     Lang. 168 pp.
          One essay on Daniel Deronda. Cited in ELL(1970).

2   BEDIENT, CALVIN. "Middlemarch: Touching Down." Hudson Re-
     view, 22: 70-84.
          Middlemarch is the epitome of realism itself. It belongs
     to the negative province of the mind, where greatness is
     attained through renunciation. It embodies a kind of ar-
     tistic humility. The novel is a prolonged protest of the
     dissatisfied ego, a lamentation on the darkness of life
     without fame. This egoistic dissatisfaction accounts for
     the deep sadness of the book. This feverish yearning for

fame makes George Eliot our contemporary. She substitutes
the good opinion of posterity for Christian immortality.
Therefore there is nothing more calamitous than the col-
lapse of aspiration.

3   CATE, HOLLIS L. "The Initial Publication of George Eliot's
     Novels in America." Ball State University Forum, 10
     (Spring), 65-69.
         Before the establishment of an Anglo-American copyright
     agreement in 1891, some American publishers paid British
     authors a specified sum for the privilege of having a head
     start on other American publishers. George Eliot received
     £3630 from Harpers for the initial American rights for six
     of her novels. The difference in the £30 she was given for
     Adam Bede in 1859 and the £1700 she received for Daniel
     Deronda in 1876 is an accurate gauge of her steadily in-
     creasing popularity in America during her lifetime.

4   DAHL, CURTIS. "When the Deity Returns: The Marble Faun and
     Romola." Studies in American Literature in Honor of Robert
     Dunn Faner, 1906-1967. Papers on Language and Literature,
     5, supp. (Summer), 82-100.
         There are many striking similarities between The Marble
     Faun, 1860, and Romola, which was begun only a few days
     after George Eliot commented on Hawthorne's novel. Both
     employ the idea of a classical deity who returns in later
     times. Both authors believe that the essential human ex-
     periences recur. As Virgin-figure Romola is comparable to
     Hawthorne's Hilda. Both women leave their lofty towers and
     descend into the hurly-burly of active life. They are
     tales of two Italian cities; both were conceived from biog-
     raphy. Both are melodramatic in some instances. Hawthorne
     stresses moral psychology; George Eliot stresses ethical
     imperatives.

5   DAICHES, DAVID. Some Late Victorian Attitudes: The Ewing
     Lectures, University of California at Los Angeles, 1967.
     London: Andre Deutsch; New York: Norton.
         George Eliot is frequently mentioned throughout the
     three essays. In her nonconformist conscience co-
     existed with skepticism. This points to a late Victorian
     mood of stoicism, of heroic endurance for its own sake.
     The value lies in the endurance rather than in any moral
     end. Her skepticism was never disillusion; she found a way
     of combining unbelief with moral fervor.

6   DAMM, ROBERT F. "Sainthood and Dorothea Brooke." Victorian
     Newsletter, No. 35, pp. 18-22.

Dorothea transcends her original narrow view of sainthood. Her conception changes from attainment of abstract
ideals to pursuit of ideals which are defined in terms of
human values in a physical world. When she marries Mr.
Casaubon, he is at that time the ideal husband for her.
She is unaware of her own latent capacity for sensuous passion. Will Ladislaw recognizes that the ascetic-saint role
she is playing is not in consonance with her nature.
Through Will, Dorothea's major reassessment of values begins. She loses her enchantment with the sensuous possibilities of life. She arrives at a humanistic middle
ground, balancing her ascetic and sensuous tendencies.
With Will she works toward social reform, not a pedantic
compilation of antiquated facts.

*7 DUMITRIU, G. Middlemarch si geneza Isabelei Archer. Analele
Universitatii Bucuresti Literatură universală şi Comparată,
18: 77-84.
Cited in ELL(1970).

8 FELTES, N. N. "George Eliot's 'Pier-Glass': The Development
of a Metaphor." Modern Philology, 67: 69-71.
Herbert Spencer apparently explained the meaning of the
optical illusion to George Eliot which she uses in the
metaphor which begins chapter 27 of Middlemarch. She calls
him "an eminent philosopher" in the passage. Ruskin used
the illustration simply for the facts; Spencer used it as
a metaphor for the obstacles which beset scientific soci-
ology; George Eliot makes it a metaphor with a specifically
moral weight of the blindness of egoism.

9 GRIFFIN, ROBERT P. "Image and Intent: Some Observations on
Style in Middlemarch." Ball State University Forum, 10:
iii, 60-63.
Consistently through Middlemarch George Eliot uses patterns and clusters of images to dramatize the moral choices
her characters struggle among. Dorothea is afraid her
shortsightedness will allow her to tread on small things.
She comes to see the significance of the avenue of limes
outside her window; her vision comes to transcend the personal.

10 HAIGHT, GORDON S. "George Eliot and John Blackwood." Blackwood's, 306: 385-400.
Except for Lewes, no one did more than John Blackwood to
develop and sustain George Eliot's genius as a novelist.
Reviews their acquaintance with excerpts from their letters.

11 HARDY, BARBARA. "Mrs. Gaskell and George Eliot." The Victo-
    rians. Edited by Arthur Pollard. London: Cresset; New
    York: Bantam, pp. 169-195.
        Mrs. Gaskell's Mary Barton is revelatory fiction such as
    George Eliot was trying to write in Scenes of Clerical
    Life, but its materials have a horror, pity, and passionate
    hysteria which find no place in George Eliot. And Mrs.
    Gaskell is much more socially and politically didactic, de-
    spite her conservatism, than George Eliot. George Eliot is
    much closer to the very unmodern Shavian character who is
    certain of the difference between right and wrong, both in
    political and personal morality. George Eliot is perhaps
    the greatest psychologist in the English novel. Her char-
    acters have a complex psyche, but they have a certain fixi-
    ty. They do show the need to idealize, to dream, and to
    transform.

12 HURLEY, EDWARD T. "Death and Immortality: George Eliot's
    Solution." Nineteenth Century Fiction, 24: 222-227.
        George Eliot explains death without God by allowing the
    family to become the focus and bearer of continuing life,
    which masters time, history, and death. The family's past
    is immortal when it is a continuous chain stretching back
    into the past, carrying out a common task or occupying the
    same land. The past is irrevocable but will be extended
    into the future only by the free choice of father and child.
    By this method George Eliot circumvents her own doctrine of
    determinism and makes immortality a personal choice within
    the family. A man's image may be carried forward in his
    children or in the transformation of the past that he
    achieves.

13 INGLIS, FRED. An Essential Discipline. London: Methuen.
        Elaborates on basic principles of literary appreciation.
    References are to Dickens and George Eliot. Recognizes
    Middlemarch as "surely the greatest novel in English" and
    quotes from it and discusses it as such.

14 LEVENSON, SHIRLEY FRANK. "The Use of Music in Daniel Deronda."
    Nineteenth Century Fiction, 24 (December), 317-334.
        The theme of music becomes a technique for revealing
    Gwendolen's essential character faults. The huge flaw in
    her character is egoism. Deronda, through his great gifts
    of feeling, sympathy, and musical appreciation, is raised
    to an almost mystical perception of the world. He enlarges
    his already large sympathies to identify with a people and
    to find a mission in life. Nearly all of the truly natural
    musicians in the novel are Jews. Being able to enjoy their

1969

music raises Gwendolen beyond the bounds of her narrow, personal lot.

15   NELSON, RAYMOND S.   "Fanny's First Play and The Mill on the Floss." Shaw Review, 12: 59-65.
         Shaw detects in Eliot an ambivalence which he deplores. She wishes to establish a rational moral order, but she also champions various orthodoxies of social and religious thought. Yet he is deeply indebted to her. Fanny's First Play, 1910, seems to be an ironic adaptation of The Mill on the Floss. It is the same story with a different conclusion. The two selections also make clear the differences Shaw saw between the liberalism of the sixties and of the eighties. He wanted to scrap the old order entirely and build new institutions based on creative evolution.

16   PARIS, BERNARD J.   "The Inner Conflicts of Maggie Tulliver: A Horneyan Analysis." Centennial Review, 13: 166-199.
         Feels that a psychological study of the novel will show a disparity between the novel's representation of Maggie and the novel's interpretation of Maggie. He analyzes Maggie in the light of Karen Horney's theories of neurosis in Neurosis and Human Growth: The Struggle Toward Self-Realization (New York, 1950). Paris feels that he can discover what the experience of Maggie Tulliver means, intellectually and emotionally, to a consciousness like that of the implied author. He feels that George Eliot did not possess the qualifications necessary for conducting such experiments in life.

*17 SABISTON, ELIZABETH J.   "The Provincial Heroine in Prose Fiction: A Study in Isolation and Creativity." DA, 30: 1150A. (Cornell University).
         Emma, Madame Bovary, Middlemarch, and The Portrait of A Lady all render an imaginative provincial woman trying against insurmountable odds to realize her own ideal conception of her personality. They attempt to impart form and beauty to the mediocre life surrounding them.

*18 SINGH, BRIJRAJ.   "The Changing Concepts of 'Charm' in Leslie Stephen's Criticism of George Eliot." University of Rajasthan Studies in English, 4: 7-12.
         Cited in MLA(1970).

*19 SQUIRES, MICHAEL GEORGE.   "The Pastoral Novel: Studies in George Eliot, Thomas Hardy, and D. H. Lawrence." DA, 31: 370A-1A. (University of Maryland).
         In Adam Bede and Silas Marner Hayslope and Raveloe are

sequestered self-sufficient pastoral communities despite
human suffering. George Eliot develops the relationships
between man and nature through figurative language.

*20 STĂNCULESCU, LIANA. Mit şi leitmotif in George Eliot's: The
Mill on the Floss. Analele Universitătii Bucuresti.
Literatară universală şi comparată, 18: 107-117.
Cited in ELL(1970:

21 SWANN, BRIAN. "Eyes in the Mirror: Imagery and Symbolism in
Daniel Deronda." Nineteenth Century Fiction, 23: 434-445.
The novel is a drama of damnation and salvation, of the
acquisition of selfhood and the establishment of standards
and values. The most interesting group of images and metaphors are those of eyesight, and the most meaningful group
of symbols are those of reflecting glass. Gwendolen's
career is set forth in terms of images of visual perception
and reflection. The quality of her beauty is shown through
her eyes. She is unable to see beyond her self. Through
the symbolism of mirrors she becomes an image only, an art
object. She undergoes tragic despair and illumination.
Deronda shows Gwendolen the process by which she can change
from an egoistic animal to a submissive soul. The process
is symbolized in the movement from reflecting mirrors to
transparent windows. Her eyes at last find a response in
Deronda's eyes.

22 WADE, ROSALIND. "George Eliot: Journalist (Mary Ann Evans
1819-80)." Contemporary Review, 215: 88-92.
Reviews the relationship with Chapman and the days of her
writing articles to help earn an income for her and Lewes.
Lewes persuaded her to attempt fiction in 1856. Her com-
mentators should not overlook "the raffish, stimulating
young intellectual, with hair falling over her shoulders,
and her feet on the arm of a chair, correcting 'proof' in
the dark book-lined, paper-strewn office at 142 Strand."

23 WATSON, GEORGE ed. The New Cambridge Bibliography of English
Literature. Volume 3: 1800-1900. Cambridge: University
Press, pp. 899-911.
Contains a list of both primary and secondary sources.

24 WATSON, KATHLEEN. "George Eliot and Mrs. Oliphant: A Comparison in Social Attitudes." Essays in Criticism (Oxford), 19: 410-419.
George Eliot denied any connection with the novels of
Mrs. Oliphant. George Eliot looks regretfully back to the
old days when class distinctions were so clear that an

unembarrassed familiarity was possible between people of
different ranks. Mrs. Oliphant saw the men and women of
Victorian England as severely limited by their class.

25 WILLEY, FREDERICK. "Appearance and Reality in Middlemarch."
Southern Review, 5: 419-435.
Throughout her fiction George Eliot instinctively coun-
sels the reader to understand and to sympathize, to look
beneath the appearance to a deeper reality within. A sub-
sidiary theme is the classical novelist's interest in language itself. One of the main themes is the elaborate and
intriguing ways in which each character constructs his intellectual beliefs in order to explain reality satisfac-
torily to himself. Those who are deeply deceived wish
even to hide truths they subconsciously suspect. Others
face disenchantment, and, though sacrificing ideals to
stubborn facts, find a painful lesson in self-understanding.
These are the ones most likely to share in the spontaneous
feelings of life that George Eliot hopes to awaken in the
reader. The dramatic changes in political and social history parallel the pattern of development in the lives of
individual members of the Middlemarch community.

26 WILLIAMS, RAYMOND. "The Knowable Community in George Eliot's
Novels." Novel, 2: 255-268.
George Eliot's connections with the farmers and crafts-
men can be heard again and again in their language. She
presents them mainly through speech and uses the rural in-
habitants of rural England as a landscape. Her central
seriousness, and yet her acute consciousness of other and
often congenial tones, is at once a paradox of language and
community. It is part of a crucial history in the development of the novel that the extended and emphatic world of
an actual rural and then industrial England can come to be
known primarily as a problem of relationship. The separated individual, with a divided consciousness of belonging
and not belonging, makes his own moral history.

27 WILSON, JACK H. "Howells' Use of George Eliot's Romola in
April Hopes." Publications of the Modern Language Association, 84: 1620-1627.
In Chapter 43 of April Hopes, 1888, the heroine declares
to her fiancé that he is "a fatherless man." Howells as
narrator adds, "These were the words of Romola in the romance, to Tito." A knowledge of Howells' fascination with
Tito and of his close study of Romola suggests an important
avenue to the interpretation of his novel. Many secondary
characters, as well as the main characters, may be clearly

comprehended through the recognition that <u>Romola</u> is a presence on different levels in a variety of ways.

1970 A BOOKS

1   ADAMS, KATHLEEN. <u>George Eliot: A Brief Biography</u>. Nuneaton, Warwickshire: Nuneaton Borough Council, 28 pp.
    This is written by the secretary of the George Eliot Fellowship.

2   AUSTER, HENRY. <u>Local Habitations: Regionalism in the Early Novels of George Eliot</u>. Cambridge: Harvard University Press.
    First argues the validity of regarding George Eliot as a regional novelist. Examines next George Eliot's first four novels in terms of her view of provincial existence, her presentation of physical environment and communal activity, and the significance of the natural and social contexts in the moral and psychological life of the individual.

*3 BONAPARTE, FELICIA. "George Eliot: Tragedy in a Minor Key." DA, 31: 2374A. (New York University).
    In George Eliot's determined world, moral judgment is not made by man but by the consequences of his actions. Thus actions are not sins but errors of judgment about the workings of natural law. Her view was essentially that of Greek tragedy.

4   CREEGER, GEORGE R. ed. <u>George Eliot: A Collection of Critical Essays</u>. Englewood Cliffs, N. J.: Prentice-Hall, Inc.
    In his introduction Creeger states that there is a persistent and petulant desire to have George Eliot different from what she was. She was characterized by a conservatism balanced by strong liberal-reforming tendencies. Her mind had a pronounced moral cast, and she felt the tension resulting from the intellectual malaise of her century. Egoism is man's greatest vice; one can be redeemed by sensing his kinship with mankind. Each of the ten essays is listed and annotated separately in this bibliography.

*5 DEEGAN, THOMAS F. "George Eliot's Historical Thought and Her Novels of the Historical Imagination." DA, 31: 3500A. (Northwestern University).
    <u>Scenes of Clerical Life</u>, <u>Adam Bede</u>, <u>The Mill on the Floss</u>, <u>Felix Holt</u>, and <u>Middlemarch</u> are novels of the historical imagination. They explicitly link the life of their characters with that of the national community in a previous generation.

1970

*6   DE MERITT, WILLIAM. "George Eliot as a Tragic Novelist: Her
     Theory and Practice." DA, 31: 4114A-15A. (Rutgers Uni-
     versity).
          The study concentrates on George Eliot's constant theme
     of the close relation between "art" and "life." As "ar-
     tists of life" her characters use tragic experience to cre-
     ate morally realistic worlds.

 7   FULMER, CONSTANCE MARIE. "She Being Dead Yet Speaketh: A
     Study of George Eliot's Moral Aesthetic." DA, 31: 2875A-
     6A. (Vanderbilt University).
          Shared characteristics of George Eliot's religion and of
     her literary theory are defined to be "solidarity" and
     "continuity." The terms and their definitions are taken
     from a note entitled "Historic Guidance," which is in her
     notebook, Huntington Library, MS. HM 12993.

 8   HARDY, BARBARA ed. Critical Essays on George Eliot. New
     York: Barnes and Noble, Inc.
          In the "Introduction" Professor Hardy points out that
     George Eliot's art is at once too realistically humane and
     too intellectually analytic to make it good material for
     the creative activity of interpretative critics. These
     essays deal with the relation between form and content as a
     means whereby a certain impression is created. Each of the
     ten essays is listed and annotated separately.

*9   HENNELLY, MARK M. "Sibyl and the Gloom: A Study of Guilt in
     the Life and Novels of George Eliot." DA, 32: 920A.
     (St. Louis University).
          Looks at George Eliot: A Biography (1968.A3) by Haight,
     and finds that the chief motivating factor in her psychic
     history seems to be a deep-seated guilt syndrome which was
     ultimately caused by her early estrangement from her mother.

*10 HOFFMAN, BRUCE H. "The Credibility of George Eliot's Major
     Characters: A Study of Character, Moral Patterns and the
     Nature of Society in Her Novels." DA, 31: 4718A. (State
     University of New York, Buffalo).
          The major flaw in The Mill on the Floss, Romola, Felix
     Holt, and Daniel Deronda is a result of George Eliot's
     attempting to impose the pattern of moral development in
     her rustic novels on one major character in these non-
     rustic novels.

*11 HUDSON, STEWART M. "George Henry Lewes's Evolutionism in the
     Fiction of George Eliot." DA, 31: 6059A. (University of
     Southern California).

190

The study undertakes the exposition of Lewes's evolutionary doctrines as humanistic progressivism and the demonstra-
tion that his evolutionary philosophy and psychology had
considerable influence on George Eliot's fiction.

12   JONES, R. T. George Eliot. British Authors: Introductory
     Critical Studies. Cambridge: University Press.
          After a brief introduction, discusses Adam Bede, The Mill
     on the Floss, Silas Marner, Felix Holt, Middlemarch, and
     Daniel Deronda in order to suggest the texture of thought
     and feeling and the quality of experience offered by the
     whole. Also attempts to draw attention to the central con-
     cerns of the novels and the principal critical problems that
     they raise.

13   KENYON, F. W. The Consuming Flame: The Story of George Eliot.
     New York: Dodd, Mead; London: Richmond; Victoria: Hut-
     chinson.
          This is a fictionalized account of George Eliot's life
     with much dialogue. The emphasis is on the earlier part of
     her life.

*14 ROUNDS, STEPHEN R. "George Eliot's Progressive Alienation
     From English Life." DA, 31: 6567A. (Indiana University).
          George Eliot's evaluation of the possibilities of change
     in the world grew steadily more dark and doubtful, and her
     evaluation is revealed in the darkening view of social and
     political England reflected in her novels.

*15 SULLIVAN, WILLIAM J. "George Eliot and the Fine Arts." DA,
     31: 4736A. (University of Wisconsin, Madison).
          Beginning with The Mill on the Floss, George Eliot regu-
     larly introduced into her novels a figure whose emotional
     and spiritual characteristics were identical to his aes-
     thetic principles and whose vocation or profession was that
     of the practising artist.

*16 SWANN, BRUCE STANLEY FRANK. "George Eliot and Realism: The
     Development of a Concept of Symbolic Form." DA, 31:
     6635A. (Princeton University).
          George Eliot's career moves from monistic moralism to
     symbolic or pluralistic symmetry. In the later novels she
     creates the novel of thoughtful action as opposed to the
     romantic novel of unusual activity.

*17 VILLGRADTER, RUDOLF. Die Darstellung des Bösen in den Romanen
     George Eliot's. Aus dem Nachlass hrsg. von Thomas Finken-

1970

staedt und Helmut Heidenreich. Saarbrücken: Universitäts-
bibliothek. 136 pp.
Cited in ELL(1970).

1970 B SHORTER WRITINGS

1   ALEXANDER, WILLIAM. "Howells, Eliot, and the Humanized Read-
     er." The Interpretation of Narrative: Theory and Practice.
     Edited by Morton Bloomfield. Harvard Studies in Litera-
     ture. Vol. 1. Cambridge, Mass.: Harvard University
     Press, pp. 149-170.
        Shelley's ethical understanding of the sympathetic imagi-
     nation in A Defense of Poetry finds an echo at the center
     of the fictional theories and purposes of George Eliot and
     William Dean Howells. For George Eliot the greatest bene-
     fit the reader owes the artist is extension of his sympa-
     thies. Like Howells George Eliot was concerned to reveal
     subtle ways men harm one another by small, even unconscious,
     egoisms and hypocrisies. She works environmental study
     more thoroughly than Howells. She is also more concerned
     with primal emotions and basic impulses. She is wiser and
     deeper in her knowledge of the human condition and in her
     judgments and sympathies.

2   ARMSTRONG, ISOBEL. "Middlemarch: A Note on George Eliot's
     'Wisdom,'" in 1970.A8.
        "Wisdom" is a set of philosophical or intellectual be-
     liefs which George Eliot pronounces for her readers. She
     intends for these comments to be bridges between the world
     of the novel and the world of the reader. This is moraliz-
     ing and preachy. Yet she gives the impression of having
     pondered and of being able to manipulate the reader. In
     this way she seems to share her own experience and to ask
     the reader to discover the truth about life in the novel.

*3   AUERBACH, NINA V. "Reality as Vision in the Novels of Jane
     Austen and George Eliot." DA, 31: 4701A-02A. (Columbia
     University).
        Both writers handle the commonplace in such a way that
     the realistic contains a sense of the visionary. In George
     Eliot's novels there is a profound tension between the
     domestic and the mythic.

4   BAGLEY, JOHN. "The Pastoral of Intellect," in 1970.A8.
        George Eliot explored and individualized the historical
     pastoral. She recreates and refeels history as a part of
     her own mental life. The inner lives of her most effective

characters are framed and typified as she frames her <u>genre</u> scenes. <u>Daniel Deronda</u> is an example of her use of the historic pastoral. The novel becomes a graphic model of sexual and national emancipation.

5 BENVENUTO, RICHARD. "At a Crossroads: The Life and The Thought of George Eliot." <u>Studies in the Novel</u>, 2: 355-361.

George Eliot emerges from Haight's biography (1968.A3) as a deeply depressed, anxious woman, hypersensitive to criticism and the passing of time, and as a courageous and dedicated artist. Unfortunately there is little more than an intimation of what went on underneath the surface of her life or of what moved inside the public figure. And Knoepflmacher's study (1968.A10) provides a spiritual correlative for George Eliot's life and takes the reader across the landscape of her ideas.

*6 BREASTED, BARBARA. "I: 'Comus' and the Castlehaven Scandal. II: Public Standards in Fiction: A Discussion of Three Nineteenth-Century Novels: George Eliot's <u>Middlemarch</u> and Jane Austen's <u>Pride and Prejudice</u> and <u>Emma</u>. III. <u>Antony and Cleopatra</u>: Theatrical Uses of the Self." DA, 31: 4112A. (Rutgers University).

In <u>Middlemarch</u> the narrator undertakes a massive investigation of the characters in which their public lives play only a part. George Eliot imagines a private hidden "center" in the self; a character's social role and the public standards by which his society assesses him are often irrelevant.

7 BURNSHAW, STANLEY. <u>The Seamless Web</u>. New York: George Braziller.

Includes discussion of most Victorian writers. Mentions George Eliot as a philosophical positivist who was interested in changing people.

8 CURRY, MARTHA, R.S.C.J. "<u>Middlemarch</u>: Unity and Diversity." <u>Barat Review</u>, 5: 83-92, 101-103.

Turns to the letters and notebooks to show George Eliot's concern for working out the structure of <u>Middlemarch</u>. Then an examination of its division into books follows with generous quotations. Dorothea passes through a moral crisis and completes her moral journey when she accepts the burden of her limited possibilities and widens the interests of her life to include others.

1970

*9 FARNHAM, MARY D. "Henry James on Three Victorian Novelists:
Concepts of the Novel." DA, 31: 6054A. (University of
North Carolina, Chapel Hill).
    From 1866 to 1885 James wrote ten notes and articles on
George Eliot's work including five major essays. Reading
George Eliot's novels as well as those of Anthony Trollope
and Robert Louis Stevenson helped him to see extended pos-
sibilities for the novel as art.

*10 FREEMAN, JOHN. "George Eliot's Great Poetry." The Cambridge
Quarterly, 5: 25-40.
    Cited in ELL(1970).

11 GOLDFARB, RUSSELL M. "Robert P. Warren's Tollivers and George
Eliot's Tullivers." University Review, 36: 209-213.
    The Brad and Maggie Tolliver brother-sister relationship
that is central to Flood recalls Maggie and Tom in The Mill
on the Floss. Warren points out through his narrative that
the key to understanding Maggie and Tom is the incestuous
attraction that patterns their lives. This article outlines the importance of incest in Flood.

12 ____. "Warren's Tollivers and Eliot's Tullivers, II." University Review, 36: 275-279.
    The Tolliver signature, the importance of the flood and
the theme of incest all suggest a relationship between
Robert Penn Warren's Flood and The Mill on the Floss.
Flood renders a service of literary criticism. Maggie's
ruling passion throughout her life is her feeling for Tom.
Maggie rejects Stephen Guest because of her love for Tom.
Paradoxically, the flood purifies their incestuous relationship and signals a return to their innocence. Incest
in The Mill on the Floss amounts to a recollection of lost
innocence.

13 GOODE, JOHN. "Adam Bede," in 1970.A8.
    Discusses her reasons for choosing the 1790's; against
the historical changes is a presentation of Adam's evolutionary process of development. In the contrasting stories
of Hetty and Adam there is an evolutionary drama of alienation and individuation which can only take place on a
"pastoral" stage. Social convention becomes natural law
in another transformation. George Eliot also realizes
through Dinah the "validity" of a religion which escapes
the apparently unchanging secular world.

14 GREENE, MILDRED S. "Isolation and Integrity: Madame de Lafayette's Princesse de Clèves and George Eliot's Dorothea
Brooke." Revue de Littérature Comparée, 44: 145-154.

Does not attempt to prove a direct literary influence but
to point out striking resemblances of character. The main
point of comparison is that they both have been brought up
on the Pensées of Pascal. They must reject Pascalianism if
they are to express their womanliness in sexual love.
Their similar heroic but often self-defeating search for
happiness is analyzed.

15 HADDAKIN, LILIAN. "Silas Marner," in 1970.A8.
    Silas Marner perhaps gives more unalloyed pleasure to the
    modern reader than any of George Eliot's works. Nothing
    essentially poetic is lost by Silas's being presented in
    prose. There is no line between fact and symbol in the
    novel. The Wordsworthian affinities go far beyond the epi-
    graph from "Michael." She insists on the power of memory
    to work the affections and to bind the life of the individu-
    al into a unity. Eppie's education is the work of nature.
    The book is about feelings and the forms in which they in-
    corporate themselves. Religion, viewed as part of "real
    life," crosses the threads of fairy tale.

16 HARDY, BARBARA. "The Mill on the Floss," in 1970.A8.
    The Mill on the Floss explores the realities of character
    and event by exposing human beings to life without opiate,
    but in the end succumbs, as a work of art, to the kind of
    unreality it has been criticizing. She finds a toughness
    and openness, a successful and transforming use of the
    personal experience of religious crisis and conversion,
    and a final unsuccessful resort to solution by fantasy.
    There is no progress in character; Maggie ascends and de-
    scends. The climaxes are reached and then denied. The
    climax of vision and decision is not utterly undone, but
    its effects are largely erased.

17 HARVEY, W. J. "Idea and Image in the Novels of George Eliot,"
    in 1970.A8.
    Tries to show the ways that the formula "ontogeny reca-
    pitulates plylogeny" is transmuted into George Eliot's art.
    There are three ways this may be explained in terms of the
    ways adults recapitulate their origins and growth. First,
    the adult may contain within him his individual childhood.
    Second, the individual may contain the historical past of
    his culture. Third, the individual may contain the whole
    of the evolutionary past. These separate skeins are woven
    together in the fiction.

18 HEYWOOD, CHRISTOPHER. "A Source for Middlemarch: Miss Brad-
    don's The Doctor's Wife and Madame Bovary." Revue de
    Littérature Comparée, 44: 184-194.

1970

Supposes George Eliot to have critically and imaginative-
ly adapted Miss Braddon's bowdlerized version of Madame
Bovary. George Eliot sought to provide a more convincing
version of the pattern of relationships derived from Flaubert and made familiar by Miss Braddon's tale.

19 HIGDON, DAVID L. "George Eliot and the Art of the Epigraph."
Nineteenth Century Fiction, 25: 127-151.
The epigraphs or mottoes represent George Eliot's use of
all types of literary sources. Thirty-one come from Shakespeare; Wordsworth supplied nine. But the primary source
is George Eliot herself. She composed ninety-six of them.
She had a consistent aesthetic purpose in using them. They
create ironies, stress abstract content, evaluate meta-
phorically, and maintain an authorial stance. The article
includes an appendix which gives the locations and sources
of the epigraphs.

20 IFE, B. W. "Idealism and Materialism in Clarín's La Regenta:
Two Comparative Studies." Revue de Littérature Comparée,
44: 273-295.
George Eliot herself makes frequent references in The
Mill on the Floss to her reading of natural science and the
way in which it helped her clarify her thinking about society. Ife gives a detailed comparison of Ana in Clarin's
La Regenta to Maggie. Clarin works with the same problems
and follows the same themes.

21 INGHAM, PATRICIA. "Dialect in the Novels of Hardy and George
Eliot." Literary English Since Shakespeare. Edited by
George Watson. London: Oxford University Press, pp. 347-
363.
George Eliot makes use of standard and non-standard
speech to place her characters in relation to one another.
The effectiveness of her use depends on the reader's grasp
of its relation to her concern with human aspirations and
self-deceit.

*22 IONESCU-MATACHE, LILIANA. "Studiu tipologic asupra lui Silas
Marner." Studiu de literatură universală, 15: 79-90.
Cited in MLA(1971).

23 KAPOOR, S. D. "An Ideal Come True: Hale White's Search for
An Ideal Woman Character in His Novels." Calcutta Review,
1: 411-418.
In an article in the University of Toronto Quarterly
(1956.B12) Wilfred H. Stone attempts to prove that Hale
White was in love with George Eliot. This article argues

that at no stage of his career was Hale White emotionally
inclined toward George Eliot. He felt a "literary enthusiasm" which hoped for "intellectual companionship."

24   LEVINE, GEORGE. "Introduction." Felix Holt, the Radical.
New York: W. W. Norton and Company, Inc., pp. ix-xxi.
Felix Holt is based on a vision of the vital interconnec-
tion of all human experience. George Eliot was testing her
vision of individual responsibility within an organic society against the practical exigencies of public life.
Felix's idealism hovers between conservatism and radicalism. He is half-politician and half-moralist, and as
George Eliot sees the world, the two aspects are irrecon-
cilable. The novel is a great imaginative struggle against
the destruction of traditional moral norms and of individual personality.

25   _____. "Romola as Fable," in 1970.A8.
It is inescapable that Romola is a failure. The picture
is always strained, always gives the impression of being
artificially contrived, and as a result, the "diagram"
shows through with clarity. Yet this novel most clearly
marks the transition from "early" to "late" George Eliot.
The belief that it is possible somehow to escape the consequences of one's actions and act without reference to one's
relations to the larger community becomes a crucial moral
blindness and a central thematic preoccupation. The novel
is a fable and moves in the direction of a vision more com-
plicated than any she has used before. Coincidences are
central. The novel, through Savonarola, is speaking
against the purity of romance and pleading for tolerance.

26   LUND, MARY G. "George Eliot and the Jewish Question." Dis-
course, 13: 390-397.
Outlines George Eliot's references to the Jewish question
in her essays and letters. The Jewish state advocated in
Daniel Deronda seized the imagination of a young man named
Balfour, who met George Eliot and praised Deronda's aim.
Forty years later he established the Palestine Mandate.
"The Legend of Jubal" also presents the irony of the
world's acceptance of the Jews' contributions to knowledge
and science while repudiating the inventor.

27   McCARTHY, PATRICK J. "Lydgate, 'The New Young Surgeon' of
Middlemarch." Studies in English Literature, 10: 805-816.
Lydgate's training, class position, and advanced methods
make him different from previous doctors in fiction, and
the importance and validity of his researches, conducted in

1970

a realistic world, give him a special interest at a time
when the public esteem for medicine was growing. George
Eliot's interest in science had been deepened and given
direction by Lewes's studies in physiology and psychology.
The image of the web may have been derived from the scientific vocabulary common to Lydgate and Lewes.

28   MARTIN, GRAHAM. "Daniel Deronda: George Eliot and Political
      Change," in 1970.A8.
          George Eliot's characters are at times determined to con-
      tribute to the growing good of the world. In Daniel Deron-
      da the contrast between the two main characters provides the
      the key to the novel. Deronda discovers himself and also
      discovers history. His public destiny comes as a shock to
      Gwendolen. The political cause to which he dedicated his
      life has no evident bearing on English life. His relation-
      ship to Gwendolen culminates in his physical departure on
      a mission that fulfills his ideals.

29   MILNER, IAN. "The Structure of Values in George Eliot."
      Notes and Queries, 17: 355.
          Gwendolen disposes of her necklace and puts her poten-
      tially "better" self in pawn. By recovering it Deronda
      sets in motion the process of redemption. Adam's increased
      salary in Adam Bede is mentioned to emphasize the increased
      trust which is placed in his worth.

30   MOLSTAD, DAVID. "The Mill on the Floss and Antigone." Pub-
      lications of the Modern Language Association, 85: 527-531.
          The conflict between the conventions of society and indi-
      vidual judgment from Antigone is at the center of The Mill
      on the Floss. Tom, an honorable but conventional person,
      clashes with his imaginative sister. Her using this is
      evidence of George Eliot's belief in the continuity of
      man's elemental self, concerned in all ages with similar
      needs and problems, though moral codes have come and gone.

*31   NADEL, IRA BRUCE. "The Alternate Vision: Renunciation in the
      Novels of George Eliot and Thomas Hardy." DA, 31: 2929A.
      (Cornell University).
          Renunciation is at the heart of George Eliot's concept of
      the redemptive, "alternate vision" of the self. The fail-
      ure of renunciation, which to her is primarily the act of
      self-denial, is what caused her to develop the idea she
      calls "sympathy."

*32   NASH, DEANNA C. "The Web as an Organic Metaphor in The Marble
      Faun, Middlemarch, A Study of Provincial Life, and The

Golden Bowl: The Growth of Contextualism as an Aesthetic Theory in the Nineteenth Century." DA, 31: 4131A. (University of North Carolina, Chapel Hill).
   The web reflects the artist's view that all men are interconnected in a vast web of society. Since all actions ultimately affect every member of the social context, the web is in a constant state of flux.

*33   NORTH, DOUGLAS M. "Inheritance in the Novels of Jane Austen, Charles Dickens, and George Eliot." DA, 31: 5419A. (University of Virginia).
   The inheritance plot is a natural, almost inevitable, component of novels built from a vision of Comtian historical evolution. Daniel Deronda is her most profound novel of inheritance.

34   OLDFIELD, DEREK and SYBIL. "Scenes of Clerical Life: The Diagram and the Picture," in 1970.A8.
   Faulty as they were, these early tales contain real insights into personal and social relationships. The real subtlety pertains not at all to technique and less to thought than to feeling. Human wishes are not vain for George Eliot, but neither will they be fulfilled.

35   PERRY, JILL. "'Esse Videtur' in Romola." Notes and Queries, 17: 19.
   Finds an ironic misuse of a Latin ending by Scala in Romola as he poses a test for Tito. Tito fails to correct his misquotation.

36   SEDGLEY, ANNE. "'Daniel Deronda.'" Critical Review, 13: 3-19.
      In Daniel Deronda George Eliot moves outward from the moral and social certainties of Middlemarch towards a recognition of those complex uncertainties that find expression in Gwendolen's ambiguity. The novel begins in a way that dislocates any sense of unifying social identity. It is in relation to her mother that Gwendolen is most fully and freely revealed. Although George Eliot is writing in a tradition that did not encourage a direct interest in sexuality, her profound insight into Gwendolen's psyche includes sexuality as it includes her susceptibility to terror and her fits of spiritual dread.

37   SUDRANN, JEAN. "Daniel Deronda and the Landscape of Exile." English Literary History, 37: 433-455.
      In Daniel Deronda George Eliot experiments to give expression to that "individual" and major "experience" which

had been tested on the very pulses of her own life: her
complex and long continued isolation from society. The
mode of Daniel Deronda is "descriptive brooding upon the
doubt situation." She makes the subject of the novel the
self's awareness of the self's dissolution and its subsequent struggle to re-form an identity. Melodrama functions
as a way of evoking horror and dread, essential responses
to the necessary terror of the descent into the self. Like
her creator Gwendolen passes through a crisis of alienation
so that she may possess her self.

*38   WADDEN, ANTHONY T. "The Novel as Psychic Drama: Studies of
       Scott, Dickens, Eliot, and James." DA, 31: 4737A. (Uni-
       versity of Iowa).
          The feminine personality of the narrator is first irri-
       tated and distressed by the "animus" images of the Tulliver
       men in The Mill on the Floss before finally integrating
       their influence, an event which is dramatized through the
       imagery of the drowning in the River Floss.

39   WILLIAMS, RAYMOND. The English Novel from Dickens to Lawrence.
       London: Chatto and Windus; New York: Oxford Press, pp.
       75-94.
          Discusses George Eliot in terms of the relations in feel-
       ing and form and educated and customary life and thought.
       She extends the community of the novel and develops the
       idiom of individual moral analysis into a world in which
       morality is both individual and social.

40   WILSON, JACK H. "Eggleston's Indebtedness to George Eliot in
       Roxy." American Literature, 42: 38-49.
          Roxy, 1878, owes a considerable debt to both Romola and
       Middlemarch. The character of Roxy Adams is a composite
       of the characters of Dorothea and Romola. Mark Bonamy is
       modeled directly on Tito Melema. The theme of growth by
       suffering into a wider sympathy and deeper humanity is a
       persistent George Eliot theme. George Eliot made a great
       contribution to many American writers during the 1870's.

41   WISENFARTH, JOSEPH. "Demythologizing Silas Marner." English
       Literary History, 37: 226-244.
          The two most important events in Silas Marner are the
       theft of the gold and the coming of the child. Both are
       legendary. Even Silas's catalepsy is taken as a certain
       sign of occult powers derived from communication with
       Satan. All of this legend is used to enhance its realism
       as the action is best seen as demythologizing; of divesting
       men, their actions, and institutions of mythological or

legendary attributes in an attempt to appraise them more accurately. All that is ascribed to extra-human agencies is eventually seen to be caused by human actions, and all that is legendary is used to demonstrate how human joy and sorrow stem from moral feeling and human action.

1971 A BOOKS

*1 ALTHAUS, DONALD C. "The Love Triangle as a Structural Principle in the Novels of George Eliot." DA, 32: 2631A. (Ohio University).
      George Eliot's love triangles are arranged to enable the author to present the interaction of several narrative, structural, and human elements which together make up the "form" of each novel.

2 CARROLL, DAVID ed. George Eliot: The Critical Heritage. New York: Barnes and Noble; London: Routledge and Kegan Paul.
      Carroll's introduction contains a detailed analysis of the reception of each novel and prints a series of letters from George Eliot and from George Henry Lewes to and from John Blackwood. Throughout the volume other pertinent letters are printed in connection with the articles. All of these letters are reprinted from Haight's volumes. The writer of each review is identified, if possible, and a few facts are given about him.

3 FOULDS, ELFRIDA VIPONT. Toward a High Attic: The Early Life of George Eliot, 1819-1880. New York: Holt.
      Reprint of 1950.A1.

*4 HARRIS, MASON D., JR. "George Eliot and the Problems of Agnosticism: A Study of Philosophical Psychology." DA, 32: 1513A. (State University of New York, Buffalo).
      This study seeks to link ideas from Feuerbach's Essence of Christianity with specific aspects of George Eliot's criticism. Lewes's Study of Psychology and other contemporary works also are examined as influencing her.

1971 B SHORTER WRITINGS

1 BEETON, D. R. "Aspects of Adam Bede." English Studies in Africa (Johannesburg), 14: 13-36.
      Adam Bede deals with four young people in the process of shaping their adult lives. Two weak characters are destroyed or negated. Two strong characters are led to moral

refinement and happiness. Arthur is weak, selfish, and pleasure-grasping. It is hard to tell whether the characters are to be blamed for their weakness or not, for man's nature is more than his weakness or strength; "Our deeds determine us as much as we determine our deeds."

2   BLUMBERG, EDWINA J. "Tolstoy and the English Novel: A Note on Middlemarch and Anna Karenina." Slavic Review, 30: 561-569.
    In the famous train ride scene of Anna Karenina, Anna reads "an English novel" and imagines herself the heroine. This novel has not been identified. Suggests that it could be Middlemarch. At any rate there are many similarities. "Kitty" Brooke is like Kitty Shcherbatskaia in her function in the novel as a foil to the major heroine. Dorothea and Anna share an "eye affliction" which is metaphorical. The motif of philanthropy and the activity of book writing are common. This idea of book writing in Middlemarch and Anna Karenina objectifies the strivings of each character. All of the honeymooning couples vacation in Italy and examine the art there. The specific material borrowed seems less significant than the way it is used by Tolstoy. He borrows images which telescope complex moral situations.

3   CUNNINGHAM, VALENTINE. "George Eliot, Julian Fane and Heine." Notes and Queries, 18: 252-254.
    Julian Fane complained of the unpatriotism of Heine's satire in the Saturday Review, November, 1855. George Eliot took up Fane's argument in her articles for the Westminster Review, 1856. She endorsed some of his suggestions, but finally offered her own magisterial correctives.

4   DI PASQUALE, PASQUALE, JR. "The Imagery and Structure of Middlemarch." English Studies, 52: 425-435.
    Studies imagery in Middlemarch as it functions to fuse the elements of plot, character, and setting. The "dim lights and tangled circumstance" combined with the sense of sight become the "organizing figure" of the novel. At the center is the web, but the important thing is seeing the web in the proper light.

5   FABER, RICHARD. "George Eliot." Proper Stations. London: Faber and Faber, pp. 50-58.
    Assembles details about class in mid-nineteenth-century English fiction. All George Eliot's novels look back to the early 1830's or earlier except for Daniel Deronda. It is set in the 1860's. Takes each novel and shows how it fits into the social system; none preaches the need for a

new system. She thought the working class should save itself by its own exertions.

6   FLEISHMAN, AVROM. The English Historical Novel: Walter Scott
     to Virginia Woolf. Baltimore: Johns Hopkins Press, pp.
     155-163.
          Romola, like other George Eliot novels, is written ac-
     cording to a concept of historical development as well as a
     moral-psychological theory of persons. She expresses a
     Comtian view of history as the progress from the theologi-
     cal domination of mankind to its liberation in a religion
     of humanity. Her historical imagination fails to unite her
     real background with her individual characters or to sus-
     tain the steps by which political change is reached.

7   FRENCH, A. L. "A Note on Middlemarch." Nineteenth Century
     Fiction, 26: 339-347.
          French interprets the fifth paragraph of chapter 20 as a
     metaphor of extraordinary complexity which gives inexplicit
     but intimate (and highly painful) insight into the effect
     on a passionate but wholly innocent girl of entering into
     physical relations with Mr. Casaubon. Being humane as well
     as intelligent, George Eliot perceives those sexual rela-
     tions as focusing, but not as constituting, the whole mar-
     riage relationship. To set this piece of Middlemarch
     against an average modern novel is to wonder whether the
     price paid for outspokenness has not become cripplingly
     high.

*8   FRIEBE, FREIMUT. "'Che faro' bei George Eliot und John Gals-
     worthy: Der englische Gentleman und die Musik im 19. Jahr-
     hundert." Literatur in Wissenschaft und Unterricht (Kiel),
     4: 251-264.
          Cited in MLA(1971).

9   HAIGHT, GORDON S. "The George Eliot and George Henry Lewes
     Collection." Yale University Library Gazette, 46: 20-23.
          In 1968 Mrs. E. C. Ouvry, Lewes's granddaughter, trans-
     ferred the copyright of the unpublished writings of George
     Eliot and George Henry Lewes to the Librarian of Yale Uni-
     versity. Among them are George Eliot's school notebook and
     manuscripts of poems. Many letters are also included.

*10 IVĂSEVA, V. "Ot Džordž Eliot K anglijsokmu roman u 60-x
     godov." Voprosy Literatury, 15: 98-119.
          Cited in MLA(1971).

11   KEARNEY, JOHN P. "Time and Beauty in Daniel Deronda: 'Was
     she beautiful or not beautiful?'" Nineteenth Century

Fiction, 26: 286-306.
  Beauty is a function of time in Daniel Deronda. The
novel begins with the question: "Was she beautiful or not
beautiful?" An answer does not come in full until Gwendolen's letter to Daniel in the last chapter. Daniel cannot
decide whether Gwendolen's physical beauty is Lamia-like or
is infused with the "ideas" which are the necessary founda-
tion for true beauty. George Eliot determines to keep
Gwendolen's failure, a disintegration within private, objective time, rigorously subordinate to Daniel's success,
which is an integration within public, objective time.

12 KNOEPFLMACHER, U. C. "Middlemarch: Affirmation Through Com-
    promise." Laughter and Despair: Readings in Ten Novels of
    the Victorian Era. Berkeley: University of California
    Press, pp. 168-201.
      Middlemarch exposes the misconceptions of characters who
    are inevitably limited in their perceptions just as they
    are inevitably buffeted by time and change. It is a novel
    without a hero. George Eliot's realism severely circum-
    scribes Dorothea's triumph. At least she puts forth an
    effort to find sanity in a disturbed and disquieting world.
    But the novel closes on a note of mixed hope and despon-
    dency, acceptance and revulsion.

13 KRIEGER, MURRY. The Classic Vision: The Retreat from Extrem-
    ity in Modern Literature. Baltimore: Johns Hopkins Press,
    pp. 197-220.
      Includes a discussion of Adam Bede; it is called "Adam
    Bede and the Cushioned Fall: The Extenuation of Extremity."
    The pains and the sorrow of Adam's fall persist. George
    Eliot is aware of all the urgent drives that lead to moral
    catastrophe. The retreat from the fall has modest gains,
    for Adam is converted into choral man and earns the right
    to sing sad songs with a communal joy. The change comes
    in Adam when he feels that he has been too hard and that
    he must repent. The nature of Loamshire works its healing
    powers on him.

14 KROEBER, KARL. Styles in Fictional Structure: The Art of
    Jane Austen, Charlotte Brontë, George Eliot. Princeton:
    Princeton University Press.
      The book is concerned with fictional style. One chapter
    contrasts a passage from Middlemarch, chapters 40-42, with
    passages from Emma and Villette. George Eliot describes
    internal connections but also uses similes to relate the
    specific situation to other possibilities. All of the
    "happenings" are bound together by the language which

represents them. Several appendices include various tabu-
lations relating to the authors' usage of specific types of
words and of the various parts of speech.

*15   KUMAR, ANITA S. "Recurring Patterns of Behavior in the Women
      Characters of George Eliot." Triveni, 40: i, 21-26.
      Cited in MLA(1971).

16   MANTON, JO. Sister Dora: The Life of Dorothy Pattison. Lon-
     don: Methuen.
     A book about the sister of Mark Pattison and a possible
     original for George Eliot's Dorothea Brooke.

17   MASON, MICHAEL Y. "Middlemarch and History." Nineteenth Cen-
     tury Fiction, 25: 417-431.
     Middlemarch is a historical novel. It covers a clearly
     dated period and has a concern for the proper representa-
     tion of the past as an end in itself. There is also the
     juxtaposition of the past and the author's present; she
     clearly does not like some of the things she sees. The
     theme of progress in knowledge is one of a number of com-
     ponents of Middlemarch's "intellectual background."

18   _____. "Middlemarch and Science: Problems of Life and Mind."
     Review of English Studies, 22: 151-169.
     George Eliot's attitudes to science were intelligently
     developed, and in Middlemarch the use of science is largely
     coherent, and certainly related to the book's deep con-
     cerns. She was in contact with science through Lewes; his
     specific accomplishments are outlined. In Middlemarch
     there are three researchers: Lydgate, Casaubon, and Fare-
     brother. Casaubon is habitually contrasted, to his dis-
     credit, with Lydgate. Farebrother is a true contrast to
     both. As an amateur entomologist he has no shaping concep-
     tion to transform his classifications into laws. His hab-
     its of mind are related to the habits of his moral life.
     The areas of science and morality also share the imagery
     of light radiating from the individual. Each individual
     organism must adapt to its environment.

19   ROBERTS, LYNNE T. "Perfect Pyramids: The Mill on the Floss."
     Texas Studies in Language and Literature, 13: 111-124.
     The Mill on the Floss contains logical structure, ra-
     tional sequence, and clear spatial definition. It assumes
     that the external world is real and that there is a clear
     relationship between cause and effect. The past is linked
     to the present through the notion of causality. In such a
     world the pyramid falls because the foundation is weak.

The last pages ravage the reader's expectations of a well-ordered world. George Eliot forces the reader to see the limitations of every rational structure he has ever created.

20 SEALY, R. J. "Brunetière, Montégut--and George Eliot." Modern Language Review, 66: 66-75.
    Brunetière applied his criterion of aesthetic excellence first to George Eliot. The origin of his concept of literary sympathy is indubitably here in his study of George Eliot. It seems beyond question that he was led to appreciate its value by Montégut.

21 STEIG, MICHAEL. "Anality in The Mill on the Floss." Novel, 5: 42-53.
    George Eliot's insights into both characters and culture in The Mill on the Floss are at times startlingly concrete artistic anticipations of Freudian psychology. The presentation of the four extreme representatives in the older generation of Dodsonism are Mr. and Mrs. Glegg, Mrs. Pullet, and Mrs. Tulliver. The presentation of these characters adds up to a portrait of a community dominated by traits typical of the "anal" personality. According to Freud, the infantile concerns with the process and products of excretion can result in parsimony, obstinacy, and excessive orderliness and cleanliness. One who is an egoist is inwardly unclean; imagery bears this out in the novel. The predominant images of the last two books of The Mill on the Floss are vibration and water. The vibration suggests sexual arousal.

22 WADDINGTON, PATRICK. "Turgenev and George Eliot: A Literary Friendship." Modern Language Review, 66: 751-759.
    In France, where the reputations of Turgenev and George Eliot reached a height unprecedented for foreigners, they were held up as twin models of an ideal "objectivity." Outlines their acquaintance with each other and prints their letters.

23 WATSON, KATHLEEN. "Dinah Morris and Mrs. Evans: A Comparative Study of Methodist Diction." Review of English Studies, 22: 282-294.
    During the period in which the novel is set, the diction of Methodists differed from the standard English of the day in vocabulary, grammar, and use of quotation. Dinah's speech, like that of her prototype, Mrs. Elizabeth Evans, George Eliot's aunt, shows her familiarity with the organizational terms of Methodism. Both claimed their actions were directed by the Lord. George Eliot also recognized

the important part played by the Bible and by hymns in
Methodist life and speech. In Dinah George Eliot uses the
part of the Methodist ethos which coincides with her own.
The doctrinal element to which she was antipathetic is ignored. She created a character which fulfilled the necessary redemptive role in the novel without affirmation of
beliefs which were unacceptable to her.

24   WATT, IAN ed. The Victorian Novel: Modern Essays in Criti-
      cism. New York: Oxford University Press.
         This collection of essays on the Victorian novelists
      represents their greatness and suggests their relevance.
      Four of the essays are on George Eliot; they are reprints
      of 1958.B18, 1964.B9, 1967.B15, and a section from 1968.A10.

Index to George Eliot's Works

Middlemarch (continued) B15,
    B18–B19, B27, B37, B41–
    B42, B44; 1968.A8, B2–B3,
    B5, B9, B13, B18–B20, B25,
    B29–B31; 1969.A6, B2, B6–
    B9, B13, B17, B25; 1970.B2,
    B6, B8, B14, B18, B27, B32,
    B40; 1971.B2, B4, B7, B12,
    B14, B16–B18

The Mill on the Floss, 1860.B1–
    B10, B12–B17; 1861.B1,
    B13–B14; 1880.B6;
    1881.B35; 1913.B3;
    1918.B2; 1922.B5; 1926.B1;
    1943.B4; 1945.B1; 1953.B7;
    1954.B5; 1955.B17; 1956.B8,
    B10; 1957.B6, B21; 1959.B18;
    1960.B3; 1961.B8;
    1962.B24; 1963.B3, B17;
    1964.B3, B16; 1965.B2–B3,
    B11, B21, B27; 1966.B2,
    B22; 1967.B7, B35;
    1968.A12, B19; 1969.B15–
    B16, B20; 1970.B11–B12,
    B16, B20, B30, B38;
    1971.B19, B21

Poetry, 1866.B11; 1868.B10–B11,
    B19–B20; 1874.B1, B3–B4,
    B6–B7; 1876.B29; 1878.B7;
    1880.B5; 1885.A2; 1918.B1;
    1957.B4; 1959.B13;
    1963.B20; 1968.A14;
    1969.A10; 1970.B10

Romola, 1863.B1–B6, B8–B9;
    1866.B9; 1874.B2; 1887.B2;
    1897.A1; 1902.A1; 1903.A1;
    1921.A1; 1925.B1; 1930.B4;
    1931.B1, B4; 1947.A2;
    1953.B1, B9; 1956.A3, B13;
    1957.B14; 1958.B5; 1959.B11;
    1962.A4, B19; 1964.B24–
    B25; 1966.B5, B19;
    1967.B38; 1968.B12;
    1969.B4, B27; 1970.B25,
    B35, B40; 1971.B6

Scenes of Clerical Life, 1858.B1–
    B7; 1859.B7; 1860.B16;
    1861.B13; 1919.B6;
    1959.B9; 1962.B13;
    1965.A4, B7; 1967.B24;
    1968.B11; 1969.B11;
    1970.B34

Silas Marner, 1861.B2–B3, B5–B12;
    1862.B1; 1863.B7, B10;
    1913.B2; 1922.B4; 1937.B3;
    1946.B8; 1951.B3; 1954.B7;
    1957.B12; 1958.B16;
    1965.B28; 1966.B13, B24;
    1967.B2; 1968.A13;
    1969.A11, B19; 1970.B15,
    B22, B41

The Spanish Gypsy, 1868.B1, B3–
    B9, B12–B18, B21; 1870.B1

Stories, 1878.B5; 1962.B20;
    1968.B14

Title Index to Writings about George Eliot and her Work

TITLE INDEX

"The Church in Nineteenth Century
  Fiction: George Eliot,"
  1939.B1
The Classic Vision: The Retreat
  from Extremity in Modern
  Literature. 1971.B13
"A Classical Reference in Hard
  Times and in Middlemarch,"
  1968.B29
"The Clergy As Drawn By George
  Eliot," 1876.B24
"A Collection of George Eliot MSS
  and Books," 1923.B1
"Comments on Daniel Deronda,"
  1947.B2
The Common Reader. 1925.B8
Considerazioni sul realismo mo-
  rale di G. Eliot. 1935.A1
The Consuming Flame: The Story
  of George Eliot. 1970.A13
"Contemporary Literature: Novel-
  ists," 1879.B17
"The Cool Gaze and the Warm
  Heart," 1960.B9
Corrected Impressions: Essays on
  Victorian Writers. 1895.B4
"The Counterpoint of Characters
  in George Eliot's Early
  Novels," 1968.B21
"The Country of George Eliot,"
  1885.B20
The Credibility of George Eliot's
  Major Characters: A
  Study of Character, Moral
  Patterns and the Nature of
  Society in Her Novels.
  1970.A10
A Critical Commentary on George
  Eliot's "Adam Bede."
  1968.A6
A Critical Edition of George
  Eliot's "Silas Marner."
  1968.A13
Critical Essays and Literary
  Notes. 1880.B8
Critical Essays on George Eliot.
  1970.A8
A Critical History of English
  Literature. 1960.B4
The Critical Reception of the
  English Novel: 1830–1880,
  1968.B3

A Critical Study of George Eli-
  ot's "Middlemarch,"
  1956.A4
"Criticism of the Novel: Con-
  temporary Reception,"
  1967.B14
"Critic's Poll--Eighteen Fifty-
  Nine," 1959.B19
Critiques and Essays in Modern
  Fiction. 1952.B1
"Cross, Mary Ann, or Marian
  (1819-1880)," 1888.B8
"Cross's Biography of George
  Eliot," 1950.B2
Culture and Society, 1780-1950.
  1958.B18

"Daniel Deronda," 1876.B3, B27,
  B33, B35; 1878.B6; 1889.B5;
  1939.B3; 1951.B5; 1970.B36
"Daniel Deronda: A Conversation."
  1876.B34; 1888.B6
"Daniel Deronda and the Land-
  scape of Exile," 1970.B37
"Daniel Deronda and the Question
  of Unity in Fiction,"
  1959.B3
"Daniel Deronda and William
  Shakespeare," 1961.B10
Daniel Deronda from a Jewish
  Point of View. 1877.A1
"Daniel Deronda: George Eliot
  and Political Change,"
  1970.B28
"Daniel Deronda or Gwendolen
  Harleth?" 1965.B10
"Daniel Deronda: 'Organ Stop,'"
  1935.B3
"'Daniel Deronda': The Dar-
  kened World," 1957.B20
Die Darstellung der Charaktere
  in George Eliot's Romanen.
  1929.A1
Die Darstellung des Bösen in den
  Romanen George Eliot's.
  1970.A17
"Death and Immortality: George
  Eliot's Solution,"
  1969.B12
"The Deaths of Thomas Carlyle and
  George Eliot," 1881.B44

213

The Form of Victorian Fiction: Thackeray, Dickens, Trollope, George Eliot, Meredith, and Hardy. 1968.B26

Formative Influences on George Eliot with Special Reference to George Henry Lewes. 1963.A1

Formes du Roman Anglais de Dickens a Joyce. 1949.B5.

Forms of the Novel in the Nineteenth Century: Studies in Dickens, Melville, and George Eliot. 1966.B23

Four English Humourists of the Nineteenth Century. 1895.B3

Die Frau bei George Eliot. 1915.A1

The Free Spirit: A Study of Liberal Humanism. 1963.B2

French Criticism of George Eliot's Novels. 1956.A2

"From Abstract to Concrete in Adam Bede," 1955.B9

From 'Amos Barton' to 'Daniel Deronda': Studies in the Imagery of George Eliot's Fiction. 1959.A1

From Dickens to Hardy. 1958.B1

From Jane Austen to Joseph Conrad. 1958.B8, B10

From Shylock to Svengali: Jewish Stereotypes in English Fiction. 1960.B12

"The Genesis of Felix Holt," 1959.B17

"The Genesis of George Eliot's Address to Working Men and Its Relation to Felix Holt, the Radical," 1963.B13

"The Genius of George Eliot," 1873.B9; 1881.B19; 1909.B1

"George Eliot," 1866.B10; 1868.B2; 1872.B19-B21; 1875.B3, B5; 1876.B26, B40; 1878.B1; 1879.B14; 1880.B3, B8; 1881.B1-B3, B5-B6, B12-B18, B20, B22, B26, B31-B33, B37-B42; 1883.B8, B13; 1885.B7-B8, B12, B21-B22; 1886.B3, B5-B6; 1887.B3, B6; 1888.B1; 1889.B2, B6; 1891.B1; 1899.B2; 1909.B2; 1919.B1, B7; 1921.B3; 1922.B1; 1925.B8; 1932.B4; 1937.B1; 1938.B2; 1946.B1; 1958.B9; 1964.B11; 1971.B5

George Eliot. 1883.A1; 1901.A1; 1902.A2; 1904.A1; 1930.A2; 1933.A2; 1936.A3; 1954.A3; 1964.A1; 1968.A15

"George Eliot: A Bibliography," 1880.B7

George Eliot: A Biography. 1968.A3, A16

George Eliot: A Brief Biography. 1970.A1

George Eliot: A Collection of Critical Essays. 1970.A4

George Eliot: A Critical Study. 1883.A2

"George Eliot: A Higher Critical Sensibility," 1967.B36

"George Eliot: A Moralizing Fabulist," 1955.B14

George Eliot: A Paper Read Before the Portsmouth Literary and Scientific Society. 1881.A1

George Eliot: A Study in Conflicts. 1932.A2

George Eliot: A Study in Mid-Victorian Pessimism. 1936.A1

George Eliot: A Study of the Omniscient Point of View in Her Fiction. 1964.A3

"George Eliot als Gelehrte, Dichterin und Frau," 1922.B7

"George Eliot als Übersetzerin," 1956.B7

"George Eliot and Bedford College," 1949.B2, B6.

"George Eliot and Carlyle," 1881.B23

"George Eliot and Charles Dickens," 1946.B2

"George Eliot and Comtism," 1877.B4

TITLE INDEX

TITLE INDEX

Title Index

"An Image of Disenchantment in the Novels of George Eliot," 1960.B1

"The Image of the Opiate in George Eliot's Novels," 1957.B10

"The Imagery and Structure of Middlemarch," 1971.B4

"Imagery in George Eliot's Last Novels," 1955.B6

"Imagery in the Scenes of Clerical Life," 1965.B7

Imagined Worlds: Essays on Some English Novels and Novelists in Honour of John Butt. 1968.B8

"Implication and Incompleteness: George Eliot's Middlemarch," 1964.B9

"In Florence with Romola," 1887.B2

"In Search of George Eliot," 1954.B8

"In Search of George Eliot: An Approach Through Marcel Proust," 1933.B1

"Incest Patterns in Two Victorian Novels," 1965.B27

"Inconsistencies and Inaccuracies in Adam Bede," 1959.B8

The Industrial Revolution in Coventry. 1960.B10

"The Influence of Contemporary Criticism on George Eliot," 1933.B3

"An Ingenious Moralist: George Eliot," 1877.B9

Inheritance in the Novels of Jane Austen, Charles Dickens, and George Eliot. 1970.B33

"The Initial Publication of George Eliot's Novels in America," 1969.B3

"The Inner Conflicts of Maggie Tulliver: A Horneyan Analysis," 1969.B16

The Inner Life of George Eliot. 1912.A1

"Innocence in the Novels of George Eliot," 1961.B16

"The Intellectual Background of the Novel: Casaubon and Lydgate," 1967.B15

"Intelligence as Deception: The Mill on the Floss," 1965.B21

"Intent and Fulfillment in the Ending of The Mill on the Floss," 1955.B17

"An Interpretation of Adam Bede," 1956.B2

"The Interpretation of Adam Bede," 1954.B2

The Interpretation of Narrative: Theory and Practice. 1970.B1

"'Into the Irrevocable': A New George Eliot Letter," 1958.B3

"Introduction," Adam Bede. 1968.B27

"Introduction," Daniel Deronda. 1961.B12

"Introduction," Essays of George Eliot. 1963.A4

"Introduction," Felix Holt, the Radical. 1970.B24

"Introduction," Middlemarch. 1956.B4; 1965.B13

"Introduction," Middlemarch: Critical Approaches to the Novel. 1967.A2

"Introduction," The Mill on the Floss. 1961.B8

"Introduction," Feuerbach's The Essence of Christianity. 1957.B17

An Introduction to the English Novel: From Defoe to George Eliot. 1951.B4; 1960.B7

"The Intruder Motif in George Eliot's Fiction," 1962.B22

"Is George Eliot Salvageable?" 1961.B2

"Isabel, Gwendolen, and Dorothea," 1963.B10

"Isolation and Integrity: Madame de Lafayette's Princesse de Clèves and George Eliot's Dorothea Brooke," 1970.B14

223

TITLE INDEX

Title Index

"Mill and Middlemarch: The Pro-
gress of Public Opinion,"
1967.B41
The Mill on the Floss. 1860.B13-
B14; 1970.B16
"The Mill on the Floss and Anti-
gone," 1970.B30
"'The Mill on the Floss' and Kel-
ler's 'Romeo and Julia
auf dem Dorfe,'" 1960.B3
"The Mill on the Floss: Maggie
Tulliver and the Child of
Nature," 1967.B7
The Mind of George Eliot.
1966.A1
"Miss Austen and George Eliot,"
1883.B10
"Miss Evans, Miss Mulock, and
Hetty Sorrel," 1965.B6
"A Missing Month in Daniel Deron-
da," 1961.B9
Mit si leitmotif in George Eli-
ot's: The Mill on the
Floss. 1969.B20
"Mme. Laure and Operative Irony
in Middlemarch: A Struc-
tural Analogy," 1963.B5
"The Moment of Disenchantment in
George Eliot's Novels,"
1954.B4
The Moral and the Story. 1962.B7
Moral Growth in the Heroines of
George Eliot. 1960.A4
"The Moral Influence of George
Eliot," 1881.B46-B47
"Moral Problems and Moral Philos-
ophy in the Victorian
Period," 1965.B26
The Moral-Aesthetic Problem in
George Eliot's Fiction.
1969.A2
"Morale psychologie, destinée
dans La moulin sur la
Floss," 1965.B2
Morality in the Novel: A Study
of Five English Novelists.
1968.B24
"The Morality of George Eliot,"
1885.B4
"The Morality of Thackeray and
George Eliot," 1883.B9

"Mordecai: A Protest Against the
Critics," 1877.B10-B11
"More Leaves from George Eliot's
Notebook," 1966.B18
"Du Moulin sur la Floss à Jean
Santeuil," 1953.B7
Movement and Vision in George
Eliot's Novels. 1959.A5
"Mr. Browning and George Eliot,"
1965.B5
"Mrs. Gaskell and George Eliot,"
1969.B11

La narrativa di George Eliot.
1969.A5
"The Natural Historian of Our
Social Classes," 1963.B16
"Das Naturgefühl bei George Eliot
und Thomas Hardy," 1928.B1
The New Cambridge Bibliography of
English Literature.
1969.B23
"The 'New' Novel: George Eliot,"
1943.B5
"The New School of Fiction,"
1883.B15
"The Nineteenth Century and Af-
ter," 1948.B3; 1967.B3
"Nineteenth-Century Holdings at
the Folger," 1962.B10
Nineteenth Century Studies:
Coleridge to Matthew Ar-
nold. 1949.B7; 1966.B25
A Note on Charlotte Brontë.
1877.B15
"A Note on Daniel Deronda,"
1960.B6
"A Note on George Eliot," 1920.B4
"A Note on George Eliot's 'Amos
Barton'--Reticence and
Chronology," 1959.B9
"A Note on Hegel and George Eli-
ot," 1965.B23
"A Note on Literary Indebted-
ness," 1955.B11
"A Note on Middlemarch," 1971.B7
Notes and Reviews. 1921.B2
"Notes on George Eliot," 1954.B9;
1957.B18; 1958.B13

226

"The Politics of George Eliot,"
1885.B14-B15
Poor Monkey: The Child in Liter-
ature. 1957.B6
Portraits de Femmes: Madame Car-
lyle, George Eliot, Une
Detraquee. 1887.B1
Portraits d'Outre-Manche. 1886.B6
"'Possibilities' in George Eli-
ot's Fiction," 1968.B22
"The Post-Romantic Imagination:
Adam Bede, Wordsworth and
Milton," 1967.B25
"Povedom Eliotova 'Sajlez Mar-
nera,'" 1951.B3
Pozdnee tvorchestro Dzhord Eliot:
Roman Middlemarch.
1967.B27
"A Preface to Middlemarch,"
1955.B16
The Present Past: The Origin and
Exposition of Theme in the
Prose Fiction of George
Eliot. 1961.A1
"The Private Life of George Eli-
ot," 1885.B30
The Problem of Evil: A Correla-
tive Study in the Novels
of Nathaniel Hawthorne and
George Eliot. 1967.B40
"Problems of Adjustment in George
Eliot's Early Novels,"
1963.B9
Profiles in Literature: George
Eliot. 1969.A1
Proper Stations. 1971.B5
Prophets of This Century.
1898.B1
Prose Styles: Five Primary Types.
1966.B3
"Proust, Bergson, and George Eli-
ot," 1945.B1
The Provincial Heroine in Prose
Fiction: A Study in Iso-
lation and Creativity.
1969.B17
"The Psychological Novel: George
Eliot, Middlemarch,"
1946.B7
"Die Psychologie der Charaktere
in George Eliot's The Mill
on the Floss," 1913.B3

II: Public Standards in Fiction:
A Discussion of Three
Nineteenth-Century Novels:
George Eliot's Middlemarch
and Jane Austen's Pride and
and Prejudice and Emma.
1970.B6
The Puritan Element in Victorian
Fiction. 1940.B1
"Purpose in George Eliot's Art,"
1930.B3

"Qualities of George Eliot's Un-
belief," 1948.B8; 1955.B7
Quarry for Middlemarch. 1950.A2
Quest and Vision: Essays in Life
and Literature. 1886.B5
"The Quest for Community in The
Mill on the Floss,"
1967.B35

A Reader's Guide to the Nine-
teenth Century British
Novel. 1954.B13
Reality As Vision in the Novels
of Jane Austen and George
Eliot. 1970.B3
"Recent Criticism of the Novel,"
1962.B11
Recollections of Eminent Men.
1887.B10
"Recurring Patterns of Behavior
in the Woman Characters of
George Eliot," 1971.B15
"The Red Haired Lady Orator.
Parallel Passages in The
Bostonians and Adam Bede,"
1961.B15
"The Reflection of English Char-
acter in English Art,"
1877.B11
"Reflections on Rarity," 1948.B2
A regényiro George Eliot és XX.
szazadi atertekelesenck
problémai. 1965.A3
"Religion in the Novels of George
Eliot," 1954.B10
"The Religion of George Eliot,"
1885.B1
The Religion of Our Literature.
Essays upon Thomas Car-
lyle, Robert Browning,

Title Index

Alfred Tennyson; Including Criticisms Upon the Theology of George Eliot. 1875.B4

Religious and Moral Ideas in the Novels of George Eliot. 1963.A2

The Religious Background of George Eliot's Novels. 1966.A8

"Religious Changes in Cheshire, 1750-1850," 1966.B24

Religious Humanism and the Victorian Novel: George Eliot, Walter Pater, and Samuel Butler. 1965.B19

"Religious Influences in Current Literature: George Eliot," 1875.B1

"Religious Tendencies of George Eliot's Writings," 1881.B21

"Remembrance of George Eliot," 1913.B1

Representative English Novelists: Defoe to Conrad. 1946.B7

"Resolution and Independence: A Reading of Middlemarch," 1960.B14

"Restoration Through Feeling in George Eliot's Fiction: A New Look at Hetty Sorrel," 1962.B1

"The Return of George Eliot," 1962.B5

"Return to Raveloe: Thirty Five Years After," 1957.B12

"Revaluations (XV): George Eliot, I," 1945.B3

"Revaluations (XV): George Eliot, II," 1945.B4

"Revaluations (XV): George Eliot, III," 1946.B5

Review of Adam Bede. 1859.B1-B6, B10-B11; 1861.B4

Review of Daniel Deronda. 1876.B1-B2, B4-B18, B20-23, B25, B28, B30, B37-B39; 1877.B6-B7, B13-B14, B16

Review of Felix Holt. 1866.B1-B2, B4-B8, B14, B21-B23

Review of Impressions of Theophrastus Such. 1879.B1-B2, B4-B5, B7-B10, B13, B15-B16, B18

Review of J. W. Cross, George Eliot's Life as Related in Her Letters and Journals. 1885.B17

Review of J. W. Cross, The Life and Letters of George Eliot. 1885.B3

Review of The Legend of Jubal and Other Poems. 1874.B1, B6-B7

Review of Maria Tosello's Le Fonti Italiane de la "Romola" di George Eliot. 1959.B11

Review of Middlemarch. 1871.B1-B3; 1872.B1-B18; 1873.B1-B6, B10-B13, B16-B17, B19-B20; 1874.B8

Review of The Mill on the Floss. 1860.B1-B10, B12, B15, B17; 1861.B1

Review of Poems. 1874.B3; 1878.B7

Review of Romola. 1863.B1-B2, B4-B6, B8-B9; 1866.B9

Review of Scenes of Clerical Life. 1858.B1-B6

Review of Scenes of Clerical Life and Adam Bede. 1859.B7

Review of Scenes of Clerical Life, Adam Bede, and The Mill on the Floss. 1860.B16; 1861.B13

Review of Silas Marner. 1861.B2, B5-B8, B10-B11; 1862.B1; 1863.B7

Review of The Spanish Gypsy. 1868.B1, B4-B9, B12, B14-B15, B21; 1870.B1

Review of Three Novels. 1861.B13

The Rise of the Novel: Studies in Defoe, Richardson, and Fielding. 1957.B22

"The River and the Web in the Works of George Eliot," 1967.B10

TITLE INDEX

Title Index

Symbolic Setting in the Novel: Studies in Goethe, Stendhal, and George Eliot. 1965.B11

Take Her Up Tenderly: A Study of the Fallen Woman in the Nineteenth-Century Novel. 1962.B3

"The Text of the Novel: A Study of the Proof," 1967.B1

"'Thee' and 'You' in Adam Bede," 1959.B7

"The Theme of Alienation in Silas Marner," 1965.B28

The Theory of the Novel in England, 1850-1870. 1958.B15; 1959.B15

"The Thorn Imagery in Adam Bede," 1962.B21

"The Three Georges," 1963.B18

"Three Giants: Charlotte Brontë, Mrs. Gaskell, and George Eliot," 1952.B3

"Three Letters to Professor D. Kaufmann," 1881.B7

"Time and Beauty in Daniel Deronda: 'Was she beautiful or not beautiful?'" 1971.B11

Time-Levels and Value-Structures in George Eliot's Novels. 1965.A1

Time Present and Time Past: Autobiography as a Narrative of Duration. 1968.A12

"The Tinker Collection of George Eliot Manuscripts," 1955.B4

"Tolstoy and the English Novel: A Note on Middlemarch and Anna Karenina," 1971.B2

Toward a High Attic: The Early Life of George Eliot. 1950.A1; 1971.A3

"Toward a Revaluation of George Eliot's The Mill on the Floss," 1956.B8

"The Tragic Vision," 1963.B2; 1965.B8

Tragik Bei George Eliot. 1969.A12

"The Treatment of Florence and Florentine Characters in George Eliot's Romola," 1957.B14

"The Treatment of Time in Adam Bede," 1957.B11

The True Story of George Eliot in Relation to "Adam Bede" Giving the Real Life History of the More Prominent Characters. 1905.A1; 1906.A1

The Truthtellers: Jane Austen, George Eliot, D. H. Lawrence. 1967.B29

"Turgenev and George Eliot: A Literary Friendship," 1971.B22

Twelve Original Essays on Great English Novels. 1960.B14

"Two Cities: Two Books," 1874.B2

"Two Talkative Authors: Orzeszkowa and George Eliot," 1965.B30

The Unbelievers: English Agnostic Thought, 1840-1880. 1964.B5

"The Unity of Daniel Deronda," 1959.B5

"The Unity of Middlemarch," 1968.B2

"The Unity of The Mill on the Floss," 1964.B16

"Unity Through Analogy: An Interpretation of Middlemarch," 1959.B6

"Unpublished Letters," 1922.B2

"The Use of 'Concreteness' as an Evaluative Term in F. R. Lewis' The Great Tradition," 1965.B18

"The Use of Music in Daniel Deronda," 1969.B14

"The Uses of Context: Aspects of the 1860's," 1965.B31

The Uses of Melodrama in George Eliot's Fiction. 1962.A3

A valóságábázolas problémai George Eliot regényeiben. 1969.A9

Title Index

"A változó világ George Eliot regényeiben," 1965.B16

A Victorian Apocalypse: A Study of George Eliot's "Daniel Deronda" and Its Relation to David F. Strauss' "Das Leben Jesu." 1966.A7

The Victorian Debate: English Literature and Society 1832-1901. 1968.B4

Victorian Era: Queens of Literature of the Victorian Era. 1886.B3

Victorian Essays. 1962.B23

Victorian Essays, A Symposium: Essays on the Occasion of the Centennial of the College of Wooster in Honor of Emeritus Professor Waldo H. Dunn. 1967.B36

Victorian Fiction: A Guide to Research. 1964.B11

The Victorian Frame of Mind. 1957.B13

The Victorian Idea of Realism: A Study of the Aims and Methods of the English Novel Between 1860 and 1875. 1962.B2

Victorian Lady Novelists: George Eliot, Mrs. Gaskell, the Brontë Sisters. 1933.B4

Victorian Literature: Modern Essays in Criticism. 1961.B19

"A Victorian Masterpiece," 1962.B8

"Victorian Morals and the Modern Novel," 1958.B14

The Victorian Novel: Modern Essays in Criticism. 1971.B24

The Victorian Novel of Religious Humanism: A Study of George Eliot, Walter Pater, and Samuel Butler. 1961.B11

"A Victorian Novelist," 1925.B2

Victorian Novelists. 1899.B1

Victorian Prose Masters. 1901.B1

The Victorian Sage: Studies in Argument. 1953.B6; 1962.B9; 1965.B14

The Victorian Temper: A Study in Literary Culture. 1951.B2

The Victorian Vision: Studies in the Religious Novel. 1961.B13

The Victorians. 1969.B11

Die Vierpersonenkonstellation im Roman: Strukturuntersuchungen zur Personenfühurung. 1969.B1

Views and Reviews. 1908.B1

"Village Life According to George Eliot," 1881.B27-B28

Vision and the Role of the Past in the Novels of George Eliot. 1959.A2

Vision as Imagery, Theme, and Structure in George Eliot's Novels. 1957.A1

"Visions and Revisions: Chapter 81 of Middlemarch," 1957.B3

"Visions are Creators: The Unity of Daniel Deronda," 1955.B1

"A Visit to George Eliot," 1879.B12

"Warren's Tollivers and Eliot's Tullivers, II," 1970.B12

The Web as an Organic Metaphor in "The Marble Faun," "Middlemarch, A Study of Provincial Life," and "The Golden Bowl": The Growth of Contextualism as an Aesthetic Theory in the Nineteenth Century. 1970.B32

"A Week with George Eliot," 1885.B5, B11-B12

"Weekend with Middlemarch," 1945.B2

The Wellesley Index to Victorian Periodicals. 1956.B6

"When the Deity Returns: The Marble Faun and Romola," 1969.B4

Title Index

The Wider Life: A Study of the Writings of George Eliot. 1964.A2

"A Woman's Arm: George Eliot and Rhoda Broughton," 1954.B5

The Women Novelists. 1919.B2; 1967.B21

Women Novelists from Fanny Burney to George Eliot. 1934.B2; 1967.B33

"The Women of George Eliot's Novels," 1922.B3

Women-Writers of the Nineteenth Century. 1923.B2

Wordsworth's Influence on George Eliot. 1960.A5

"The Work of George Eliot," 1878.B4

"Writing in Bohemia," 1964.B22

Author Index to Writings about George Eliot and her Work

AUTHOR INDEX

Francillon, R. E., 1876.B28;
    1880.B4
Freeman, John, 1970.B10
Fremantle, Anne, 1933.A2
French, A. L., 1971.B7
Friebe, Freimut, 1971.B8
Fujita, Seiji, 1969.A6
Fukuhara, Rintaro, 1947.A2
Fulmer, Constance Marie, 1970.A7
Furuya, Senzo, 1966.A4
Fyfe, Albert J., 1954.B2

G., E., 1943.B2
Gardener, Charles, 1912.A1
Gardner, Charles, 1919.B1;
    1925.B1
Garrett, Peter K., 1967.B12
Gary, Franklin, 1933.B1
Geibel, James W., 1969.A7
Gelley, Alexander, 1965.B11
Gerould, Gordon Hall, 1942.B1
Gillespie, Harold R., Jr.,
    1964.B7
Goldberg, Hannah, 1957.B9
Goldfarb, Russell M., 1964.B8;
    1970.B11-B12
Goode, John, 1970.B13
Gosse, Edmund, 1922.B1
Gottheim, Lawrence Robert,
    1965.B12
Gould, George M., 1904.B1
Greenberg, Robert A., 1961.B5
Greene, Mildred S., 1970.B14
Greene, Philip Leon, 1962.B6
Greenhut, Morris, 1948.B5-B6
Gregor, Ian, and Brian Nicholas,
    1962.B7
Griffin, Robert P., 1969.B9
Griswold, Hattie Tyng, 1887.B6
Groot, H. B. de, 1968.B7
Groot, J. C. J., 1921.B1

H., J., 1937.B3
Haddakin, Lilian, 1970.B15
Hagan, John, 1961.B6
Haight, Gordon S., 1940.A2;
    1942.B2; 1949.B2; 1950.B2;
    1954.A1, B3; 1955.A2, B3-B4;
    1956.B3-B4; 1958.B9-B10;
    1960.B5; 1961.B7-B8;
    1965.A2; 1968.A3, B8-B9;
    1969.A8, B10; 1971.B9

Haldane, Elizabeth S., 1925.B2;
    1927.A1
Hall, Roland, 1968.B10
Halstead, Frank G., 1946.B3
Hamely, E. B., 1868.B13
Hamley, E., 1889.B3
Handley, Graham, 1960.B6; 1961.B9
Hanson, Lawrence and Elizabeth
    Hanson, 1952.A3
Hardwick, Elizabeth, 1955.B5
Hardy, Barbara, 1954.B4; 1955.B6;
    1956.B5; 1957.B10;
    1959.A3; 1964.B9; 1967.A2,
    B13; 1969.B11; 1970.A8,
    B16.
Harris, Mason D., Jr., 1971.A4
Harris, R. J., 1953.B5
Harris, Stephen LeRoy, 1964.B10
Harrison, Frederic, 1886.B7;
    1895.B1-B2; 1901.B2
Harvey, W. J., 1957.B11;
    1958.B11; 1961.A2;
    1964.B11; 1965.B13;
    1966.B7; 1967.B14-B15;
    1970.B17
Hastings, Robert, 1963.B7
Hatton, Joshua [Guy Roslyn],
    1875.B3, B5; 1876.A1-A2
Hazeltine, Mayo Williamson,
    1883.B8
Heagarty, Mary Alice, 1964.B12
Heilman, Robert B., 1957.B12
Hellman, George Sidney, 1922.B2
Hennelly, Mark M., 1970.A9
Henry, John, 1943.B3
Henry, Maria Louise, 1883.B9
Herrick, Mrs. S. B., 1873.B9
Hester, Waverly Erwin, 1961.A3;
    1966.B8; 1967.B16
Heywood, Christopher, 1970.B18
Heywood, Joseph Converse, 1877.B9
Higdon, David Leon, 1968.A4, B11;
    1970.B19
Hill, Donald L., 1968.B12
Hinkley, Laura L., 1946.B4
Hirshberg, Edgar W., 1967.B17
Hoffman, Bruce H., 1970.A10
Hoggart, Richard, 1962.B8
Holloway, John, 1953.B6;
    1962.B9; 1965.B14
Holmstrom, John and Laurence
    Lerner, 1966.A5

238

Author Index

Steig, Michael, 1971.B21
Steiner, F. George, 1955.B16
Steinhoff, William R., 1955.B17; 1961.B17
Stephen, Leslie, 1881.B39–B41; 1888.B8; 1899.B2; 1902.A2
Stevenson, Lionel, 1959.B16; 1960.B15
Stone, W. H., 1956.B12
Stowell, R. S., 1903.A1
Strachan, L. R. M., 1938.B5
Stump, Reva Juanita, 1957.A1; 1959.A5
Sudrann, Jean, 1970.B37
Sullivan, Margaret F., 1881.B42
Sullivan, William J., 1970.A15
Sully, James, 1881.B43
Supp, Dorothee, 1969.A12
Sutton, Charles W., 1880.B7
Svaglic, Martin J., 1954.B10
Swann, Brian, 1968.B21
Swann, Bruce Stanley Frank, 1970.A16
Swanson, Roger M., 1968.B33
Swinburne, Algernon Charles, 1877.B15; 1881.B44
Szirotny, June Marjorie, 1966.A8

Taylor, Bayard, 1880.B8
Templin, Lawrence Howard, 1964.A3
Thale, Jerome, 1954.B11; 1955.B18; 1957.B20–B21; 1958.B16; 1959.A6
Thomson, Clara, 1901.A1
Thomson, Fred C., 1959.B17; 1961.B18; 1965.B28; 1967.B43
Thomson, J. R., 1885.B29
Thomson, Patricia, 1963.B18
Tick, Stanley, 1966.B23
Tilley, Arthur, 1883.B15
Tillotson, Geoffrey and Kathleen, 1965.B29
Tillotson, Kathleen, 1949.B6
Tomlinson, May, 1918.B2–B3; 1919.B6; 1920.B3
Tomlinson, T. B., 1963.B19
Tompkins, J. M. S., 1967.B44
Tosello, Maria, 1956.B13
Towne, Edward C., 1887.B9
Toyoda, Minoru, 1931.A3

Trollope, Anthony, 1883.B16
Troughton, Marion, 1951.B6
Tucker, Houston Clay, 1960.A8
Tuckerman, Bayard, 1882.B9
Turner, William Henry, 1969.A13
Tye, J. R., 1967.B45
Tytler, Sarah, 1889.B6

Van Ghent, Dorothy, 1953.B11
Venables, G. S., 1866.B22–B23
Villgradter, Rudolf, 1970.A17
Vincent, Leon H., 1920.B4

Wachi, Seinosuke, 1966.A9
Wadden, Anthony T., 1970.B38
Waddington, Patrick, 1971.B22
Wade, Mabel Claire, 1925.B6
Wade, Rosalind, 1963.B20; 1969.B22
Wagenknecht, Edward, 1943.B5
Walker, Hugh, 1921.B4
Walker, R. B., 1966.B24
Walters, Gerald, 1958.B17
Ward, R., 1881.B45
Ward, Sir A. W., 1917.B2
Ware, L. G., 1860.B17
Watson, George, 1969.B23
Watson, Kathleen, 1969.B24; 1971.B23
Watt, Ian, 1957.B22; 1971.B24
Wedgwood, J., 1881.B46–B47
Welsh, Alexander, 1959.B18
Welsh, Alfred H., 1882.B10
Welsh, D. J., 1965.B30
Wenley, R. W., 1922.B6
West, Anthony, 1954.B12
Westermarck, H., 1894.A1
Weygandt, Cornelius, 1925.B7
Wheatley, James Holbrook, 1960.A9
Whipple, Edwin P., 1877.B16; 1885.B30; 1887.B10
Whiting, Mary Bradford, 1892.B1
Wilkinson, W. C., 1874.B9–B10
Willey, Basil, 1949.B7; 1950.B4; 1966.B25
Willey, Frederick William, 1962.A5; 1969.B25
Williams, Blanche Colton, 1935.B4; 1936.A3; 1938.B6
Williams, Orlo, 1926.B2
Williams, Raymond, 1958.B18; 1969.B26; 1970.B39

Subject Index to Secondary Writings

Morality (Continued)
1949.B7; 1951.A2; 1954.B10;
1955.A3, B7, B13; 1957.B17;
1958.A1; 1959.A4, B1;
1960.A4, B5; 1961.B11, B13;
1962.B14-B15, B17; 1963.A2.
B2; 1964.B5, B13-B14;
1965.A5, B1, B19, B21, B26,
B31; 1966.A1, A7-A8, B7,
B16; 1967.A3-A4, B4, B16,
B29, B40; 1968.A11, B24,
B28; 1969.A2, B5, B9, B12;
1970.A3, A7, A9-A10, B29,
B39; 1971.A4

Theories of Art, 1893.B1;
1930.B3; 1952.A1; 1953.B2;
1955.B10; 1956.B3, B11;
1957.B15, B19; 1963.B12;
1965.B22-B24; 1967.B30;
1969.A2; 1970.A7, B1